OCS EIS/EA
MMS 2001-099

Programmatic Environmental Assessment for Grid 10

Site-Specific Evaluation of BP Exploration and Production, Inc.'s Joint Initial Development Operations Coordination Document, N-7216

Holstein Project
Green Canyon Blocks 644 and 645

Prepared by

Minerals Management Service
Gulf of Mexico OCS Region

U.S. Department of the Interior
Minerals Management Service
Gulf of Mexico OCS Region

New Orleans
November 2001

PROGRAMMATIC ENVIRONMENTAL ASSESSMENT FOR GRID 10 AND SITE-SPECIFIC EVALUATION FOR BP'S HOLSTEIN PROJECT

Finding of No Significant Impact

BP Exploration and Production, Inc.'s Joint Initial Development Operations Coordination Document (DOCD) and its amendments propose to drill and complete 15 wells, re-enter and complete the existing appraisal well (for a total of 16 wells in the proposal), install a truss spar, and commence production in Green Canyon, Blocks 644 (OCS-G 11080) and 645 (OCS-G 11081) have been reviewed. Our programmatic environmental assessment (PEA) and site-specific evaluation of the proposed action (N-7216) is complete and results in a Finding of No Significant Impact (FONSI). Based on the conclusions of this PEA, there is no evidence that the proposed action will significantly (40 CFR 1508.27) affect the quality of the marine and human environments. Preparation of an environmental impact statement is not required.

J. Hammond Eve
Regional Supervisor, Leasing and Environment
GOM OCS Region

Date: 11/30/01

Pat Roscigno
Acting Chief, Environmental Assessment Section
Leasing and Environment, GOM OCS Region

Date: 11/30/01

Dennis Chew
Supervisor, NEPA/CZM Coordination Unit
Leasing and Environment, GOM OCS Region

Date: 11/30/01

Elizabeth Reuler
Supervisor, Physical Sciences Unit
Leasing and Environment, GOM OCS Region

Date: 11/30/01

ADVISORIES AND REMINDERS FOR N-7216

1. In response to the request accompanying your plan for a hydrogen sulfide (H_2S) classification, the area in which the proposed drilling operations are to be conducted is hereby classified, in accordance with 30 CFR 250.417(c), as "H_2S absent."

2. Within 60 days of commencing production, you must provide this office with the following information regarding you liquid hydrocarbon production:

    (1)   °API gravity,
    (2)   pour point (°C), and
    (3)   viscosity (Centipoise at 25 °C).

3. Please be advised that exploration activities were recently approved for lease OCS-G 21218, Block 601, Green Canyon Area, which could potentially interfere with your proposed activities. Therefore, you should contact Mr. Joe Schneider, Marathon Oil Company, Post Office Box 3128, Houston, TX 77253 [Phone: (713) 296-1927, Email: JJSCHNEIDER@MARATHONOIL.COM], prior to commencement of your activities, in order to avoid any potential conflicts.

4. In your plan, you have stated that your proposed activities are in the vicinity of areas that could support high-density chemosynthetic communities. Therefore, please be reminded that you will use a state-of-the-art positioning system (e.g., differential global positioning system) on your anchor handling vessel to ensure that any sea floor disturbance resulting from your use of anchors (including that caused by the anchors, anchor chains, and wire ropes) does not occur within 250 feet of such areas (see the enclosed map which depicts the areas). Additionally, you will submit plats, at a scale of 1 inch equals 1,000 feet with DGPS accuracy, to this office within 60 days after completion of operations which depict the "as placed" location of all anchors, anchor chains, and wire ropes and demonstrate that the features were not physically impacted by these anchoring activities.

TABLE OF CONTENTS

FIGURES

TABLES

INTRODUCTION

The Minerals Management Service (MMS) developed a comprehensive strategy for postlease National Environmental Policy Act (NEPA) compliance in deepwater areas (water depths of greater than 400 m) of the Central and Western Planning Areas of the Gulf of Mexico (GOM). You can find an in-depth discussion of this strategy on our Internet site at the following address:

www.gomr.mms.gov/homepg/regulate/environ/strategy/strategy.html.

The MMS's strategy led to the development of a biologically based grid system to ensure broad and systematic analysis of the GOM's deepwater region. The grid system divided the Gulf into 17 areas or "grids" of biological similarity. Under this strategy, the MMS will prepare a programmatic environmental assessment (PEA) to address a proposed development project within each of the 17 grids. These Grid PEA's will be comprehensive in terms of the impact-producing factors and environmental and socioeconomic resources described and analyzed.

Once a PEA for a grid has been completed, it will serve as a reference document to implement the "tiering" (40 CFR 1502.20) concept detailed in NEPA's implementing regulations. Future environmental evaluations may reference appropriate sections from the PEA to reduce reiteration of issues and effects previously addressed in the "grid" document. This will allow the subsequent environmental analyses for individual plans within the grid to focus on specific issues and effects related to the proposals. The PEA also addresses categorical exclusion criterion C.(10)(1) (from 516 DM 6 Appendix 10) by summarizing information to characterize the environment of the Grid.

This PEA characterizes the environment of Grid 10 and also examines the effects that may result from the site-specific activities proposed in BP Exploration and Production, Inc.'s Joint Initial Development Operations Coordination Document (DOCD) for the Holstein Project (N-7216). To the extent possible, the PEA will also evaluate other potential activities proposed or known within Grid 10.

Figure 1 shows the relationship of Grid 10 to the Gulf's coastline and to the other 17 grids. Green Canyon Blocks 644 and 645 are highlighted.

Figure 2 depicts the protraction diagrams and blocks that are contained in Grid 10. The highlighted blocks (Green Canyon Blocks 644 and 645) are the proposed location for the Holstein Project activities.

Current Status of Grid 10

The purpose of this section is to provide the reader with a "state of the grid." Information in this section is based on current MMS data and publicly announced prospects that are projected for Grid 10. See Appendix E for additional information and supportive data.

Grid 10 includes portions of the Green Canyon, Garden Banks, Keathley Canyon, and Walker Ridge Outer Continental Shelf (OCS) protraction diagrams. Table 1 provides information on the protraction diagrams, blocks, leases, and acreage in Grid 10.

Table 1

Protraction Diagram, Blocks, Leases, and Acreage in Grid 10

Protraction Diagrams	No. of Grid Blocks	Approximate Acreage in Grid	No. of Grid Blocks Leased	Percentage of Grid Blocks Leased
Green Canyon	415	2,390,400	250	60%
Garden Banks	20	115,200	10	50%
Keathley Canyon	14	80,640	3	21%
Walker Ridge	142	817,920	90	63%
Grid Totals	591	3,404,160	353	60%

Green Canyon constitutes approximately 70 percent of the total number of blocks in the grid. It also contains about 71 percent of the total number of leases in the grid. Walker Ridge is the second largest component of the grid. It contains approximately 24 percent of the total number of blocks in the grid and has slightly over 25 percent of the total leases. Garden Banks and Keathley Canyon contribute about 3 percent and 2 percent, respectively, to the total number of blocks and leases. Overall, about 60 percent of all the blocks in the grid are leased.

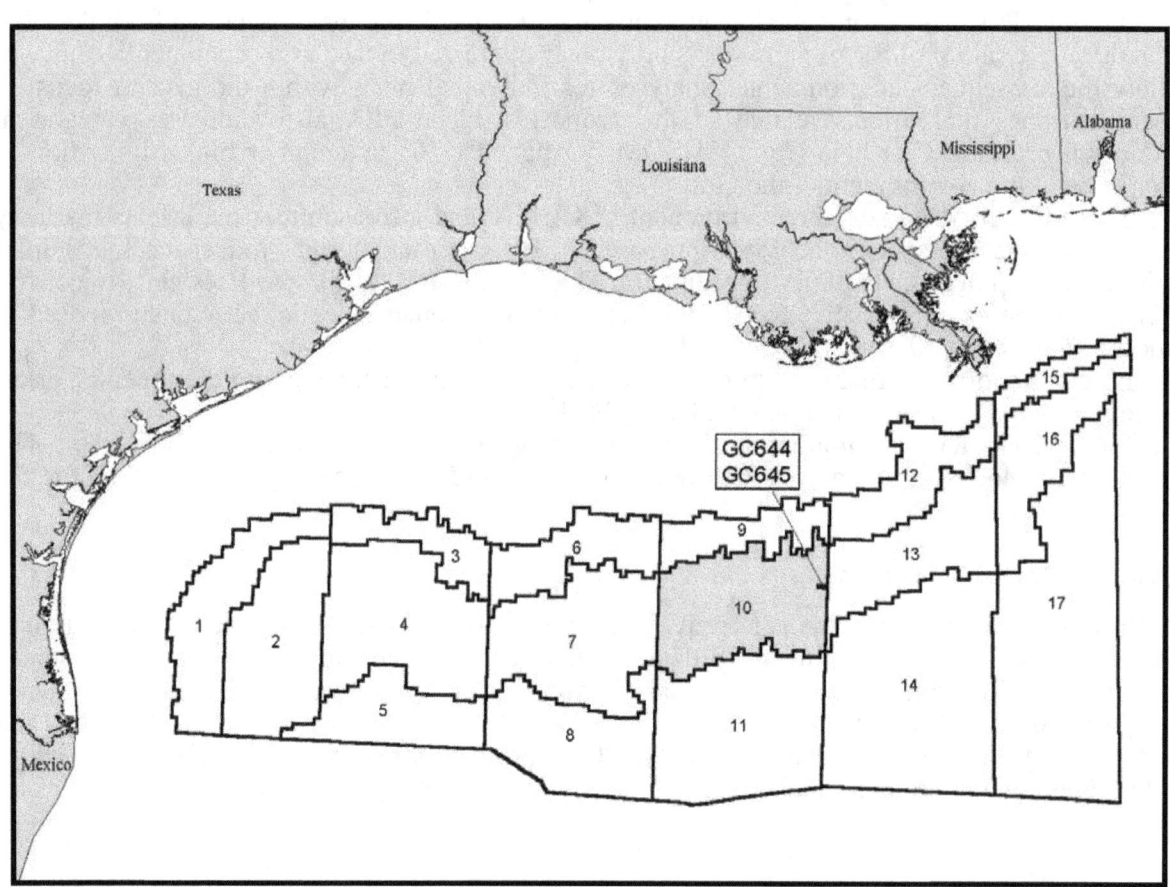

Figure 1. Grid 10 in Relationship to the Gulf Coastline and to Other Grids.

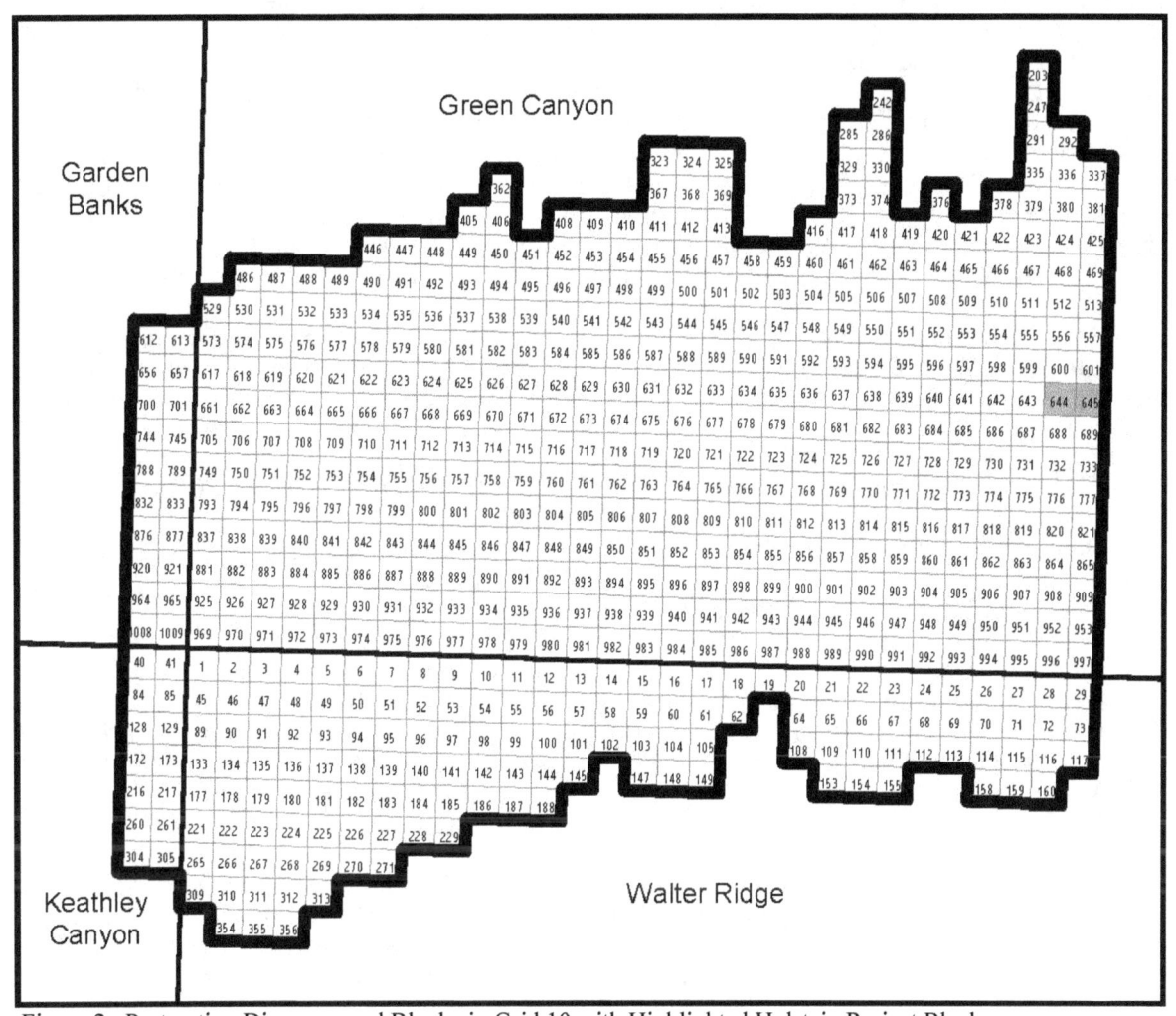

Figure 2. Protraction Diagrams and Blocks in Grid 10 with Highlighted Holstein Project Blocks.

Figure 3 depicts the bathymetry of Grid 10 in 10-meter contour intervals.

Green Canyon Blocks 644 and 645 lie in the W-92 Military Warning Area (MWA). See Figure 4 for the boundaries of this MWA. All leased blocks within the grid and that are contained within the MWA will have stipulations included within their leases regarding specific Department of Defense mitigative measures, i.e., hold and save harmless, electromagnetic emissions, and operational considerations. For additional information regarding these stipulations, see the Final Environmental Impact Statement (EIS) for Central GOM Lease Sales 169, 172, 175, 178, and 182 (USDOI, MMS, 1997a).

A portion of the Gulfmex No. 2 Lightering Zone is in Grid 10. On August 29, 1995, the U.S. Coast Guard designated four areas within the GOM for the offloading of hydrocarbons at sea from very large tankers to smaller tankers that could transport the hydrocarbons to coastal terminals. The deep draft of the fully loaded large tankers prohibits these vessels from docking at shore-based port facilities. Lightering areas are more fully discussed in the GOM Deepwater Operations and Activities Environmental Assessment (USDOI, MMS, 2000).

At present, there are 29 operators and/or leaseholders in Grid 10. These operators include

Agip Petroleum Co. Inc.
Amerada Hess Corporation
Amoco Production Company
BHP Petroleum (GOM) Inc.
BP Exploration & Production Inc.
Chevron U.S.A. Inc.
Conoco Inc.
Devon Energy Production Company, L.P.
Dominion Exploration & Production, Inc.
EEX Corporation
Exxon Asset Management Company
Exxon Mobil Corporation
Kerr-McGee Oil & Gas Corporation
Marathon Oil Company
Mariner Energy, Inc.

Maxus (U.S.) Exploration Company
Mobil Oil Exploration & Producing Southeast Inc.
Mobil Producing Texas & New Mexico Inc.
Murphy Exploration & Production Company
Nexen Petroleum Offshore U.S.A. Inc.
Ocean Energy, Inc.
OXY USA Inc.
RME Petroleum Company
Samedan Oil Corporation
Shell Offshore Inc.
Spinnaker Exploration Company, L.L.C.
Texaco Exploration and Production Inc.
Union Oil Company of California
Vastar Resources, Inc.

Figure 5 geographically depicts the leasehold position of these operators within Grid 10.

The Grid's active lease status and plans submitted data are portrayed in Figure 6. A total of 45 (about 13%) of the leased blocks have Exploration Plans (EP's) approved by the MMS. There is one DOCD filed on two blocks within the Grid, BP's Holstein Project, Green Canyon, Blocks 644 and 645. No leases are currently producing within the grid.

There are three publicly announced prospects contained within Grid 10: Holstein (Green Canyon, Blocks 644 and 645), Fuji (Green Canyon, Block 506), and McKinley (Green Canyon, Block 416). Figure 7 shows these prospect locations, as well as the locations of wells drilled within the Grid.

Figure 8 is a pie chart that depicts the status of wells within Grid 10.

At this time, there are no production structures or pipelines within Grid 10. BP's Holstein Project will add the first spar and pipelines to the grid.

There are numerous onshore support bases that are available along the Gulf Coast and that could serve as logistical infrastructure for Grid 10. In the current proposal, BP chose Fourchon and Venicce, Louisiana, as its onshore bases to support the proposed operations. Figure 9 shows the relationship of Grid 10 to these shorebases. The distances in miles from the Grid to the shorebases are also depicted on Figure 9.

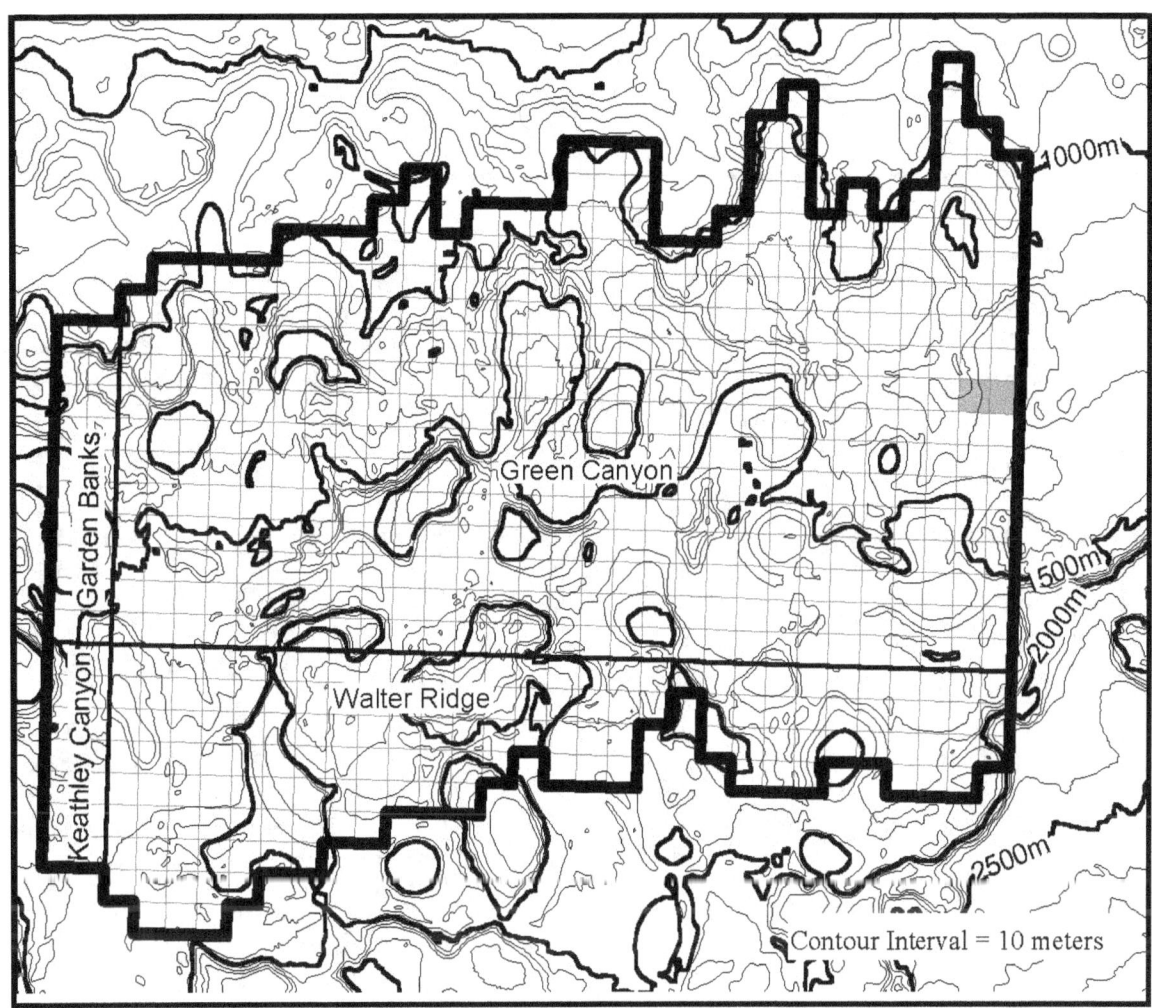

Figure 3. Bathymetry of Grid 10 (contour interval is 10 m).

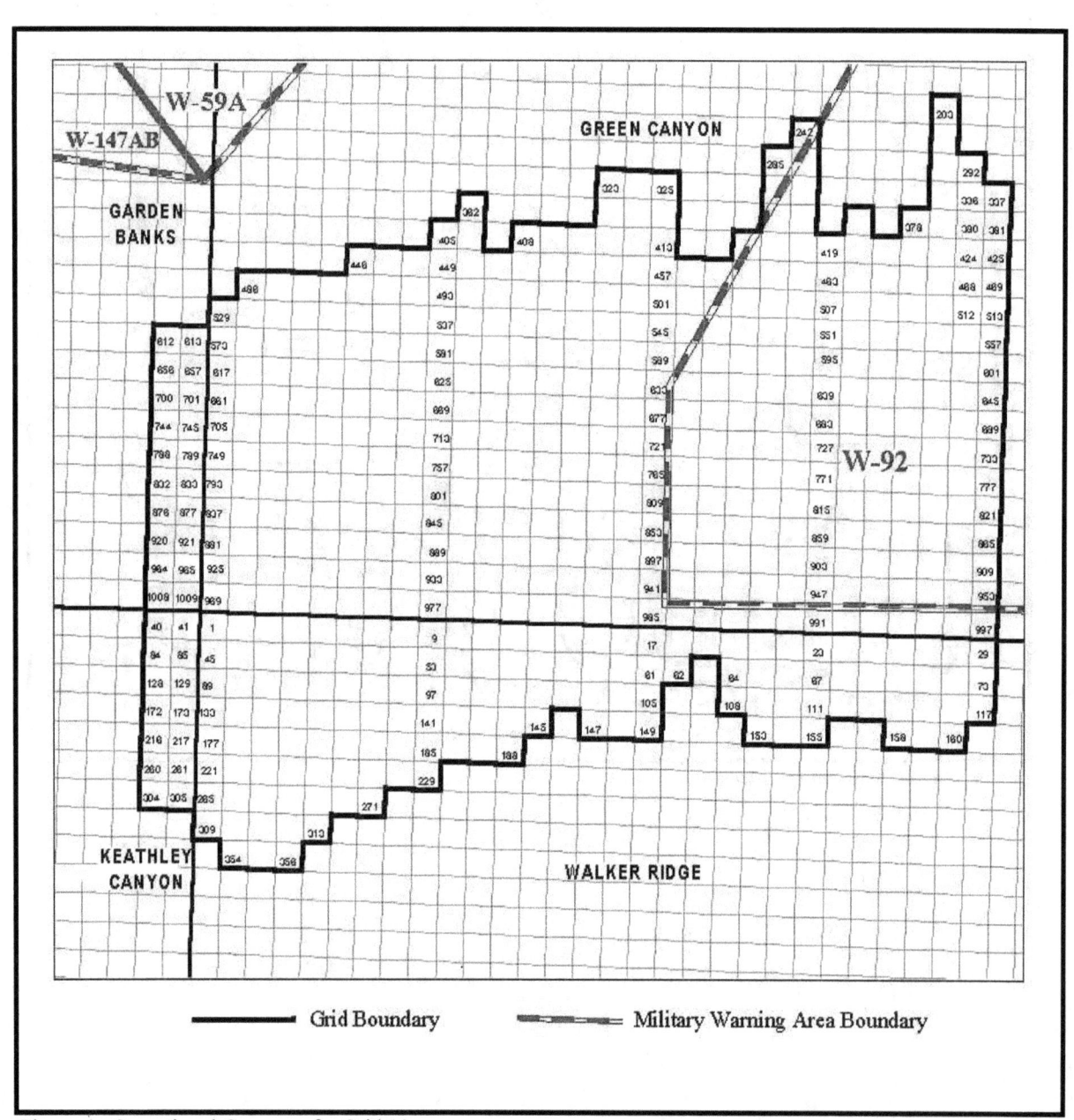

Figure 4. Operational Concerns for Grid 10.

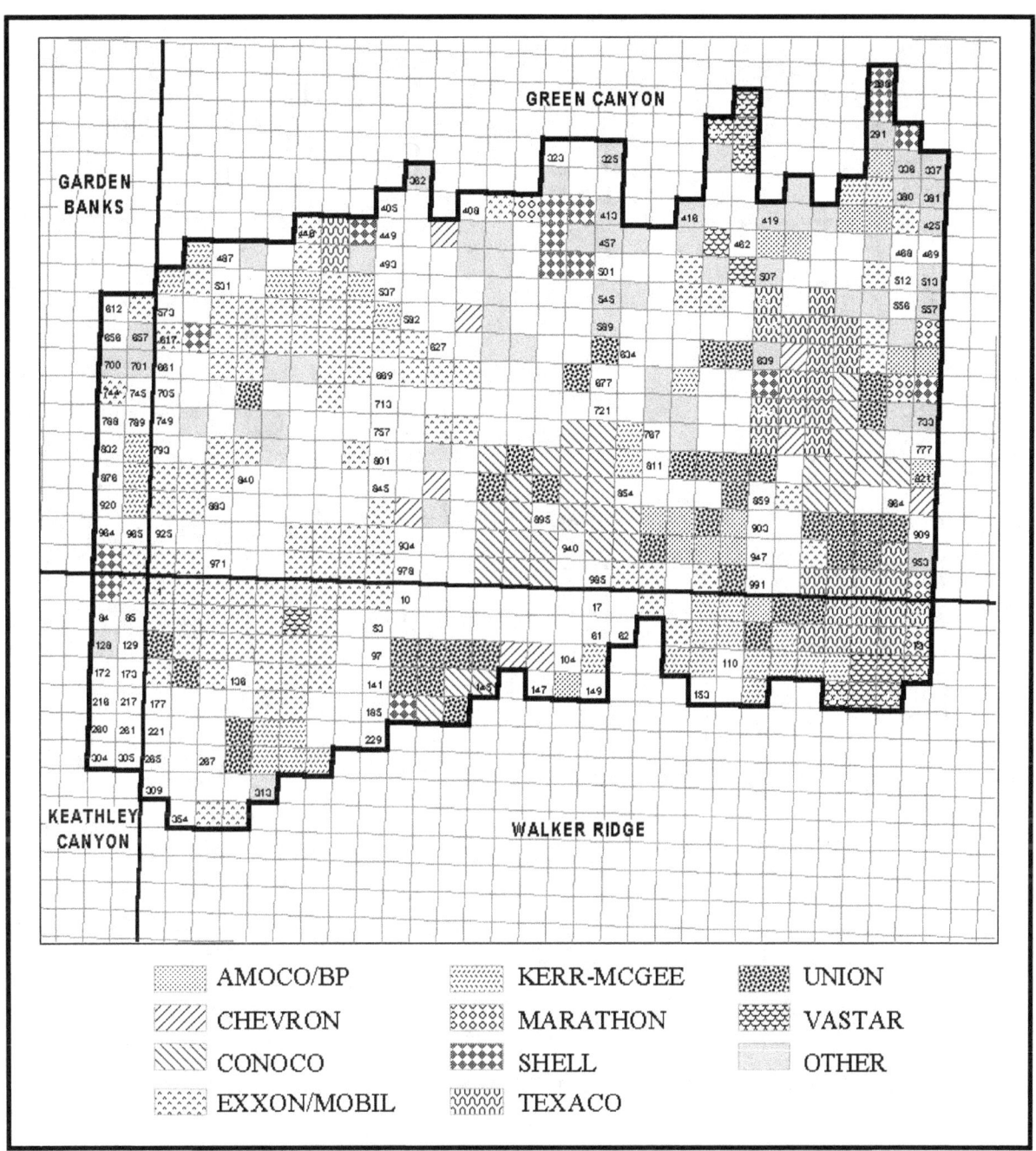

Figure 5. Leasehold Position of Operators within Grid 10.

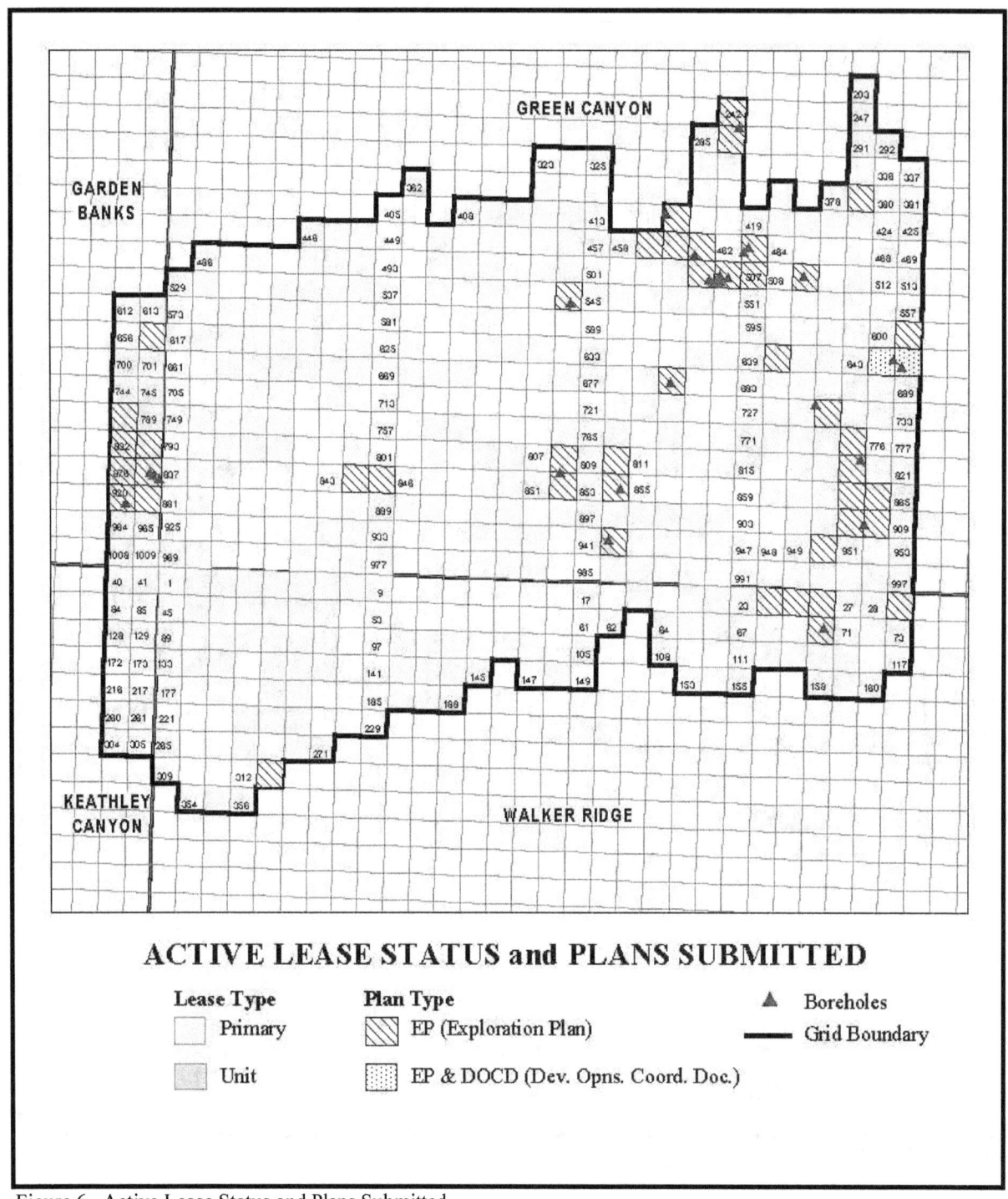

Figure 6. Active Lease Status and Plans Submitted.

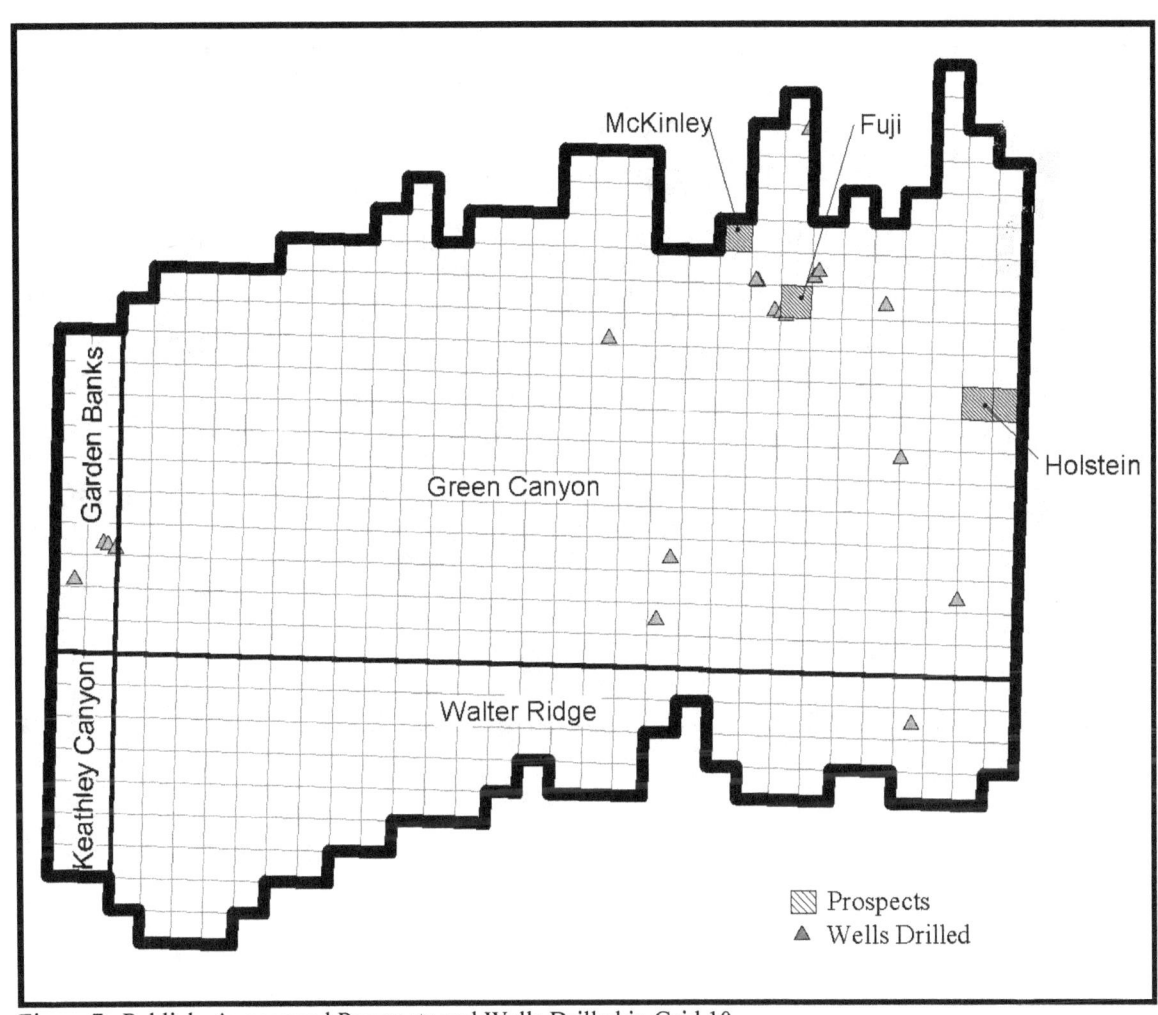

Figure 7. Publicly Announced Prospects and Wells Drilled in Grid 10.

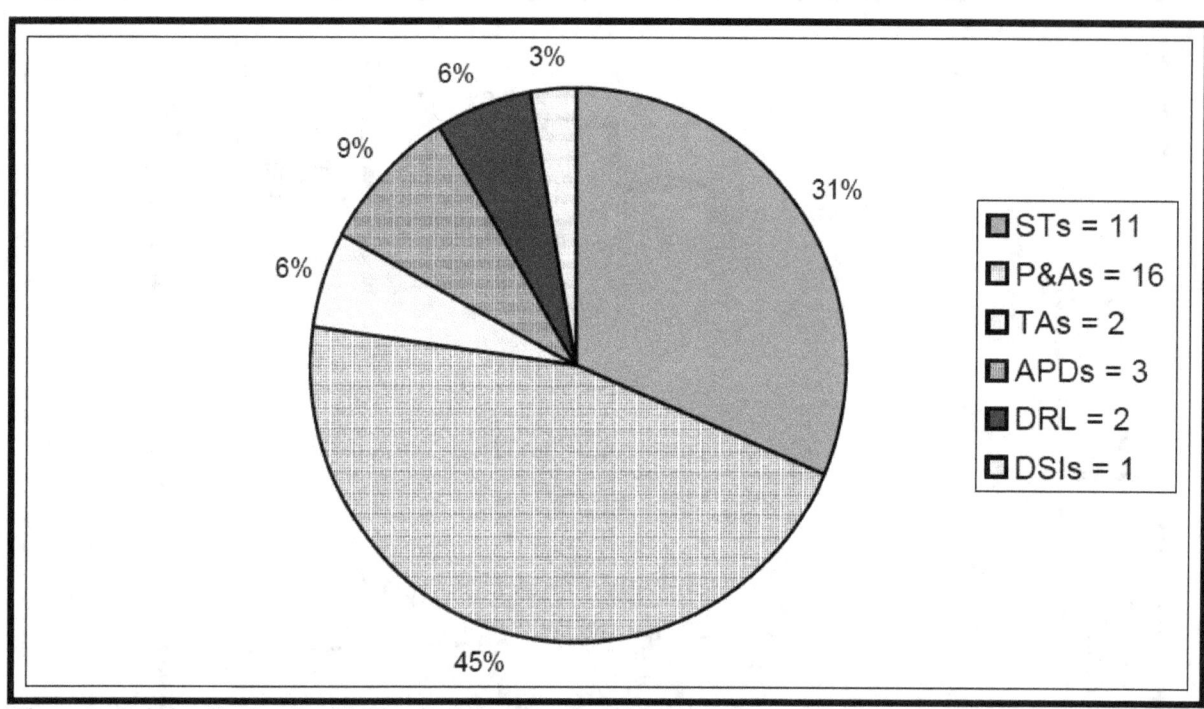

Figure 8. Existing Exploration Drilling Activities Conducted in Grid 10.

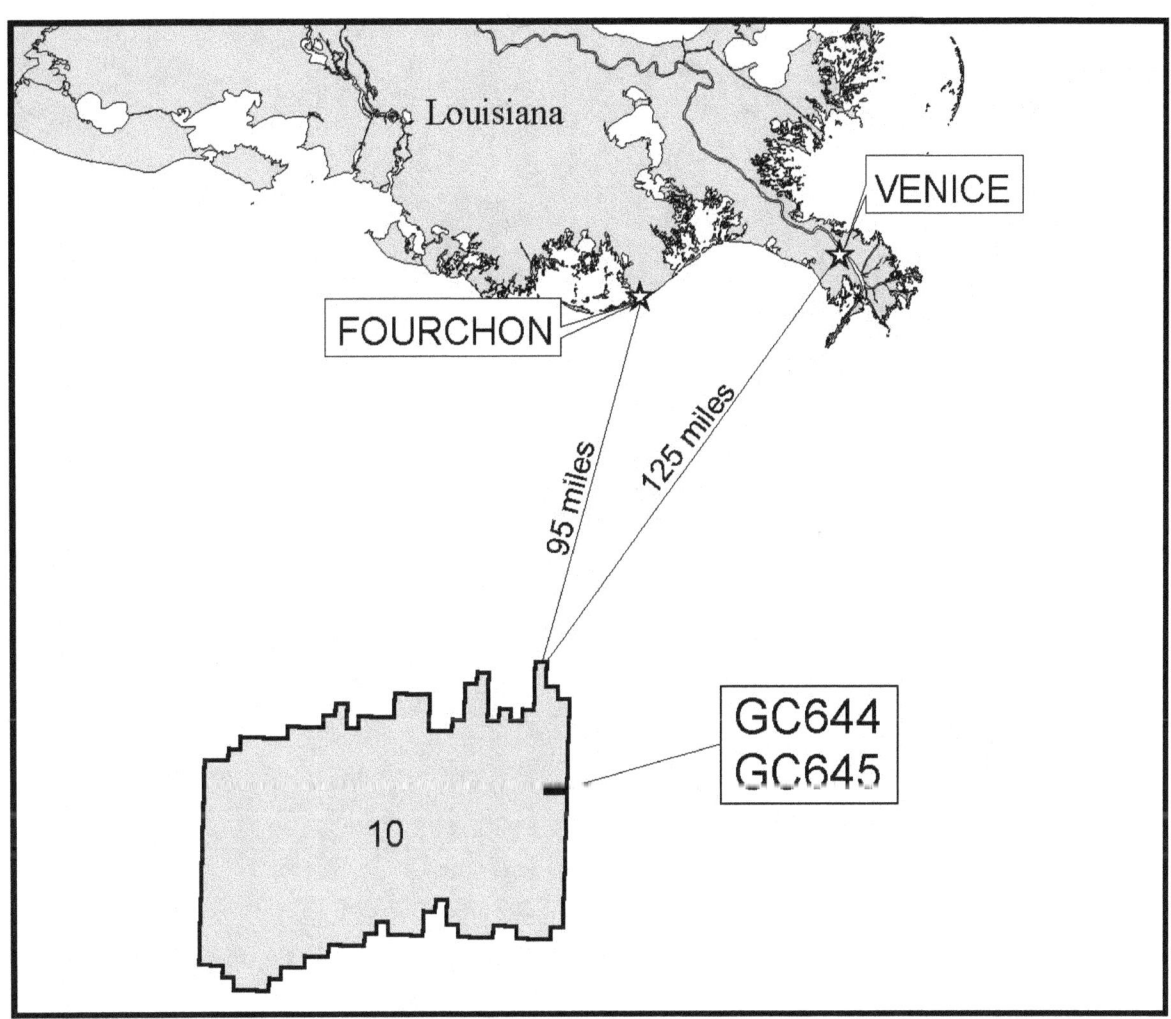

Figure 9. Distance from Grid 10 to BP's Selected Shorebase.

1. THE PROPOSED ACTION

1.1. PURPOSE AND NEED FOR THE PROPOSED ACTION

Under the Outer Continental Shelf Lands Act (OCSLA), as amended, the U.S. Department of the Interior (DOI) is required to manage the leasing, exploration, development, and production of oil and gas resources on the Federal OCS. The Secretary of the Interior oversees the OCS oil and gas program and is required to balance orderly resource development with protection of the human, marine, and coastal environments while simultaneously ensuring that the public receives an equitable return for these resources and that free-market competition is maintained.

The purpose of this programmatic environmental assessment (PEA) is two-fold. It assesses the specific and cumulative impacts associated with the proposed action and also provides information on the deepwater area within Grid 10. The document can be used as a basis to allow most subsequent activities proposed in the grid to be processed as CER's. However, if it is determined that a subsequent proposal will require preparation of a site-specific EA, the PEA provides sufficient information so it can be referenced (tiered) in the site-specific EA (SEA). The SEA will be focused on a few key issues. The grid area was determined by the MMS's implementing regulations for the National Environmental Policy Act (NEPA) to be an area of "relatively untested deep water" [516 DM Chapter 6, Appendix 10,C. (10) (1)]. To properly characterize the grid, the PEA captures all of the available environmental and operational information for the area. Chapter 3 describes the environment at the specific site of the proposed activities and in the broader grid area. Analyses within Chapter 4 examine the potential effects of the proposed action and other reasonably foreseeable activities within the grid on the environment in the vicinity of the proposal and on the broader grid area.

BP Exploration and Production, Inc.'s (BP) Initial Unit Development Operations Coordination Document (DOCD) represents an action that cannot be categorically excluded because it represents activities in relatively untested deep water [516 DM Chapter 6, Appendix 10, C. (10)(1)].

This PEA of the Grid implements the "tiering" process outlined in 40 CFR 1502.20, which encourages agencies to tier environmental documents, eliminating repetitive discussions of the same issue. By use of tiering from the most recent Final Environmental Impact Statement (EIS) for Central GOM Lease Sales 169, 172, 175, 178, and 182 (USDOI, MMS, 1997a), and by summarizing and referencing related environmental documents, this PEA concentrates on environmental effects and issues specific to the proposed action and proposed activities within the Grid.

1.2. DESCRIPTION OF THE PROPOSED ACTION

The MMS GOM Region, Office of Field Operations, received an Initial Unit DOCD from BP that proposes to drill and complete 15 wells, re-enter and complete the existing appraisal well, install a truss spar, and commence hydrocarbon production in the Green Canyon Blocks 644 Unit (Unit Agreement Number 754399004) composed of Blocks 644 (OCS-G 11080) and 645 (OCS-G 11081). Previous plans on these leases include N-6263 (Exploration Plan) and R-3298 (Revised Exploration Plan). BP's Deepwater Operations Plan, Conceptual Phase, was approved by the MMS with an effective date of June 28, 2001. The planned wells will share a common surface location (a truss spar floating production system) in Green Canyon Block 645. Table 1-1 depicts the spar's proposed location.

Table 1-1

Proposed Location of the Holstein Truss Spar in Green Canyon Block 645

Surface Location	Distance from Lease Lines	Lambert X-Y Coordinates	Latitude/Longitude
Holstein Truss Spar	FWL 1,149 ft FSL 6,235 ft	X = 2,440,510 Y = 9,922,076	Lat. 27° 19' 16.43" N. Long. 90° 32' 07.67" W.

Note: FWL is from the west line of the lease.
FSL is from the south line of the lease.

The design premise for BP's Holstein Field also includes provisions for up to three subsea tiebacks to the spar.

The Holstein truss spar is a manned, floating production facility that will be permanently anchored on location by a 16-line (4 by 4 spread), semi-taut leg mooring system composed of conventional steel spiral strand wire, chain, and anchor (suction) piles. The hull portion of the spar measures approximately 45.5 m (149 ft) in diameter and has an overall length of approximately 214.9 m (705 ft). The spar and associated equipment have a 30-year design life. The spar will be installed with a dynamically positioned derrick barge.

Batch/pre-drill operations will be performed from a mobile offshore drilling unit (MODU) and then a platform rig will be installed onto the truss spar for all subsequent operations. The spar's rig will be both drilling and completion capable, and designed to operate independently of the rest of the platform and to be removable. This rig will be used for the initial completion operations and for performing any necessary well re-completions, sidetracks, or workovers. Water injection operations are planned for enhancing hydrocarbon production. BP plans to inject the produced water as a part of these operations.

The spar is designed to accommodate a normal complement of 140-150 personnel. However, the maximum capacity is 260 personnel.

The water depth at the truss spar location is approximately 1,324 m (4,344 ft). The deepwater development is located approximately 191 km (118.7 mi) from the nearest Louisiana shoreline. The project will use existing onshore support bases in Fourchon and Venice, Louisiana, to support the proposed activities [about 201 km and 245 km (125 mi and 152.5 mi), respectively, to the proposed spar location].

Hydrocarbon production from the Holstein Project will be transported off lease by two proposed right-of-way pipelines. A proposed 24-in liquid hydrocarbon right-of-way pipeline will tie into a yet to be determined existing platform location in shallow water. From there, production will enter the existing pipeline infrastructure for shipment to the shore. A proposed 20-in natural gas right-of-way pipeline will depart the spar and tie into the existing gas pipeline infrastructure for transport to the shore. The environmental effects from these proposed transportation operations will be evaluated in MMS-prepared environmental documents when the pipeline applications are received. Mitigative measures may be included in these evaluations to minimize or eliminate potential environmental effects from the proposed activities.

1.2.1. Activity Schedule

Table 1-2 shows the activity schedule proposed by BP for their Holstein Project.

Table 1-2

Proposed Activity Schedule for the Holstein Project

Activity	Start Date	End Date
MODU OPERATIONS		
Batch set casing strings on 15 wells	12/01/01	06/11/02
Predrill 5 wells to their total depth	06/11/02	01/03/03
INSTALLATION OPERATIONS		
Pre-set moorings	07/01/03	08/01/03
Upend hull and set temporary work deck	11/08/03	11/14/03
Connect moorings and fixed ballast	11/15/03	12/19/03
Remove temporary work deck	12/20/03	12/20/03
Install spar-supported vertical risers (SSVR)	12/20/03	12/21/03
Install south and north modules and helideck	12/22/03	01/06/04
Install spar rig	01/07/04	01/09/04
Hook-up and commissioning	01/07/04	06/08/04
SPAR RIG OPERATIONS		
Reenter and tie-back 5 predrilled wells	03/26/04	05/26/04
Complete first predrilled well	05/26/04	06/30/04
Commence first production	06/30/04	N/A
Complete four predrilled wells	06/30/04	10/20/04
Drill to TD and complete 10 wells	10/20/04	02/05/06
Reenter and complete GC 645 Well No. 1	02/06/06	03/24/06

1.2.2. New or Unusual Technology

BP has proposed the use of two new or unusual technologies in its DOCD. They are as follows: (1) spar supported vertical risers and (2) specially designed well casing programs. See BP's DOCD submittal for a full discussion of these technologies (BP, 2001).

An alternative riser tensioning system, a spar supported vertical riser system, is being proposed for the Holstein Project. The wells will be connected to the topside facilities by vertical risers. Dual casing risers are proposed (a 14 3/4-in outer riser and a 11 3/4-in inner riser). Production and injection tubing are 5 1/2-in tubulars.

Each riser will be supported by a dedicated hydropneumatic tensioner assembly that is mounted on the spar's deck. These tensioners will be similar to units currently in service to support a drilling riser on a GOM spar facility.

The use of tensioners on all the vertical risers is believed to be a new application of this technology on a spar development. All spar developments to date have used air can systems to tension the production risers. A key feature of the new system is the "tuned" tensioner stiffness that limits the risers' stroke, relative to the spar, to typically less than 1 ft in all but the most extreme conditions. This low stroke movement will permit the use of a conventional access deck around the surface well trees, thus providing increased safety during tree installation, routine operations, and well intervention activities.

Limiting the risers' stroke is achieved by permitting higher riser loads than typically generated by air can tensioning systems. Studies performed to date have demonstrated that these higher riser system loads can be accommodated by currently available riser and equipment designs.

Environmental review of the vertical riser system determined that the spar-supported vertical riser system will not interact with the environment any differently than the traditional air can system. Increased safety may be realized during certain well activities with this technology.

3

BP is proposing two well design casing programs: (1) "unitized drilling riser" and (2) "combo riser." For both cases, the MODU will batch set the 36-in conductors, the 20-in surface casing, and the 13 3/8-in intermediate casing prior to the installation of the truss spar. BP's "unitized drilling riser" case uses the traditional inner and outer drilling risers with the advantage that the risers need to be run only once for the initial drilling and completion program. After the spar installation, drilling below the 13 3/8-in casing to the wells' total depth will be carried out through the drilling risers in dedicated drilling slots in the well bay. The "unitized drilling riser" is then "parked" and the rig is skidded to the relevant well slot for running the production risers and carrying out the well completion operations.

The "combo riser" case allows BP to eliminate the traditional drilling riser. All spar drilling would be done through the production risers. After the spar's installation, the rig would run the outer production riser and drilling would then continue through setting of the 11 3/4-in liner and the 9 5/8-in drilling liner. Either the 11 3/4-in or the 9 5/8-in liner will then be tied back to the surface and will serve as the inner production riser. Further deepening of wells and all well completions will be carried out through the inner production riser.

The "combo riser" case will result in the largest overall rig loads. The rig has to be designed for the higher loads associated with drilling, with the rotary table centered over all well bay slots.

Environmental review of both riser cases determined that neither of the proposals will interact with the environment any differently than "conventional" technology.

2. ALTERNATIVES TO THE PROPOSED ACTION

2.1. NONAPPROVAL OF THE PROPOSAL

BP would not be allowed to drill, complete, and produce the 16 wells proposed in its Joint Initial DOCD. This alternative would result in no impact from the proposed action but could discourage the development of much needed hydrocarbon resources, and thereby result in a loss of royalty income for the United States and energy for America. Considering these aspects and the fact that we anticipate very minor environmental and human effects resulting from the proposed action, this alternative was not selected for further analysis.

2.2. APPROVAL OF THE PROPOSAL WITH EXISTING AND/OR ADDED MITIGATION

Measures that BP proposes to implement to limit potential environmental effects are discussed in their Joint Initial DOCD. The MMS's lease stipulations, Outer Continental Shelf Operating Regulations, Notices to Lessees and Operators, and other regulations and laws were identified throughout this environmental assessment as existing mitigation to minimize potential environmental effects associated with the proposed action. Additional information can be found in the Final EIS for Central GOM Lease Sales 169, 172, 175, 178, and 182 (USDOI, MMS, 1997a). Considering the above mitigative measures, this alternative was selected for evaluation in this PEA.

3. DESCRIPTION OF THE AFFECTED ENVIRONMENT

3.1. PHYSICAL ELEMENTS OF THE ENVIRONMENT

3.1.1. Water Quality

3.1.1.1. Coastal Waters

Although the Holstein development is over 161 km (100 mi) from the Louisiana coastline, nearshore water quality is addressed in this document for the following three reasons:

- the service bases for the development are located on or near the coast;

- marine transportation to and from the site will traverse coastal waters; and

- there is a low probability that accidental spills may make landfall in this region.

The bays, estuaries, and nearshore coastal waters of the Gulf are highly important in that they provide feeding, breeding, and/or nursery habitat for many commercially-important invertebrates and fishes, sea turtles, birds, and mammals. Water quality governs the suitability of these areas for animal as well as human use. Furthermore, the egg, larval, and juvenile stages of marine biota dependent upon these areas are typically more sensitive to the degradation of the water quality than are their adult stages. The quality of coastal waters is, therefore, an important issue. A comprehensive assessment of water quality in coastal and estuarine waters of the GOM is contained in USEPA (1999).

The water quality in the coastal waters of the GOM is highly influenced by season. For example, salinity in open water near the coast may vary between 29 and 32 parts per thousand (ppt) during fall and winter, but falls to 20 ppt during spring and summer due to increased runoff (USDOI, MMS, 2001a). Oxygen and nutrient concentrations also vary seasonally.

More than 30 percent of the estuaries along the Gulf have impaired water quality to the point that they cannot support beneficial uses such as aquatic life support, and recreational and commercial fisheries (USEPA, 1999). Some of the industries and activities contributing to water quality degradation include petrochemical, agricultural, power production, pulp and paper, fish processing, municipal waste, shipping, and dredging. There are over 3,700 point sources of contamination that flow into the Gulf (Weber et al., 1992, in USDOI, MMS, 2001a), with municipalities, refineries and petrochemical plants accounting for the majority of these point sources (USDOI, MMS, 2001a). Most of the industrial sources are in Texas and Louisiana with much lesser numbers in the remaining Gulf States. Vessels from the shipping and fishing industries as well as recreational boaters add a significant amount of contaminants to coastal waters in the form of bilge water, waste, spills, and leaching from anti-fouling paints. Many millions of cubic feet of sediments are moved each year in coastal areas in channelization, dredging, dredge disposal, shoreline modification in support of shipping, oil and gas, and other activities. Water quality may be affected by these activities as they can facilitate saltwater intrusion, increased turbidity, and release of contaminants.

Nonpoint sources of contamination such as forestry, agriculture, and urban runoff are difficult to regulate and probably have the greatest impact on coastal water quality (USDOI, MMS, 2001a). Inland cities, farms, ranches, and various industries drain into waterways that empty into the GOM. About 80 percent of U.S. cropland drains into the Gulf. The GOM coastal area alone used 10 million pounds of pesticides in 1987 (USDOI, MMS, 2001a). Nutrient enrichment (nitrogen and phosphorus), mostly from river runoff, is another major water quality problem that can lead to noxious algal blooms, reduced seagrasses, fish kills, and oxygen depletion. The Mississippi River alone has been estimated to contribute more than 341,000 pounds of phosphorus and approximately 1.68 million pounds of nitrogen to the Gulf per day.

Biological indicators of poor coastal water quality are evident in the GOM area. Approximately 50 percent of the largest U.S. fish kills between 1980 and 1989 occurred in Texas and 50 percent of shellfish beds in Louisiana are closed annually because of contamination (USDOI, MMS, 2001a). Although the Gulf States had a number of "hot spots" for certain locations and contaminants, they did not fare that badly when compared to other U.S. coastal waters during the major NOAA National Status and Trends Mussel Watch Program (USDOI, MMS, 2001a).

3.1.1.2. Offshore Waters

The five watermasses identified in the physical oceanography section of this document (Appendix D) can be recognized by their chemical characteristics, e.g., salinity, dissolved oxygen (DO), nitrate, phosphate, and silicate. Offshore marine waters in the GOM are characterized by higher salinity concentrations (36.0 to 36.5 ppt) than coastal and inshore waters (USDOI, MMS, 2001a).

The distribution of DO and nutrients in the waters of the Gulf vary with depth. The DO concentrations are highest at the surface due to photosynthesis and exchange with the atmosphere and generally decreases with depth due to respiration by various organisms (including bacteria). However, higher DO concentrations may be encountered in cold watermasses. Nutrient concentrations show an inverse relationship to the DO concentrations. Nutrients reach their lowest levels in the upper water layers where they become depleted by photosynthetic activity. They reach their highest levels in the Gulf's deepwater areas. Nutrient and oxygen concentrations in the open water of the deep Gulf are not usually measurably affected by anthropogenic inputs.

There are several phenomena that occur in the Gulf and that dramatically effect the area's water quality. Examples of these include hypersaline basins (e.g., 250 ppt in the Orca Basin) and the nepheloid layer, a thin, near-bottom, highly turbid zone that may play a role in transporting material, including contaminants, from nearshore to offshore waters. Another example is hypoxic or oxygen-depleted bottom waters that may occur in the northern Gulf off the mouth of the Mississippi River. This hypoxic area may become very large (16,500 km^2) and stretch from the river delta area to Freeport, Texas. This phenomenon is probably exacerbated by human inputs (USDOI, MMS, 2001a). Near-hypoxic conditions, unrelated to the river plume, may also be observed in oceanic zones of oxygen minimums at depths between 200 and 400 m (656-1,312 ft). These conditions have low enough DO concentrations (2.5-3.0 ml/l) to affect the biota (USDOI, MMS, 2001a).

Land-derived material is widespread in the Gulf due to large riverine inputs and transport across the shelf to the slope by slumping, slope failure (Gallaway et al., 2001), and other processes. Natural seepage is considered to be a major source of petroleum hydrocarbons in the Gulf slope area (Kennicutt et al., 1987; Gallaway et al., 2001; USDOI, MMS, 2001a).

The Northern Gulf of Mexico Continental Slope Study (NGMCS) (1988) found that the concentration of hydrocarbons in slope sediments (except in seep areas) was lower than previous reports for shelf and coastal sediments, but no consistent decrease with increasing water depth was apparent below 300 m or 984 ft (Gallaway et al., 2001). In general, the Central Gulf had higher levels of hydrocarbons, particularly those from terrestrial sources, than the Western Gulf (Gallaway and Kennicutt, 1988). Total organic carbon was also highest in the Central Gulf. Hydrocarbons in sediments have been determined to influence biological communities of the Gulf slope, even when present in trace amounts (Gallaway and Kennicutt, 1988).

3.1.2. Air Quality

The proposed operations would occur west of 87.5 degrees west longitude and hence fall under the MMS's jurisdiction for enforcement of the Clean Air Act. The air over the OCS water is not classified, but it is presumed to be better than the National Ambient Air Quality Standards for all criteria pollutants. The blocks involved, Green Canyon Blocks 644 and 645, are offshore, south of Terrebonne Parish, Louisiana. Terrebonne Parish is in the attainment of the National Ambient Air Quality Standards (USEPA, 2001).

The primary meteorological influences upon air quality and the dispersion of emissions are the wind speed and direction, the atmospheric stability, and the mixing height. The general wind flow for this area is driven by the clockwise circulation around the Bermuda High, resulting in a prevailing southeasterly to southerly flow. Superimposed upon this circulation are smaller scale effects such as the sea breeze effect, tropical cyclones, and mid-latitude frontal systems. Because of the various factors, the winds blow from all directions in the area of concern (USDOI, MMS, 1988).

Not all of the Pasquill-Gifford stability classes are routinely found offshore in the GOM. Specifically, the F stability class is rare. This is the extremely stable condition that usually develops at night over land with rapid radiative cooling; this large segment of the GOM is simply incapable of loosing enough heat overnight to set up a strong radiative inversion. Likewise, the A stability class is also rare. It is the extremely unstable condition that requires a very rapid warming of the lower layer of the atmosphere, along with cold air aloft. This is normally brought about when cold air is advected in aloft and strong insolation rapidly warms the earth's surface that, in turn, warms the lowest layer of the atmosphere. Once again, the ocean surface is incapable of warming rapidly; therefore, you would not expect to find stability class A over the GOM. For the most part, the stability is slightly unstable to neutral.

The mixing heights offshore are quite shallow, generally 900 m (2,953 ft) or less. The exception to this is close to shore, where the influence of the land penetrates out over the water for a short distance. Transient cold fronts also have an impact on the mixing heights; some of the lowest heights can be expected to occur with frontal passages and on the cold air side of the fronts. This effect is caused by the frontal inversion.

BP's estimated air emissions for this proposed project are summarized below in Table 3-1. These estimates represent the worst case scenario for the proposed project. The MMS' exemption levels are also shown for comparison.

Table 3-1

Projected Emissions for the Holstein Project

Year	PM	SO$_x$	NO$_x$	VOC	CO
2001	3.34	15.24	114.28	3.44	24.93
2002	23.33	106.31	797.28	24.08	173.95
2003	104.77	480.62	3601.41	108.04	785.76
2004	86.14	389.81	3302.69	105.41	880.82
2005	30.16	127.75	1714.58	64.00	691.95
2006	9.04	30.87	988.61	42.22	533.55
2007-2024	3.96	7.55	813.88	36.97	495.43

Note: The MMS's exemption levels for PM, SO$_x$, NO$_x$, and VOC is 3,952.71 tons, while the exemption level for CO is 82,119.46 tons.

3.2. BIOLOGICAL RESOURCES

3.2.1. Sensitive Coastal Environments

General information on the types and status of coastal landforms in the central and western Gulf is contained in USDOI, MMS (2001a). A brief description of that information is summarized below.

Barrier landforms include islands, spits, dunes, and beaches. They are usually long and narrow in shape, having been formed by reworked sediment transported by waves, currents, storm surges, and winds. Barrier landforms are in a state of constant change and they can be classified into two main types:

- Transgressive—where shorelines move inland and marine sediment deposits overlay terrestrial sediments. This type is usually rapidly eroding, low profile, with numerous washover channels.

- Regressive—where shorelines move seaward and terrestrial sediment deposits overlay marine sediments. This type is characterized by higher profile dunes, with few if any washover channels (USDOI, MMS, 2001a).

Both types are important ecologically. Barrier systems, particularly vegetated ones with fresh- and/or saltwater pools, may serve as habitat for a variety of fairly specialized species, including birds. The islands and spits protect the bays, lagoons, estuaries, salt marshes, seagrass beds, and other wetlands, some of which may contain threatened or endangered species.

The shorebases to be used by the activity, Port Fourchon and Venice, Louisiana, are located in transgressive areas, where rates of shoreline retreat are the highest of those around the Gulf.

3.2.1.1. Wetlands

Wetlands are virtually continuous along the Gulf Coast, especially along the Louisiana coast. Wetlands include seagrass beds, mudflats, mangroves, marshes (fresh, brackish, and salt), and hardwood and cypress-tupelo swamps. They may occur as isolated pockets, narrow bands, or large areas (USDOI, MMS, 2001a).

High-productivity, high-detritus input and extensive nutrient recycling characterize coastal wetlands. They are important habitats for a large number of invertebrate, fish, reptile, bird, and mammal species, including rare and endangered species, and high-value commercial and recreational species for at least part of their life cycles.

The GOM coastal wetlands represent about half of the Nation's wetland area. These wetlands help support the exceptionally productive coastal fisheries (e.g., Gulf ports account for four of the top five ports in the U.S. in terms of landed weight) and about 75 percent of the migratory waterfowl traversing the country (Johnston et al., 1995). The USDOC, NOAA (1991) and (Johnston et al., 1995) estimated that, although wetland area has decreased substantially over the last 30 years, about 1.3 million ha of marshes, estuarine shrub-scrub, and freshwater forested/shrub-scrub remain on the Gulf Coast. Of these three categories, 80 percent is marsh, 19 percent estuarine scrub-shrub, and 1 percent forested wetland. Louisiana has the greatest area with 55 percent of the total (representing 69% of total marsh) followed by Florida (18%) (including 97% of total scrub-shrub, mostly mangrove), Texas (14%), and Mississippi (2%) (Johnston et al., 1995).

The National Biological Service (NBS) provides calculations of wetland losses that are more recent than the NOAA data. The NBS updates its wetland loss data every three years. Based on satellite imagery, NBS suggests that wetland losses are greater than previously thought although the rate of loss appears to be declining (Johnston et al., 1995). Since the 1980's, wetland areas have declined significantly around the Gulf (USDOI, MMS, 2001a). For these reasons, wetlands are an important issue when assessing impacts of coastal developments and/or accidental spills, in situations where spills may impinge on the coast. The shorebases to be used by the proposed activity, Port Fourchon and Venice, Louisiana, are located in areas where rates of wetland loss are the highest around the Gulf.

3.2.1.2. Seagrasses

Seagrass ecosystems are extremely productive and provide important habitat for wintering waterfowl, and spawning and feeding habitat for several species of fish and shellfish, and some endangered and threatened species of manatee and sea turtles. Seagrass losses in the Gulf have been extensive over the last 50 years. Although found in isolated patches and narrow bands along the entire Gulf Coast in shallow, clear, estuarine areas, seagrasses mostly occur in the eastern portion of the GOM between Mobile Bay and Florida Bay. Florida contains about 693,000 ha (about 68%) of the 1.02 million ha estimated for all the Gulf States (Handley, 1995).

Louisiana has a large amount of submerged vegetation but only a small area of seagrass (about 5,657 ha in 1988) (Handley, 1995). The shorebases to be used by the activity, Port Fourchon and Venice, Louisiana, are located in areas where seagrasses are very uncommon.

3.2.2. Deepwater Benthic Communities/Organisms

3.2.2.1. Chemosynthetic Communities

Deep-sea chemosynthetic communities are biological ecosystems that rely on carbon sources derived independent of photosynthetic processes. They are supported symbiotically by bacteria that oxidize compounds such as hydrogen sulfide (H_2S) and methane (CH_4) in the absence of light. These bacteria produce complex organic compounds including proteins and carbohydrates that support higher level organisms such as Vestimentiferan tube worms, infaunal lucinid or thasirid clams, and mytilid mussels (MacDonald et al. 1990). Bacteria live within specialized cells in these invertebrate organisms and are supplied with oxygen and chemosynthetic compounds by the host via specialized blood chemistry (Fisher, 1990). The host, in turn, lives off the organic products subsequently released by the chemosynthetic bacteria and may even feed on the bacteria themselves. Free-living chemosynthetic bacteria may also live in the substrate within the invertebrate communities and may compete with their symbionts for sulfide and methane energy sources.

The reliance of deep-sea chemosynthetic communities on nonphotosynthetic carbon sources limits their distribution in the Gulf to areas where hydrocarbon sources are available. Within the northern Gulf, chemosynthetic communities are generally associated with slow oil and gas seeps, rapid expulsion mud volcanoes, and mineral seeps (Roberts and Carney, 1997). The most common hydrocarbon source is associated with seeps. Oil reservoirs beneath the Gulf include faults within source rock that have allowed oil and gas to migrate upward to the seafloor over the past several million years (Sassen et al., 1993). Hydrocarbons seeping to the surface diffuse through overlying sediments where bacterial degradation creates the chemosynthetic substrate taken up by symbiotic invertebrates. Vestimentiferan tube worms and lucinid and vesicomyid clams rely on H_2S, whereas mytilid mussels utilized dissolved CH_4. Mud volcanoes and mineral seeps provide similar chemosynthetic source material, but their occurrence in the Gulf is far less extensive than oil and gas seeps.

Hydrocarbon seep communities in the Gulf have been reported to occur at water depths between 290 and 2,000 m (Roberts et al., 1990; MacDonald, 1992). A total of 43 significant chemosynthetic communities are known to exist in OCS lease blocks between depths of 300 and 1,000 m, including 18 in Green Canyon (USDOI, MMS, 2000 and 2001a). However, none of these occur in Grid 10 (Figure 3-1). The total number of these communities in the Gulf is now known to exceed 50 (Gallaway et al., 2000). The densest aggregations occur in waters deeper than 500 m. Future identification of chemosynthetic communities would likely rely on a combination of broad-scale geophysical sensing surveys followed by more detailed site-specific protocols including visual surveys by submersibles or remotely-operated vehicles (ROV's). The MMS (USDOI, MMS, 2000) suggests that maps of hydrocarbon discovery and production sites enhanced by the use of seismic and side-scan sonar could be used to identify general localities where chemosynthetic communities might exist. However, direct observation would be required to identify the existence of communities at scales of 1 km or less.

3.2.2.2. Coral Reefs

Coral reefs are particularly sensitive to human disturbance from increased sediment (e.g., from dredging), nutrient inputs (e.g., from sewage effluents), and physical damage (e.g., from anchoring). In the GOM, shallow-water coral reefs are associated with topographic highs such as the well-known East and West Flower Gardens and a number of others in the CPA (Figure 3-1). None of these are located in the deepwater areas of Grid 10.

Deepwater coral reefs appear to be very rare in the Gulf, albeit little studied (USDOI, MMS, 2000). Moore and Bullis (1960) collected more than 136 kg (300 lb) of scleractinian coral, Lophelia prolifera, from a depth of 421-512 m (1,381-1,680 ft), about 20 nmi from Viosca Knoll Block 907 (USDOI, MMS, 2000). This block is some 257 km (160 mi) from Grid 10. Hard bottoms supporting potential unknown coral reef habitat are avoided as a consequence of the MMS's Chemosynthetic Community NTL (NTL No. 2000-G20).

3.2.2.3. Deepwater Benthos

Marine benthic communities consist of a wide variety of single-celled organisms, plants, bacteria, invertebrates, and to some extent, even fish. Their lifestyles are extremely varied as well and can include absorption of dissolved organic material, symbiosis (e.g., chemosynthetic communities), collection of food through filtering, mucous webs, seizing, or other mechanisms.

It is convention in the Gulf region to classify benthic animals according to size as megafauna (large, usually mobile animals on the surface), macrofauna (retained on 0.25- to 0.50-mm mesh size sieve), meiofauna (0.063-mm screen; mostly nematode worms), and microfauna (protists and bacteria). The four types are discussed briefly below.

Megafauna

Animals of a size typically caught in trawls and large enough to be easily visible (e.g., crab, shrimp, benthic fish, etc.) are called megafauna. In the Gulf, most are crustaceans, echinoderms, or benthic fish. Benthic megafaunal communities in the central Gulf appear to be typical of most temperate continental slope assemblages found at depths from 300 to 3,000 m (984 to 9,843 ft) (USDOI, MMS, 2001a). Exceptions include the chemosynthetic communities discussed previously.

Megafaunal invertebrate and benthic fish densities appear to decline with depth between the upper slope and the abyssal plain (Pequegnat 1983; Pequegnat et al., 1990). This phenomenon is generally believed to be related to the low productivity in deep, offshore Gulf waters (USDOI, MMS, 2001a). Megafaunal communities in the offshore Gulf have historically been zoned by depth strata which are typified by certain species assemblages (Menzies et al., 1973; Pequegnat, 1983; Gallaway et al., 1988; Gallaway, 1988a-c; Pequegnat et al., 1990; and USDOI, MMS, 2001a). These zones include the following:

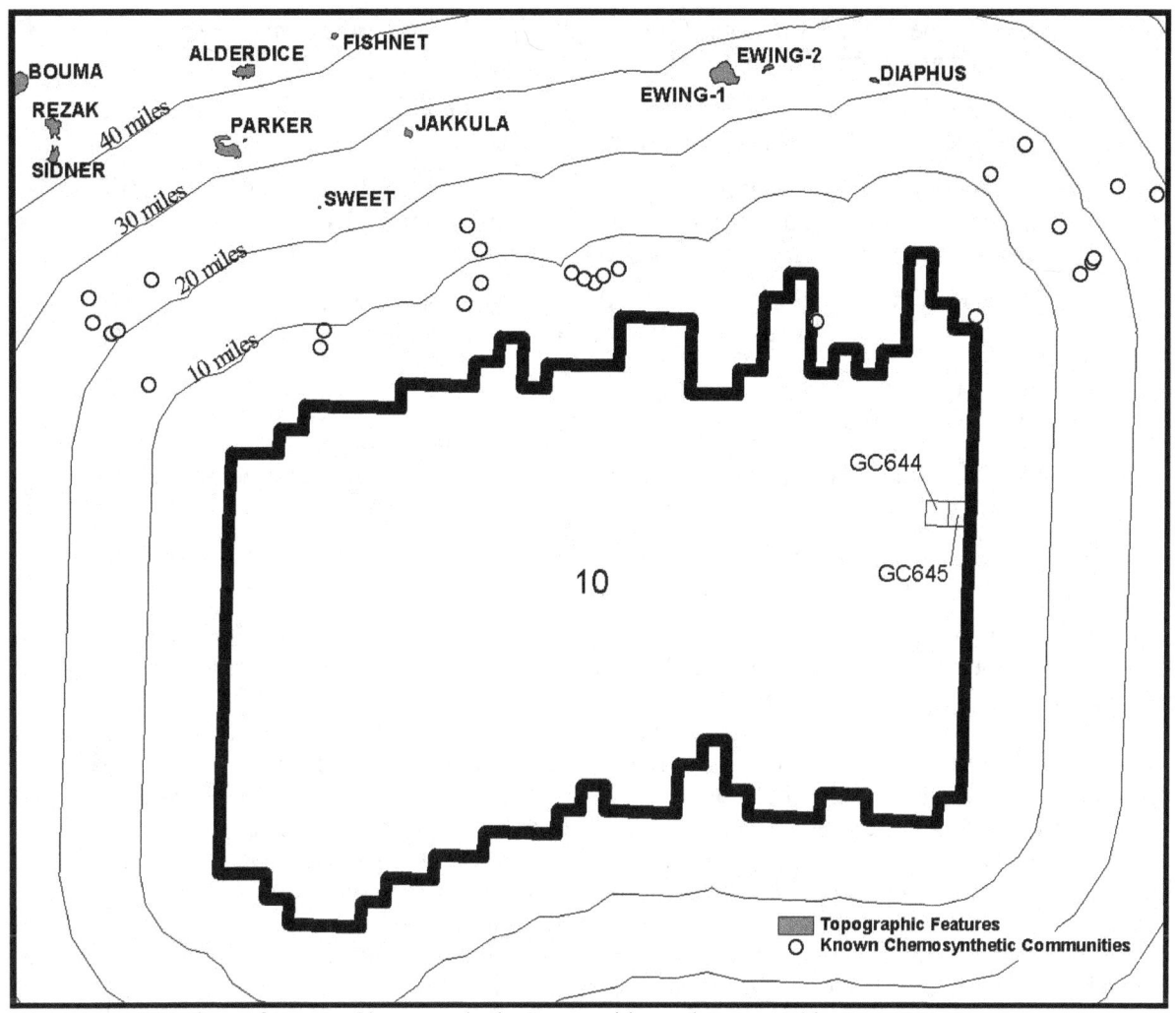

Figure 3-1. Locations of Known Chemosynthetic Communities and Topographic Features.

Shelf/Slope Transition Zone (100-500 m) — Echinoderms, crustaceans, and several species of abundant fish.

- Archibenthal Zone (Horizon A) (500-775m) — Galatheid crabs, rat tail fishes, large sea cucumbers, and sea stars are abundant.

- Archibenthal Zone (Horizon B) (800-1,000 m) — Galatheid crabs and rat tail fishes are abundant; fishes, echinoderms, and crustaceans decline; characterized by the red crab, Chaceon quinquedens.

- Upper Abyssal Zone (1,000-2,000 m) — Number of fish species decline while the number of invertebrate species appear to increase; sea cucumbers, Mesothuria lactea and Benthodytes sanguinolenta are common; galatheid crabs include 12 species of the deep-sea genera Munida and Munidopsis, while the shallow brachyuran crabs decline.

- Mesoabyssal Zone (2,300-3,000 m) — Fish species are few and echinoderms continue to dominate the megafauna.

- Lower Abyssal Zone (3,200-3,800 m) — Large asteroid, Dytaster insignis, is the most common megafaunal species.

Carney et al. (1983) postulated a simpler system of zonation having three zones: (1) a distinct shelf assemblage in the upper 1,000 m; (2) indistinct fauna between 1,000 and 2,000 m; and (3) a distinct slope fauna between 2,000 and 3,000 m.

The baseline NGMCS Study conducted in the mid- to late 1980's trawled 5,751 individual fish and 33,695 invertebrates, representing 153 and 538 taxa, respectively. That study also collected 56,052 photographic observations, which included 76 fish taxa and 193 non-fish taxa. Interestingly, the photographic observations were dominated by holothurians, bivalves, and sea pens, groups that were not sampled effectively (if at all) by trawling. Decapod crustaceans dominated the trawls and were fourth in the photos from an abundance perspective. Decapod density generally declined with depth but with peaks at 500 m and between 1,100 and 1,200 m, after which depth abundance was quite low. Fish density, while variable, was generally high at depths between 300 and 1,200 m, then declined substantially.

Gallaway et al. (2001) concluded that megafaunal composition changes continually with depth such that a distinct upper slope fauna penetrates to about 1,200 m depths and a distinct deep-slope fauna is present below 2,500 m. A broad transition zone characterized by low abundance and diversity occurs between depths of 1,200 and 2,500 m. The proposed Holstein development lies at the shallower margin of the transition zone.

Macrofauna

The benthic macrofaunal component of the NGMCS Study (Gallaway et al., 2001) included a sampling station in Grid 10, and it was at the same latitude as the proposed Holstein development. A nearby grid (Grid 13) contained a transect (the central transect) of 11 baseline stations from 305-m to below the 1,524-m (1,000 ft to below the 5,000-ft) contour. All of these data are relevant to proposed Holstein development because they were taken from the same geographic area and encompass the same depths and substrates.

The NGMCS Study examined 69,933 individual macrofauna from over 1,548 taxa; 1,107 species from 46 major groups were identified (Gallaway et al., 2001). Polychaetes (407 species), mostly deposit-feeding forms (196 taxa), dominated in terms of numbers. Carnivorous polychaetes were more diverse, but less numerous than deposit-feeders, omnivores, or scavengers (Pequegnat et al., 1990; Gallaway et al., 2001). Polychaetes were followed in abundance by nematodes, ostracods, harpacticoid copepods, bivalves, tanaidacids, bryozoans, isopods, amphipods, and others. Overall abundance of macrofauna ranged from 518 to 5,369 individuals/ m² (Gallaway et al., 1988). The central transect (4,938 individuals/ m²) had higher macrofaunal abundance than either the eastern or western Gulf transects (4,869 and 3,389 individuals/ m², respectively) (Gallaway et al., 2001).

In the GOM, macrofaunal density and biomass declines with depth from approximately 5,000 individuals/ m² on the lower shelf-upper slope to several hundred individuals/ m² on the abyssal plain (USDOI, MMS, 2001a). This decline in benthos has been attributed to the relatively low productivity of the Gulf offshore open waters (USDOI, MMS, 2001a). However, Pequegnat et al. (1990) have reported mid-depth maxima of macrofauna in the upper slope at some locations of high organic particulate matter, and Gallaway et al. (2001) noted that the decline with depth is not clear cut and is somewhat obscured by sampling artifacts.

There is some suggestion that sizes of individual macrofauna decrease with depth (Gallaway et al., 2001) and that size of individuals are generally small. Macrofaunal abundance appears to be higher in spring than in fall (Gallaway et al., 2001).

Macrofauna in the Gulf appears to have lower densities but higher diversities than the Atlantic, especially above 1,000 m, whereas at deep depths the fauna are less dissimilar in densities and very similar in diversities (Gallaway et al., 2001).

Meiofauna

Meiofauna (primarily composed of small nematode worms), as with megafauna and macrofauna, also decline in abundance with depth (Pequegnat et al., 1990; Gallaway et al., 2001; USDOI, MMS, 2001a). The overall density (mean of 707,000/ m²) of meiofauna is approximately two orders of magnitude greater than the macrofauna throughout the depth range of the slope (Gallaway et al., 1988). These authors reported 43 major groups of meiofauna with nematodes, harpacticoid copepods (adults and larvae), polychaetes, ostracods, and Kinorhyncha, accounting for 98 percent of the total numbers. Nematodes and harpacticoids were dominant in terms of numbers, but polychaetes and ostracods were dominant in terms of biomass, a feature that was remarkably consistent across all stations, regions, seasons, and years (Gallaway et al., 2001). Meiofaunal densities appeared to be somewhat higher in the spring than in the fall. Meiofaunal densities reported in the NGMCS Study are among the highest recorded worldwide (Gallaway et al., 2001). There is also evidence that the presence of chemosynthetic communities may enrich the density and diversity of meiofauna in the immediate surrounding area (Gallaway et al., 2001).

The above conclusions were partially based on the collections from the single NGMCS Study station in Grid 10 as well the adjacent stations in Grid 13 (the central Gulf transect) (see also "Macrofauna" above). The central Gulf transect appeared to contain a higher abundance of meiofauna than transects in the eastern or western Gulf, and in general (although not always, perhaps related to enrichment from chemosynthetic communities), there was a trend of decreasing meiofauna numbers with depth (Gallaway et al., 2001).

Microbiota

Less is known about the microbiota than the other groups in the GOM, especially in deepwater (USDOI, MMS, 2000). A recent MMS publication (USDOI, MMS, 2001b) provides information on this subject. An overview is provided below.

As reported by Rowe (CSA, 2000), the microbiota of the deep Gulf sediments is not well characterized. While direct counts have been coupled with some in situ and re-pressurized metabolic studies performed in other deep ocean sediments (Deming and Baross, 1993), none have been made in the deep GOM. Cruz-Kaegi (1998) made direct counts using a fluorescing nuclear stain at several depths down the slope, allowing bacterial biomass to be estimated from

13

their densities and sizes. Mean biomass was estimated to be 2.37 g C. m^{-2} for the shelf and slope combined, and 0.37 g C. m^{-2} for the abyssal plain. In terms of biomass, data indicate that bacteria are the most important component of the functional biota. Cruz-Kaegi (1998) developed a carbon cycling budget based on estimates of biomass and metabolic rates in the literature. She discovered that, on the deep slope of the Gulf, the energy from organic carbon in the benthos is cycled through bacteria.

3.2.3. Marine Mammals

Twenty-nine species of marine mammals are known to occur in the Gulf (Mullin and Hoggard, 2000). They include 7 species of baleen whales (Mysteceti), 21 species of toothed whales and dolphins (Odontoceti), and 1 species of manatee (Sirenia). Seven of these mammals are listed as endangered. The distributions of the neritic and oceanic species of marine mammals are appear related to water depth (GulfCet I program, Davis et al., 2000) and localized areas of productivity along the continental slope (GulfCet II program, Davis et al., 2000, in USDOI, MMS, 2001b).

3.2.3.1. *Nonendangered and Nonthreatened Species*

Many of the 22 nonendangered and nonthreatened species of marine mammals in the Gulf are found in oceanic water (> 200 m isobath).

Four species of beaked whales occur in the Gulf and include Sowerby's beaked whale (*Mesoplodon bidens*), Gervais' beaked whale (*M. europaeus*), Blainville's beaked whale (*M. densirostris*), and Cuviers beaked whale (*Ziphius cavirostris*). There have been few confirmed sightings of either Blainville's or Sowerby's beaked whale in the Gulf and they are therefore considered rare. Although little is known of the life histories of beaked whales in the Gulf, stomach content analysis indicates that these whales feed in deep waters on mesopelagic cephalopods and deepwater benthic invertebrates (Jefferson et al., 1993).

Of the two nonendangered baleen whales, minke whales (*Balaenoptera acutorostrata*) are rare in the Gulf, most likely representing strays from Atlantic populations (Mullin and Hoggard, 2000). Minkes feed on invertebrates and fish (Jefferson et al., 1993; Wursig et al., 2000; USDOI, MMS, 2001b). Bryde's whale (*B. edeni*) is the most frequently sighted baleen whale in the Gulf, which suggests the presence of a resident population (Jefferson and Schiro, 1997; Mullin and Hoggard, 2000). A number of Bryde's whales were sighted in the vicinity of the DeSoto Canyon Area in the north-central Gulf along the 100-m isobath (GulfCet I and II programs, USDOI, MMS, 2001b). Bryde's whales feed on fishes and invertebrates (Jefferson et al., 1993; USDOI, MMS, 2001b).

The pygmy sperm whale (*Kogia breviceps*) and the dwarf sperm whale (*K. simus*) are known to inhabit deep oceanic waters (Jefferson and Schiro, 1997). These species have been observed across a wide range of depths in the Gulf, but may be more common along the continental shelf break and the upper slope where plankton biomass is high (Baumgartner, 1995, in USDOI, MMS, 2000 and USDOI, MMS, 2001a). Little is known of their life history, but they appear to feed on deepwater cephalopods, fishes, and crustaceans (Leatherwood and Reeves, 1983; Jefferson et al., 1993).

The remaining members of nonendangered marine mammals in the Gulf are members of the dolphin family (Delphinidae). The Atlantic spotted dolphin (*Stenella frontalis*) and the bottlenose dolphin (*Tursiops truncatus*) are the only cetaceans commonly found over the continental shelf of the Gulf (Jefferson and Schiro, 1997). The spotted dolphin feeds on fishes and cephalopods, whereas the bottlenose is opportunistic, feeding on a wide variety of species (USDOI, MMS, 2001b). The short-finned pilot whale (*Globicephala macrorhynchus*) and Risso's dolphin (*Lagenodelphis hosei*) are widespread along the continental slope at depths of

200-2,000 m (Baumgartner, 1995, in USDOI, MMS, 2000 and USDOI, MMS, 2001a; Jefferson and Schiro, 1997; Mullin and Hoggard, 2000). Both species feed on cephalopods and fish, and the Risso's also feeds on crustaceans (USDOI, MMS, 2001b).

Other species are reported from the shelf break out to deeper waters of the slope. They include Frasier's dolphin (*Lagenodelphis hosei*), the orca (Orcinus orca), the false killer whale (Pseudorca crassidens), the melon-headed whale (*Peponocephala electra*), the roughed-toothed dolphin (*Steno bredanensis*), the pantropical spotted dolphin (*Stenella attenuata*), the spinner dolphin (*S. longirostris*), the striped dolphin (*S. coeruleoalba*), and the Clymene dolphin (*S. clymene*) (Davis et al., 1998; Jefferson and Schiro, 1997; Mullin and Hoggard, 2000). They all feed on fish and cephalopods. The Frasier's dolphin supplements its diet with crustaceans; the killer whale also eats marine mammals, birds, and sea turtles; and the false killer occasionally attacks cetaceans (USDOI, MMS, 2001b).

3.2.3.2. Endangered and Threatened Species

Five baleen whales (northern right, blue, fin, sei, and humpback), one toothed whale (sperm), and a subspecies of the West Indian manatee are currently listed as endangered species (50 CFR 17.11). The baleen whales are considered uncommon in the Gulf (Davis and Fargion, 1996; Jefferson and Schiro, 1997) and the few that do occasionally occur have probably strayed from normal migration routes (USDOI, MMS, 2001b). The sperm whale, an odontocete or toothed whale, is relatively common off the Mississippi River delta area and is considered the only deepwater species of marine mammal in the Gulf (Jefferson and Schiro, 1997).

The West Indian manatee (*Trichechus manatus*) consists of two subspecies, of which only the Florida manatee (*T. m. latirostris*) inhabits the northern Gulf. The Florida manatee typically ranges no farther north than the Swan River, Florida, but individuals have been reported as far west as Louisiana and west Texas (Domning and Hayek, 1986; USDOI, MMS, 2000). Because the manatee typically inhabits inland coastal areas and does not typically venture into the deeper areas of the Gulf (USDOI, FWS, 1995), development and production activities at the Holstein development are not expected to affect this endangered species.

The sperm whale (*Physeter macrocephalus*) inhabits marine waters from the tropics to the pack-ice edges of both hemispheres, although generally only large males venture to the extreme northern and southern portions of their range (Jefferson et al., 1993). In general, sperm whales seem to prefer certain areas within each major ocean basin, which historically have been termed "grounds" (Rice, 1989). As deep divers, sperm whales generally inhabit oceanic waters, but they do come close to shore where submarine canyons or other geophysical features bring deep water near the coast (Jefferson et al., 1993). Sperm whales prey on cephalopods, demersal fishes, and benthic invertebrates (Rice, 1989; Jefferson et al., 1993).

The sperm whale is the only great whale that is considered to be common in the northern Gulf (Fritts et al., 1983b; Mullin et al., 1991; Davis and Fargion, 1996; Jefferson and Schiro, 1997). Sighting data suggest a northern Gulf-wide distribution over slope waters. Congregations of sperm whales are commonly found in waters over the shelf edge in the vicinity of the Mississippi River delta in waters that are 500 to 2,000 m (1,641 to 6,562 ft) in depth (Mullin et al., 1994a; Davis and Fargion, 1996; Davis et al., 2000). Sperm whale sightings in the northern Gulf chiefly occur in waters with a mean seafloor depth of 1,105 m (3,625 ft) (Davis et al., 1998). Consistent sightings in the region indicate that there is a resident population of sperm whales in the northern Gulf consisting of adult females, calves, and immature individuals (Mullin et al., 1994b; Davis and Fargion, 1996; Sparks et al., 1996; Jefferson and Schiro, 1997; Davis et al., 2000). Also, recent sightings were made in 2000 and 2001 of solitary mature male sperm whales in the DeSoto Canyon area (Lang, personal communication). Minimum population estimates of sperm whales in the entire Gulf totaled 411 individuals, as cited in the NMFS stock assessment report for 1996 (Waring et al., 1997). Subsequent abundance estimates of sperm whales in the "oceanic northern GOM" survey area totaled 387 individuals (Davis et al., 2000). Sperm whales in the Gulf are currently considered a separate stock from those in the Atlantic and Caribbean (Waring et al., 1997).

3.2.4. Sea Turtles

All five species of sea turtles found in the Gulf are protected under the Endangered Species Act of 1973, as amended. These include loggerhead (*Caretta caretta*), leatherback (*Dermochelys coriacea*), hawksbill (*Eretmochelys imbricata*), Kemp's ridley (*Lepidochelys kempi*), and green (*Chelonia mydas*) sea turtles. The Kemp's ridley, leatherback, green, and hawksbill sea turtles are listed as endangered, while the loggerhead sea turtles are classified as threatened. Detailed biological and life history synopses of these species may be found in USDOI, MMS (2001a and 2000, pages IV-36 to IV-40).

The loggerhead (*Caretta caretta*) is a large sea turtle that inhabits the continental shelves and estuaries of temperate and tropical environments of the Atlantic, Pacific, and Indian Oceans. This species typically wanders widely throughout the marine waters of its range and is capable of living in varied environments for a relatively long time (Marquez, 1990; USDOC, NMFS and USDOI, FWS, 1991a; Ernst et al., 1994). They may remain dormant during winter months, buried in moderately deep, muddy bottoms (Marquez, 1990). Loggerheads are carnivorous and, though considered primarily predators of benthic invertebrates, are facultative feeders over a wide range of food items (Ernst et al., 1994). Loggerheads are considered to be the most abundant sea turtle in the GOM (Dodd, 1988). Loggerhead nesting along the Gulf Coast occurs primarily along the Florida panhandle, although some nesting also has been reported from Texas through Alabama (USDOC, NMFS and USDOI, FWS, 1991a). The loggerhead is currently listed as a threatened species.

The green turtle (*Chelonia mydas*) is the largest hardshell turtle and considered to be a circumglobal species. They are commonly found throughout the tropics and as stragglers in a far more extensive area, generally between latitude 40°N. and latitude 40° S. (USDOC, NMFS and USDOI, FWS, 1991b; Hirth, 1997). In the continental U.S., they are found from Texas to Massachusetts. Green turtles are omnivorous; adults prefer feeding on plants, but juveniles and hatchlings are more carnivorous (Ernst et al., 1994; Hirth, 1997). The adult feeding habitats are beds or pastures of seagrasses and algae in relatively shallow, protected waters; juveniles may forage in areas such as coral reefs, emergent rocky bottom, sargassum mats, and in lagoons and bays. Movements between principal foraging areas and nesting beaches can be extensive, with some populations regularly carrying out transoceanic migrations (USDOC, NMFS and USDOI, FWS, 1991b; Ernst et al., 1994; Hirth, 1997). Green turtles occur in some numbers over grass beds along the south Texas coast and the Florida Gulf Coast. Reports of nesting along the Gulf Coast are infrequent, and the closest important nesting aggregations are along the east coast of Florida and the Yucatan Peninsula (USDOC, NMFS and USDOI, FWS, 1991b). The green turtle is currently listed internationally as a threatened species and as an endangered species in the State of Florida.

The hawksbill (*Eretmochelys imbricata*) is a small to medium-sized sea turtle that occurs in tropical to subtropical seas of the Atlantic, Pacific, and Indian Oceans. In the continental U.S., the hawksbill has been recorded in all the Gulf States and along the Atlantic coast from Florida to Massachusetts, although sightings north of Florida are rare. They are considered to be the most tropical of all sea turtles and the least commonly reported sea turtle in the GOM (Marquez, 1990; Hildebrand, 1995). Coral reefs are generally recognized as the resident foraging habitat for juveniles and adults. Adult hawksbills feed primarily on sponges and demonstrate a high degree of selectivity, feeding on a relatively limited number of sponge species, primarily demosponges (Ernst et al., 1994). Nesting within the continental U.S. is limited to southeastern Florida and the Florida Keys. Juvenile hawksbills show evidence of residency on specific foraging grounds, although some migrations may occur (USDOC, NMFS and USDOI, FWS, 1993). Some populations of adult hawksbills undertake reproductive migrations between foraging grounds and nesting beaches (Marquez, 1990; Ernst et al., 1994). The hawksbill is presently listed as an endangered species.

The Kemp's ridley (*Lepidochelys kempi*) is the smallest sea turtle. This species occurs mainly in the GOM and along the northwestern Atlantic coast as far north as Newfoundland. Juveniles and adults are typically found in shallow areas with sandy or muddy bottoms, especially in areas of seagrass habitat. Kemp's ridleys are carnivorous and feed primarily on crabs, though they also feed on a wide variety of other prey items as well (Marquez, 1990; USDOC, NMFS and USDOI, FWS, 1992a; Ernst et al., 1994). The major Kemp's ridley nesting area is near Rancho Nuevo, along the northeastern coast of Mexico (Tamaulipas), although scattered nests have also been reported in other areas of Mexico and in Texas (e.g., within the Padre Island National Seashore), Colombia, Florida, and South Carolina (USDOC, NMFS and USDOI, FWS, 1992a; Ernst et al., 1994). Adult Kemp's ridleys exhibit extensive internesting movements but appear to travel near the coast, especially within shallow waters along the Louisiana coast. The Kemp's ridley is currently regarded as the most endangered of all sea turtle species.

The leatherback (*Dermochelys coriacea*) is the largest and most distinctive living sea turtle. This species possesses a unique skeletal morphology, most evident in its flexible, ridged carapace, and in cold water maintains a core body temperature several degrees above ambient. They also have unique deep-diving abilities. This species is also the most pelagic and most wide-ranging sea turtle, undertaking extensive migrations from the tropics to boreal waters. Though considered pelagic, leatherbacks will occasionally enter the shallow waters of bays and estuaries. Leatherbacks feed primarily on gelatinous zooplankton such as jellyfish, siphonophores, and salps, though they may, perhaps secondarily, ingest some algae and vertebrates (Ernst et al., 1994). Data from analyses of leatherback stomach contents suggest that they may feed at the surface, nocturnally at depth within deep scattering layers, or in benthic habitats. Florida is the only site in the continental U.S. where the leatherback regularly nests (USDOC, NMFS and USDOI, FWS, 1992b; Ernst et al., 1994; Meylan et al., 1995). The leatherback is currently listed as an endangered species.

3.2.5. Coastal and Marine Birds

Most species of marine birds listed as either endangered or threatened inhabit nearshore waters along the coast and the continental shelf of the Gulf of Mexico and rarely occur in deepwater areas (USDOI, MMS, 2001a). Forty-three species of seabird representing four ecological categories have been documented from deepwater areas of the Gulf: summer migrants (e.g., shearwaters, storm-petrels, and boobies), summer residents that breed in the Gulf (e.g., sooty, least, and sandwich terns), winter residents (e.g., gannets, gulls, and jaegers), and permanent resident species (e.g., laughing gull, royal and bridled terns) (Hess and Ribic, 2000; USDOI, MMS, 2001a). The most abundant species typically found in deepwater areas include terns, storm-petrels, and gulls (Hess and Ribic, 2000).

Seabirds' presence in the Gulf changes seasonally, with species diversity and overall abundance being highest in the spring and summer and lowest in fall and winter. Seabirds also tend to associate with various oceanic conditions including specific sea-surface temperatures and salinities (e.g., laughing gull and black and sooty terns), areas of high plankton productivity (e.g., laughing gulls, *pomarine jaeger*, Audubon's shearwater, band-rumped storm-petrel, and bridled tern), and particular currents (*pomarine jaeger*) (Hess and Ribic, 2000). Non-seabirds (especially passerines) that seasonally migrate over the Gulf may use offshore oil and gas structures as artificial islands for rest and shelter during inclement weather.

Shorebirds

Shorebirds are those members of the Order *Charadriiformes* generally restricted to coastline margins (beaches, mudflats, etc.). Gulf of Mexico shorebirds comprise five taxonomic families-- *Jacanidae* (jacanas), *Haematopodidae* (oystercatchers), *Recurvirostridae* (stilts and avocets), *Charadriidae* (plovers), and *Scolopacidae* (sandpipers, snipes, and allies) (Hayman et al., 1986). An important characteristic of almost all shorebird species is their strongly developed migratory behavior, with some shorebirds migrating from nesting places in the far north to the southern part of South America (Terres, 1991). Both spring and fall migrations take place in a series of "hops" to staging areas where birds spend time feeding heavily to store up fat for the sustained flight to the next staging area; many coastal habitats along the GOM are critical for such purposes. Along the Gulf Coast, 44 species of shorebirds have been recorded; only 6 species nest in the area, and the remaining species are wintering residents and/or "staging" transients (Pashley, 1991). Although variations occur between species, most shorebirds begin breeding at 1-2 years of age and generally lay 3-4 eggs per year. They feed on a variety of marine and freshwater invertebrates and fish, and small amounts of plant life.

Marsh and Wading Birds

The following families have some representatives in the northern Gulf: *Ardeidae* (herons and egrets), *Ciconiidae* (storks), *Threskiornithidae* (ibises and spoonbills), *Gruidae* (crane), and *Rallidae* (rails, moorhens, gallinules, and coots). Wading birds are those birds that have adapted to living in marshes. They have long legs that allow them to forage by wading into shallow water, while their long necks and bills are used to probe under water or to make long swift strokes to seize fish, frogs, aquatic insects, crustaceans, and other prey (Terres, 1991). Seventeen species of wading birds in the Order *Ciconiiformes* are currently known to nest in the U.S., and all except the wood stork nest in the northern Gulf coastal region (Martin, 1991). Within the Gulf Coast region, Louisiana supports the majority of nesting wading birds. Great egrets are the most widespread nesting species in the Gulf region (Martin, 1991).

Members of the *Rallidae* family have compact bodies; therefore, they are not labeled wading birds. They are also elusive and rarely seen within the low vegetation of fresh and saline marshes, swamps, and rice fields (Bent, 1926; National Geographic Society, 1983; Ripley and Beehler, 1985).

Waterfowl

Waterfowl belong to the taxonomic Order *Anseriformes* and include swans, geese, and ducks. A total of 36 species are regularly reported along the north-central and western Gulf Coast; they include 1 swan, 5 geese, 11 surface-feeding (dabbling) ducks and teal, 5 diving ducks (pochards), and 14 others (including the wood duck, whistling ducks, sea ducks, the ruddy duck, and mergansers) (Clapp et al., 1982; National Geographic Society, 1983; Madge and Burn, 1988). Many species usually migrate from wintering grounds along the Gulf Coast to summer nesting grounds in the north. Waterfowl migration pathways have traditionally been divided into four parallel north-south paths, or "flyways," across the North American continent. The GOM coast serves as the southern terminus of the Mississippi (Louisiana, Mississippi, and Alabama) flyway. Waterfowl are highly social and possess a diverse array of feeding adaptations related to their habitat (Johnsgard, 1975).

Raptors

The American peregrine falcon was "delisted" on August 20, 1999, removing it from protection under the Endangered Species Act (ESA). However, the falcon is still protected under the Migratory Bird Treaty Act. The FWS will continue to monitor the falcons' status for 13 years to ensure it stays as a recovered species.

Endangered and Threatened Species

The following coastal and marine birds species that inhabit or frequent the northern GOM coastal areas are recognized by FWS as either endangered or threatened: piping plover, least tern, roseate tern, bald eagle, and brown pelican.

Piping Plover

The piping plover (*Charadrius melodus*) is a migratory shorebird that is endemic to North America. The piping plover breeds on the northern Great Plains, in the Great Lakes, and along the Atlantic Coast (Newfoundland to North Carolina); and winters on the Atlantic and GOM coasts from North Carolina to Mexico and in the Bahamas, West Indies. Piping plovers prefer such areas as coastal sand flats and mud flats in proximity to large inlets or passes (Nicholls and Baldassarre, 1990). Similarly, nesting habitat in the north includes open flats along the Missouri River and the Great Lakes. This species remains in a precarious state given its low population numbers, sparse distribution, and continued threats to habitat throughout its range.

Least Tern

For the least tern (*Sterna antillarum*), only the population of interior nesting colonies is endangered. This applies to Louisiana for parts of the Mississippi River and tributaries north of Baton Rouge and to Mississippi for the Mississippi River. The least tern is not considered federally endangered or threatened within 50 mi of the Gulf, where numbers are not dangerously low (Patrick, personal communication, 1997).

Roseate Tern

The roseate tern (*Sterna dougalli*) is listed as threatened in Alabama and Florida. In the Florida Panhandle region, it has only been sighted five times and is a transient migratory stray (USDOI, FWS, 1989). A northeastern Atlantic breeding population is found east and north of Raritan Bay, New Jersey, and a Caribbean breeding population is found only as far north as south Florida (USDOI, FWS, 1989). The roseate tern is exclusively marine.

Bald Eagle

The bald eagle (*Haliaeetus leucocephalus*) is the only species of sea eagle that regularly occurs on the North American continent (USDOI, FWS, 1984). Its range extends from central Alaska and Canada to northern Mexico. The bulk of the bald eagle's diet is fish, though bald eagles will opportunistically take birds, reptiles, and mammals (USDOI, FWS, 1984). The general tendency is for winter breeding in the South with a progressive shift toward spring breeding in northern locations. In the Southeast, nesting activities generally begin in early September; egg laying begins as early as late October and peaks in late December. The historical nesting range of the bald eagle within the Southeast United States included the entire coastal plain and shores of major rivers and lakes. There are certain general elements that seem to be consistent among nest site selection. These include (1) the proximity of water (usually within 0.8 km or 0.5 mi) and a clear flight path to a close point on the water, (2) the largest living tree in a span, and (3) an open view of the surrounding area. The proximity of good perching trees may also be a factor in site selection. An otherwise suitable site may not be used if there is excessive human activity in the area. The current range is limited, with most breeding pairs

19

occurring in peninsular Florida and Louisiana, and some in South Carolina, Alabama, and east Texas. Sporadic breeding takes place in the rest of the southeastern states and in the Florida Panhandle. One hundred twenty nests have been found in Louisiana; only three nests occurred within 8 km (5 mi) of the coast (Patrick, written communication, 1997). The bald eagle was listed as endangered in 1967 in response to the declines due to DDT and other organochlorines that affected the species' reproduction (USDOI, FWS, 1984). In July 1995, the FWS reclassified the bald eagle from endangered to threatened in the lower 48 states (*Federal Register*, 1995).

Brown Pelican

The brown pelican (*Pelicanus occidentalis*) is one of two pelican species in North America. It feeds entirely upon fish captured by plunge diving in coastal waters. Organochlorine pesticide pollution apparently contributed to the endangerment of the brown pelican. In recent years, there has been a marked increase in brown pelican populations along its entire former range. The population of brown pelicans and their habitat in Alabama, Florida, Georgia, North and South Carolina, and points northward along the Atlantic Coast were removed from the endangered species list in 1985. Within the remainder of the range, which includes coastal areas of Mississippi, where populations are not secure, the brown pelican remains listed as endangered (*Federal Register*, 1985).

3.2.6. Essential Fish Habitat and Fish Resources

3.2.6.1. Essential Fish Habitat

The Fishery Conservation and Management Act of 1976 (Magnuson Act) established national standards for the conservation and management of exploited fish and shellfish stocks in U.S. Federal waters. Coastal waters extending 200 nmi seaward, but outside areas under State jurisdiction, were delineated as fisheries conservation zones for the U.S. and it possessions. Eight Regional Fishery Management Councils were created to manage fish stocks within those conservation zones based upon the national standards. Councils were required to prepare Fishery Management Plans (FMP's) that would provide the basis for local administration and management of regional fisheries. The FMP components generally address management objectives, alternatives and rationale; habitat issues; the benefits and adverse impacts of each alternative; and plans for the monitoring, review, and possible amendments to any action.

The Fishery Conservation and Management Act was superceded by the Magnuson-Stevens Fishery Conservation and Management Act of 1996, which required that FMP's further include the identification and description of Essential Fish Habitat (EFH). Essential fish habitat includes those waters and substrate necessary for the successful spawning, breeding, feeding, or growth to maturity of targeted species. The Act also requires that management councils consult with Federal agencies regarding any activities that may adversely affect essential fish habitat designated in specific FMP's. An adverse effect is any activity that reduces the quality of essential fish habitat whether it is direct (physical disruption) or indirect (loss of prey). Federal agencies are also required to assess actions that could conserve and enhance essential fish habitat.

In the Central and Western Gulf, essential fish habitat has been identified for 32 managed species of fish and shellfish (Gulf of Mexico Fisheries Management Council, 1998; USDOC, NMFS, 1999a and b). Of these, 21 species inhabit nearshore waters less than 200 m (656 ft) in depth. (See USDOI, MMS, 2001a, for further information on the distribution and habitat of these species.) The remaining 11 "offshore" species include the silky shark, longfin mako shark, dolphin, swordfish, skipjack tuna, yellowfin tuna, bluefin tuna, greater amberjack, king mackerel, tilefish, and red snapper. Although these species spawn in deepwater areas of the GOM, little is known about the life history and fate of pelagic larvae and fry. Bluefin larvae have been found associated with the Loop Current boundary and the Mississippi River plume (Richards et al., 1989, in USDOI, MMS, 2001b). Juvenile and adult red snapper aggregate around hard-bottom relief but seldom occur at depths >300 m (985 ft).

3.2.6.2. Description of Fish Resources

The GOM supports a great diversity of fish resources. The distribution and abundance of these resources are not random and are governed by a variety of ecological factors such as temperature, salinity, primary productivity, bottom types, and many other physical and biological factors. There are considerable inshore and offshore differences in fish resources. The majority of the GOM fisheries are dependent upon wetland, estuarine, and nearshore habitats (USDOI, MMS, 2001b).

Fish can be classified as demersal (bottom-dwelling), oceanic pelagic, or mesopelagic (midwater). Demersal (or benthic) fish have been addressed above under the megafauna descriptions (Chapter 3.2.2.3.1). There are no commercial fisheries in Grid 10 directed at demersal species. Oceanic pelagic and mesopelagic fishes are discussed briefly below. Additional life history information on important commercial invertebrate fish resources of the GOM is contained in USDOI, MMS (2000 and 2001a).

Oceanic Pelagics (Including Highly Migratory Species)

Common oceanic pelagic species include the large predatory tunas, marlins, sailfish, swordfish, dolphins, wahoo, and mako sharks. Other pelagics include halfbeaks, flyingfishes, and driftfishes (*Stromateidae*). Lesser known oceanic pelagics include opah, snake mackerels (*Gempylidae*), ribbonfishes (*Trachipteridae*), and escolar.

Oceanic pelagic species occur throughout the GOM, especially at or beyond the shelf edge. Oceanic pelagics are reportedly associated with mesoscale hydrographic features such as fronts, eddies, and discontinuities. Fishermen contend that yellowfin tuna aggregate near sea-surface temperature boundaries or frontal zones; however, Power and May (1991) (in USDOI, MMS, 2001b) found no correlation between longline catches of yellowfin tuna and sea-surface temperature (defined from satellite imagery) in the GOM. Many of the oceanic fishes associate with drifting Sargassum seaweed, which provides feeding and/or nursery habitat.

Mesopelagics (Midwater Fishes)

Mesopelagic fish assemblages in GOM collections are numerically dominated by *myctophids* (lanternfishes), with *gonostomatids* (bristlemouths) and *sternoptychids* (hatchet fishes) common but less abundant. These fishes make extensive vertical migrations during the night from mesopelagic depths (200-1,000 m; 656-3,280 ft) to feed in upper, more productive layers of the water column (Hopkins and Baird, 1985, in USDOI, MMS, 2001b). Mesopelagic fishes are important ecologically because they transfer substantial amounts of energy between mesopelagic and epipelagic zones.

The GOM appears to be a distinct zoogeographic province based upon analysis of lanternfish distribution (Bakus et al., 1977, in USDOI, MMS, 2001b). The GOM lanternfish assemblage was characterized by species with tropical and subtropical affinities. This was particularly true for the eastern GOM where Loop Current effects on species distributions were most pronounced. Gartner et al., (1987, in USDOI, MMS, 2001b) collected 17 genera and 49 species of lanternfish in trawls fished at discrete depths from stations in the southern, central, and eastern Gulf. The most abundant species in decreasing order of importance were *Ceratoscopleus warmingii*,

Notolychus valdiviae, Lepidophanes guentheri, Lampanyctus alatus, Daiphus dumerili, Benthosema suborbitale, and *Myctophum affine*. Ichthyoplankton collections from oceanic waters yielded high numbers of mesopelagic larvae as compared with larvae of other groups (Richards et al., 1989, in USDOI, MMS, 2001b). Lanternfishes generally spawn year-round, with peak activity in spring and summer (Gartner, 1993, in USDOI, MMS, 2001b).

3.2.7. Gulf Sturgeon

On September 30, 1991, the Gulf sturgeon was listed as a threatened species warranting protection under the Endangered Species Act, as amended. A subspecies of the Atlantic sturgeon, Gulf sturgeon are classified as anadromous, with immature and mature fish participating in freshwater migrations. Research netting and biotelemetry have shown that subadults and adults spend 8-9 months each year in rivers and 3-4 of the coolest months in estuaries or Gulf waters. Sturgeon that are less than about two years old remain in riverine habitats and estuaries throughout the year (Clugston, 1991). According to Wooley and Crateau (1985), Gulf sturgeon occurred in most major river systems from the Mississippi River to the Suwannee River, Florida, and in marine waters of the Central and Eastern GOM south to Florida Bay. It is not possible, at present, to estimate the size of Gulf sturgeon populations throughout its range, but extant occurrences in 1996 include the Mississippi River and Lake Pontchartrain, Louisiana, to Charlotte Harbor, Florida (Patrick, personal communication, 1996). Gulf sturgeon historically spawned in major rivers of Alabama, Mississippi, and the Florida's northern Gulf Coast. Its present spawning is limited to those rivers from the Pearl to the Suwannee. In spring, large subadults and adults that migrate from the estuaries or the Gulf into major river passes feed primarily on lancelets, brachiopods, amphipods, polychaetes, and globular molluscs. Small sturgeon that remain in river passes during spring feed on amphipods, shrimp, isopods, oligochaetes, and aquatic insect larvae (Clugston, 1991). During the riverine stage, adults cease feeding, undergo gonadal maturation, and migrate upstream to spawn. Spawning occurs over coarse substrate in deep holes. The decline of the Gulf sturgeon is believed to be due to overfishing and habitat destruction, primarily the damming of coastal rivers and the degradation of water quality (Barkuloo, 1988).

3.3. SOCIOECONOMIC CONDITIONS AND OTHER CONCERNS

3.3.1. Economic and Demographic Conditions

3.3.1.1. Socioeconomic Impact Area

The MMS defines the Gulf of Mexico impact area for population, labor, and employment as that portion of the Gulf of Mexico coastal zone whose social and economic well-being (population, labor and employment) is directly or indirectly affected by the OCS oil and gas industry. For this analysis, the coastal impact area consists of 80 counties and parishes along the U.S. portion of the Gulf of Mexico. This area includes 24 counties in Texas, 26 parishes in Louisiana, 4 counties in Mississippi, 2 counties in Alabama, and 24 counties in the Panhandle of Florida. Inland counties and parishes are included where offshore oil and gas activities are known to exist, where offshore-related petroleum industries are established, and where one or more counties or parishes within a Metropolitan Statistical Area (MSA) are on the coast; all counties and parishes within the MSA are included.

Most of the probable changes in population, labor, and employment resulting from the proposed activity would occur in the 24 counties in Texas and the 26 parishes in Louisiana because the oil and gas industry is best established in this region and the two onshore service bases associated with the proposed activity are located in Louisiana. Some of the likely changes in population, labor, and employment resulting from the proposed activity would occur to a lesser extent in the six Alabama and Mississippi counties due to having an established oil and gas industry and its proximity to the offshore location. Changes in economic factors (in minor service and support industries) from the proposed activity would occur, to a much lesser extent, in the 24 counties of the Florida Panhandle because of its proximity to the proposed activity area.

For analysis purposes, the MMS has divided the economic impact area (defined geographically in the first paragraph of this section) into the subareas listed in Table F-1 (see Appendix F). This impact area is based on the results of a recent MMS socioeconomic study, "Cost Profiles and Cost Functions for Gulf of Mexico Oil and Gas Development Phases for Input-Output Modeling." One of the objectives of this study was to allocate expenditures from the offshore oil and gas industry to the representative onshore subarea where the dollars were spent. Table F-2 (in Appendix F) presents these findings in percentage terms. In the table, the IMPLAN number is the code given to the industry (sector) by the input-output software (IMPLAN) used to calculate impacts in Chapter 4 of this document. It is analogous to the standardized industry code (SIC). As shown in the table, very little has been spent in the Florida subareas. This is to be expected given the lack of offshore leasing in this area and Florida's stance towards oil and gas development off their beaches. The table also makes clear the reason for including all of the Gulf of Mexico subareas in the economic impact area. Expenditures in Texas to several sectors are either exclusively found there or make up a very large percentage of the total. In addition, a significant percentage of total sector expenditures is allocated to each Louisiana subarea.

3.3.1.2. Population and Education

Table F-3 in Appendix F depicts baseline population projections for the potential impact area. Baseline projections are for the impact area in the absence of the proposed activity. According to Woods and Poole forecasts, most subareas in the region will experience an average annual growth in population of approximately 1-2 percent over next 25 years. On average, the percent of the population age 25 years and over completing high school only in the impact area (53.82%) is less than that for the United States (54.90%). The same holds true for college graduates (13.85% versus 20.34%). While several individual parishes, counties, and MSA's exhibit graduation percentages greater than the national average, most do not.

3.3.1.3. Infrastructure and Land Use

The GOM OCS Region has one of the highest concentrations of oil and gas activity in the world. The offshore oil and gas industry has experienced dramatic changes over recent years, particularly since 1981. Historically, most of the activity has been concentrated on the continental shelf off the coasts of Texas and Louisiana. Future activity is expected to extend into progressively deeper waters and into the EPA. The high level of offshore oil and gas activity in the Gulf of Mexico is accompanied by an extensive development of onshore service and support facilities. The major types of onshore infrastructure include gas processing plants, navigation channels, oil refineries, pipelines and pipeline landfalls, pipecoating and storage yards, platform fabrication yards, separation facilities, service bases, terminals, and other industry-related installations such as landfills and disposal sites for drilling and production wastes.

Land use in the impact area varies from state to state. The coasts of Florida and Texas are a mixture of urban, industrial, recreational beaches, wetlands, forests, and agricultural areas. Alabama's coastal impact area is predominantly recreational beaches and small residential and fishing communities. Mississippi's coast consists of barrier islands, some wetlands, recreational beaches, and urban areas. Louisiana's coastal impact area is mostly vast areas of wetlands; some small communities and industrial areas extend inward from the wetlands.

3.3.1.4. Navigation and Port Usage

A service base is a community of businesses that load, store, and supply equipment, supplies, and personnel needed at offshore work sites. Although a service base may primarily serve the OCS planning area and subarea in which it is located, it may also provide significant services for the other OCS planning areas and subareas. As OCS operations have progressively moved into deeper waters, larger vessels with deeper drafts have been phased into service, mainly for their greater range of travel, greater speed of travel, and larger carrying capacity. Service bases with the greatest appeal for deepwater activity have several common characteristics: strong and reliable transportation system; adequate depth and width of navigation channels; adequate port facilities; existing petroleum industry support infrastructure; location central to OCS deepwater activities; adequate worker population within commuting distance; and insightful strong leadership. Typically, deeper draft service vessels require channels with depths of 6-8 m. The proposed activity is expected to impact Port Fourchon (primarily) and Venice, Louisiana, the designated service bases for the Holstein development. A small amount of vessel and helicopter traffic may originate from bases other than those named above in order to address changes in weather, market, and operational conditions.

3.3.1.5. Employment

Table F-4 in Appendix F depicts baseline employment projections for the potential impact area. Baseline projections are employment estimates for the impact area in the absence of the proposed activity. According to Woods and Poole forecasts, most subareas in the region will experience an average annual growth in employment of approximately one and a half percent for the next several years and decrease steadily to one and a quarter percent during the last years of analysis. Unemployment in the impact area has averaged 4.4 percent during 2000, while the national average was 3.9 percent. Unemployment numbers varied widely by parish/county from a high of 10.5 percent to a low of 1.8 percent. Employment in the impact area by major industry sectors is shown in Table F-5 in Appendix F. Service (36.06%) and retail (21.67%) jobs dominate the area, while manufacturing follows at 12.38 percent. Payroll distribution by major industry sectors, as seen in Table F-6 (see Appendix F), reflects the employment in the impact area.

3.3.1.6. Current Economic Baseline Data

Current crude oil and natural gas prices are substantially above the economically viable threshold for drilling in the Gulf of Mexico. As of September 7, 2001, light sweet crude lists for $28.03 per barrel on the New York Mercantile Exchange (a decrease of 7.22% or $2.18 from a year ago). Henry Hub Natural Gas closed at $2.50 per million BTU (a decrease of 35.73% or $1.39 from a year ago) (www.oilnergy.com). In addition to oil and gas price, drilling rig use is employed by the industry as a barometer of economic activity. According to Offshore Data Services, the utilization rate for all marketed mobile rigs in the GOM was 78.4 percent. This breaks down as a 72.9 percent utilization rate for jackups (average day rates of $26,000-66,000); 91.7 percent for semisubmersibles (average day rates of $45,000-135,000); 100 percent for drillships (average day rates of $125,000-150,000); and 100 percent for submersibles (average day rates of $35,00-43,000). Platform rigs in the Gulf recorded a 71.9 percent utilization rate, while inland barges had a 92 percent utilization rate. (Offshore Data Services, *Gulf of Mexico Weekly Rig Locator*, 2001).

Offshore service vessel (OSV) day rates, another indicator of the industry's activity, remains strong despite the softening of the drilling rig market which most vessel operators believe will become active later this year (*WorkBoat*, vol. 58, no. 9, September 2001, page 16). The July 2001 average day rates for all three types of vessels used by the offshore oil and gas industry increased from the July 2000 averages. Anchor-handling tug/supply vessel (AHTS) average day rates for ranged from $10,500 for under 6,000-hp to $12,500 for over 6,000-hp vessels; utilization rates were 88 percent and 100 percent, respectively. Supply boat average day rates ranged from $7,718 for boats up to 61 m (200 ft) and $10,950 for 61 m (200 ft) and over; utilization was 89 percent and 100 percent, respectively. Crewboat average day rates ranged from $2,928 for boats under 38 m (125 ft) to $3,775 for boats 38 m (125 ft) and over; utilization was 100 percent and 98 percent, respectively. Another indicator of the direction of the industry is the exploration and development (E&D) expenditures of the major oil and gas companies. After substantial cutting their E&D budgets during the 1998 and 1999 fiscal years, majors are once again increasing these areas on their balance sheets. According to Global Marine Chairman, President, and CEO, Bob Rose, "the outlook for 2001 is very bullish." (www.oilandgasonline.com, January 17, 2001).

Commencing with Central GOM Lease Sale 178 Part 1 in March 2001, new royalty relief provisions for both oil and gas production in the GOM's deep and shallow waters were enacted. These rules will govern the next three years of lease sales. Central GOM Lease Sale 178 Part 1 resulted in 534 leases let (an increase of 59.88% or 200 blocks from Central GOM Lease Sale 175 in March 2000). Of these 534 leases, 348 were in shallow water (0-400 m or 0-1,312 ft). This increase of 67.30 percent from the last Central GOM lease sale largely reflects the intensified interest in natural gas due to higher prices over the last year and the new royalty relief provisions. The 186 blocks receiving bids in deepwater (greater than 400 m or 1,312 ft) reflects an increase of 47.62 percent or 60 blocks. Again, this dramatic increase in leasing could be a result of the recently issued royalty relief provisions. Western GOM Lease Sale 180 and Central GOM Lease Sale 178 Part 2, offering the newly available United States' blocks beyond the United States Exclusive Economic Zone, were held on August 22, 2001. No bids were received for blocks offered in Central GOM Lease Sale 178 Part 2. Of the 4,114 blocks offered in Western GOM Lease Sale 180, 320 received bids. About 55 percent of blocks receiving bids (or 177 blocks) in Western GOM Lease Sale 180 are in deepwater.

3.3.1.7. How OCS Development Has Affected the Impact Area

1980 - 1989

In the oil and gas industry drilling rig use is employed as a barometer of economic activity. Between the end of 1981 and mid-1983 drilling rig activity in the GOM took a sharp downturn. By 1986 the demand for mobile drilling rigs had suffered an even greater decline. Population and net migration paralleled these fluctuations in mobile drilling rig activity. Population growth rates for all coastal subareas were relatively high prior to 1983; families moved to the Gulf coast looking for work in the booming oil and gas industry. Lower rates of population growth accompanied the decline in drilling activity as workers were laid off and left the area in search of work elsewhere. After 1983, all subareas experienced several years of significant net migration out of the region. The negative impact on population continued until 1986 when the demand for mobile rigs declined to its lowest level in over a decade and the price of oil collapsed.

1990 - 1997

In the early to mid-1990's, the impact area experienced a major resurgence in oil exploration and drilling due to advances in technology and the enactment of the Deep Water Royalty Relief Act in 1995. The renewed interest in oil and gas exploration and development in the GOM produced a modest to significant recovery from the high unemployment levels experienced after the 1986 downturn. Ironically, the Gulf Coast encountered a shortage of skilled labor in the oil and gas industry due to "the restructuring of the oil industry to centralize management, finance and business services, and the use of computer technology," (Baxter, 1990). Additionally, potential oil and gas industry employees experienced the "shadow effect." Workers who previously lost high-paying jobs in the oil industry (or oil service industry) during the 1980s downturn were reluctant to return. The shadow effect, coupled with the shortage of skilled labor where the core problems were lack of education and or training for requisite skills, created a situation where temporary communities of workers from out of the area (some from out of the country) were established. Furthermore, the higher skill levels required by deep water development drilling could not be completely met by the existing impact area's labor force causing in-migration. Unemployment in the impact area, though, declined due to increased economic diversification by the region.

1998 - Present

In early 1998, crude oil prices were hovering near 12-year lows. This restrained the resurgence of exploration and development activity in the GOM. While offshore development strategy varies by company, most major oil companies, diversified firms and small independents cut back production and curtailed exploration projects. Several large integrated companies resorted to layoffs and mergers as ways to assail low prices; a redistribution of headquarter personnel from the New Orleans area to the Houston area occurred and unemployment in the impact area rose. Offshore drilling strategies focused on mega and large prospects, foregoing small prospects, and only considering medium prospects when prices rose (Rike, 1998). A few companies, though, took advantage of lower drilling rates during this period and increased their drilling. Concurrently, technological innovations (such as 3-D seismic, slim hole drilling, synthetic based drilling fluid, and hydraulic rigs) decreased the cost of extraction and thus stimulated the development of large or mega prospects that were still considered economic at low prices.

In March of 1999 OPEC, who produces 40 percent of the world's oil, announced crude oil production cutbacks. Full member compliance increased oil prices to 20-year highs encouraging moderate exploration and development spending during the 1999 fiscal year. Crude oil prices continued to increase during 2000 and now into 2001. It is generally believed that the increase in price is being driven by two major factors. First is the continued OPEC compliance to maintain prices within their current output targets of a $22 minimum and a $28 maximum barrel price. This was recently fortified by the cartel's January 17, 2001, announcement to cut production by 1.5 million barrels per day beginning February 1, 2001, in order to increase the price. The second factor, according to the Federal Reserve Bank of Dallas, is the "world capacity to supply oil has not kept pace with the growth of oil demand spurred by a resurgent world economy. [Furthermore,] a short supply of oil tankers, rising shipping rates and low inventories of refined product and crude oil have added upward pressure to spot crude oil prices." (Brown, 2000, p. 2). The low prices throughout much of the 1990's were too low to stimulate additions to capacity. In addition, many tankers were scrapped in the 1990's when weak demand, low shipping rates and increasing environmental regulation put a lot of pressure on the tanker industry. (Brown, 2000, p. 3).

High oil prices and Federal environmental clean air efforts have prompted fuel switching away from crude oil to natural gas. Like crude oil, the supply of natural gas did not keep up with demand pushing prices higher. In December 2000, natural gas broke record highs closing at $10.10. Matthew Simmons, industry analyst and president of Houston investment bank Simmons & Co., states, "in addition to heating about 53 percent of American homes, natural gas is also being used to generate about 16 percent of the country's electricity – a percentage that is still growing." (Simmons, 2001). Mr. Simmons believes, and many other analysts concur, that this is "a decade-long problem." (Simmons, 2001). However, in recent months, natural gas prices have decreased dramatically (75.25%) since its record high of $10.10. According to Kelley Doolan, a natural gas market specialist for Platts and chief editor of Inside FERC's Gas Market Report, several factors have kept a downward pressure on natural prices in recent months. These include moderate weather in most of the nation keeping demand for gas by electricity generators in check; relatively low oil prices; and the general economic slowdown which has reduced demand for gas by the industrial sector. Even without this pronounced drop in price, demand growth for natural gas is expected to be strong during the next 20 years. The 2001 Update of the Fueling the Future: Natural Gas and New Technologies for a Cleaner 21st Century report projects that natural gas demand would increase by 53 percent by the year 2020 (American Gas Foundation, 2001).

3.3.2. Environmental Justice

On February 11, 1994, President Clinton issued an executive order to address questions of equity in the environmental and health conditions of impoverished communities. The most effective way of assuring that environmental endangerment is not concentrated in minority or low-income neighborhoods is to locate and identify them from the outset of a proposed project. Low incomes also coincided with concentrations of minority populations: black, Hispanic, and/or Native American. Minority populations within the impact region include African-Americans living in all the GOM coast states and Asian-Americans in Alabama. Few Native Americans live in coastal counties, and there are no recognized tribal lands in any of the ten coastal counties from Mississippi to the Panhandle of Florida, according to maps of tribal lands and locations published in December 1998 by the Bureau of Indian Affairs. The Poarch Band of Creeks lives in Escambia County, Alabama, and the Florida Tribe of Eastern Creeks has its designated statistical area north of Appalachicola Bay near the Florida/Georgia state line (USDOI, Bureau of Indian Affairs, www.gdsc.bia.gov/pdf/usa.pdf, December 1998.). The Native American Data Center also lists these tribes as well as others in coastal Louisiana (www.indiandata.com/eastern.htm) such as the Intertribal Council (ITC). The Council was established in the early 1970's by five tribes--the Chitimacha, Tunica-Biloxi, Coushatta, Houma, and Jena Band of Choctaws. At that time, only the Coushatta tribe was federally recognized. Today, four Louisiana tribes are federally recognized. The first of these to be recognized was the Coushatta in 1973, and the last was the Jena Band of Choctaw in 1995. The United Houma Nation is still awaiting a finding on its petition. Because its citizens live principally in LaFourche Parish and close to Port Fourchon, they could be directly affected by increases in oil/gas activity from the proposed action. Low-income populations living in the impact area include fishermen and timber harvesters.

3.3.3. Commercial Fisheries

More than 26 percent (40% excluding Alaska) of commercial fish landings in the continental U.S. occur in the GOM (USDOI, MMS, 2001b). In 1999, the GOM placed second in total landed weight (almost 1 million tons) and third in value ($776 million) considering all U.S. regions (USDOC, NMFS, 2001, in USDOI, MMS, 2001b). The most important species, such as menhaden, shrimps, oyster, crabs, and drums, are all species that depend heavily on estuarine habitats and the fisheries are restricted to the continental shelf. Menhaden was the most valuable finfish landed in 1999, accounting for $78.5 million in total value. The GOM shrimp fishery, however, is the most valuable fishery in the U.S., and the Gulf fishery accounts for 71.5% of total domestic production.

Commercial fishing in deeper waters (i.e., >200 m [656 ft]) of the GOM is characterized by fewer species, and lower landed weights and values than the inshore fisheries. Historically, the deepwater offshore fishery contributes less than 1 percent to the regional total weight and value (USDOI, MMS, 2001a). Target species can be classified into three groups: (1) epipelagic fishes, (2) reef fishes, and (3) invertebrates. In general, the Holstein development is beyond the normal depth range of commercial reef fishes and invertebrates. While it is possible that new species of demersal fish or invertebrates may be pursued in the future if other fisheries fail, it appears unlikely at present because of the high cost and risk of fishing at extreme water depths. In addition, considerable time, effort and finances would have to be expended to develop new markets for new species. Thus, if new fisheries develop in the deepwater Gulf, the most likely target species would be the epipelagic fishes, normally fished using surface longlines.

Epipelagic commercial fishes include dolphin, sharks (mako, silky, and thresher), snake mackerels (escolar and oilfish), swordfish, tunas (bigeye, blackfin, bluefin, and yellowfin), and wahoo (USDOI, MMS, 2001a). These species are widespread in the Gulf and probably occur in Grid 10. Nonetheless, it does not appear likely that significant fisheries for epipelagic fishes will develop in the far offshore waters of the Gulf, including the Holstein project area, because of the generally low productivity and high costs and risks associated with these waters.

3.3.4. Recreational Resources and Beach Use

The following section on recreational resources is summarized from USDOI, MMS (2001a). Additional sportfishing data are available from the NMFS statistics (available at www.noaa.nmfs.gov).

The coastal zone of the Gulf is a major recreational region of local, state and national importance. Recreational resources include national seashores, parks, beaches, and wildlife areas as well as designated conservation areas for historic and natural sites, landmarks, wilderness areas, wildlife sanctuaries, and scenic rivers. There are also private commercial recreational facilities such as resorts, marinas, amusement parks, and botanical gardens. The region offers a diversity of recreational activities including swimming, beachcombing, picnicking, camping, nature viewing, bird watching, boating, scuba diving, fishing, hunting, and others. The value of tourism on the U.S. Gulf Coast has been estimated at $20 billion (USDOI, MMS, 2001a). Table 3-38 (in USDOI, MMS, 2001a) lists 45 major recreational areas in the coastal zones of Texas, Louisiana, and Mississippi.

Recreational fishing is a major activity in the northern GOM, mostly in inshore waters but offshore waters are fished as well. In many areas, oil platforms provide opportunities for enhanced fishing success. Western Florida alone accounted for 12 million angling trips by three million anglers in 1998 (USDOI, MMS, 2001a). The other Gulf States support sportfishing, although not as extensive as western Florida.

Important sportfish inshore species include: spotted sea trout (the top species in 1998 at over 20 million fish landed), sand sea trout, gray and red snapper, red and black drum, white grunt, Spanish mackerel, gag, Crevalle jack, and southern flounder. Florida anglers target hard bottom species such as gray snapper, white grunt and gag more so than the other states which tend toward the soft bottom species such as red drum and sand sea trout (USDOI, MMS, 2001a).

It is unlikely that sport fishers presently use the Holstein area to any extent due to the distance offshore and the generally lower productivity off the shelf.

3.3.5. Archaeological Resources

Archaeological resources are any material remains of human life or activities that are at least 50 years of age and that are of archaeological interest (30 CFR 250.2). The Archaeological Resources Regulation (30 CFR 250.26) provides specific authority to each MMS Regional Director to require archaeological resource surveys, analyses, and reports. Surveys are required prior to any exploration or development activities on leases within the high-probability areas (NTL 98-06).

3.3.5.1. Prehistoric

Available geologic evidence suggests that sea level in the northern Gulf of Mexico was at least 90 m (295 ft), and possibly as much as 130 m (427 ft), lower than present sea level, and that the low sea-stand occurred during the period 20,000-17,000 years before present (B.P.) (Nelson and Bray, 1970). Sea level in the northern Gulf reached its present stand around 3,500 years B.P. (Coastal Environments, Inc., 1986).

During periods that the continental shelf was exposed above sea level, the area was open to habitation by prehistoric peoples. The advent of early man into the GOM region is currently accepted to be around 12,000 years B.P. (Aten, 1983). According to the sea-level curve for the northern GOM proposed by Coastal Environments, Inc. (CEI), sea level at 12,000 B.P. would have been approximately 45 m (148 ft) below the present still stand (CEI, 1977 and 1982). On this basis, the continental shelf shoreward of the 45-m to 60-m (148 to 197 ft) bathymetric contours has potential for prehistoric sites dating after 12,000 B.P. Because of inherent uncertainties in both the depth of sea level and the entry date of prehistoric man into North America, the MMS adopted the 12,000 years B.P. and the 60-m (197 ft) water depth as the seaward extant of the prehistoric archaeological high-probability area. Based on the extreme water depth of these lease blocks, the proposed oil or gas development activities will not impact any prehistoric archaeological resources.

3.3.5.2. Historic

With the exception of the Ship Shoal Lighthouse structure, historic archaeological resources on the OCS consist of historic shipwrecks. A historic shipwreck is defined as a submerged or buried vessel, at least 50 years old, that has foundered, stranded, or wrecked and that is presently lying on or embedded in the seafloor. This includes vessels (except hulks) that exist intact or as scattered components on or in the seafloor. A 1977 MMS archaeological resources baseline study for the northern GOM concluded that two-thirds of the total number of shipwrecks in the northern Gulf lie within 1.5 km (0.9 mi) of shore and most of the remainder lie between 1.5 and 10 km (0.9 and 6.2 mi) of the coast (CEI, 1977). A subsequent MMS study published in 1989 found that changes in the late 19th- and early 20th-century sailing routes increased the frequency of shipwrecks in the open sea in the Eastern Gulf to nearly double that of the Western and Central Gulf (Garrison et al., 1989). The highest observed frequency of shipwrecks occurred within areas of intense marine traffic, such as the approaches and entrances to seaports and the mouths of navigable rivers and straits.

There are more than 4,000 historical shipwrecks in the northern Gulf (USDOI, MMS, 2001a). Few of them have been accurately located or mapped but most are believed to be in relatively shallow water (USDOI, MMS, 2001a). About 33 merchant vessels were sunk in the northern Gulf on the OCS by U-Boats between 1942 and 1943. Six of these are believed to be in deep water (>200 m or 656 ft) in the Lund and Mississippi Canyon protraction diagrams. There are no wrecks listed for the Holstein lease blocks (Tables 3-39 and 3-40 in USDOI, MMS, 2001a).

Review of the Garrison et al. (1989) shipwreck database lists nine shipwrecks that fall within the Green Canyon, Walker Ridge, Garden Banks, and Keathley Canyon Areas. None of these wrecks specifically fall within the Grid 10 area. All of the wrecks listed are known only through the historical record and, to date, have not been located on the ocean floor. The MMS shipwreck database should not be considered exhaustive lists of shipwrecks. Regular reporting of shipwrecks did not occur until late in the 19th century, and losses of several classes of vessels, such as small coastal fishing boats, were largely unreported in official records.

Wrecks occurring in deeper water would have a moderate to high preservation potential. In the deep water, temperature at the seafloor is extremely cold, which slows the oxidation of ferrous metals. The cold water would also eliminate the wood-eating shipworm, Terredo navalis (Anuskiewicz, 1989, page 90).

Aside from acts of war, hurricanes cause the greatest number of wrecks in the Gulf. The wreckage of the 19th century steamer, New York, which was destroyed in a hurricane in 1846, lies in 16 m (52 ft) of water and has been documented by the MMS (Irion and Anuskiewicz, 1999) as scattered over the ocean floor in a swath over 457 m (1,500 ft) long. Shipwrecks occurring in shallow water nearer to shore are more likely to have been reworked and scattered by subsequent storms than those wrecks occurring at greater depths on the OCS. Historic research indicates that shipwrecks occur less frequently in Federal waters. However, these wrecks are likely to be better preserved, less disturbed, and, therefore, more likely to be eligible for nomination to the National Register of Historic Places than are wrecks in shallower State waters.

4. POTENTIAL ENVIRONMENTAL EFFECTS

4.1. PHYSICAL ELEMENTS OF THE ENVIRONMENT

4.1.1. Impacts on Water Quality

4.1.1.1. Coastal

A number of project activities such as regulated and accidental discharges of contaminants as well as construction activities have the potential to impact water quality. The Holstein Project's Green Canyon Blocks 644 and 645 are located approximately 220 km (118.7 nmi) from the Louisiana coastline and thus, there is a very low potential for interaction between coastal waters and routine activities offshore. A large oil spill or blowout, a very rare event based on historical statistics for the GOM, constitutes a possible exception. The potential effects of a large hydrocarbon spill are discussed separately in Appendix A. The effects on coastal water quality from an offshore spill or blowout would depend on the type of accident (e.g., subsurface or surface blowout, surface spill, etc.), the volume of the hydrocarbon release, and environmental conditions at the time and place of the spill as well as along the spill trajectory, and the type and volume of dispersant that might be used, if any. Given the location of the Holstein development, it would take 20 days or more before the oil could reach coastal waters during which time much of the lighter, more toxic fractions would have evaporated. A large percentage of the oil would have dispersed naturally or with the assistance of dispersant applications.

BP will use two existing onshore support bases during drilling, completion, and production operations associated with this project: (1) the C-Port Fourchon shorebase located in Fourchon, Terrebonne Parish, Louisiana; and (2) the Venice shorebase located in Venice, Plaquemines

Parish, Louisiana. No expansion of these physical facilities is expected to result from the proposed activities.

There is some potential to affect coastal water quality from vessel activity between the shore bases and the offshore site. During the drilling/completion phase of the proposed activities, BP estimates that there will be three trips per week by the crewboat and two trips per week by the supply boat (BP, 2001). During the facility installation phase, there will be seven trips per week by both vessels; during the hook-up/commissioning phase, there will be seven and five trips, respectively, and during the production phase, there will be two and three trips by the crewboat and supply boat, respectively. No dredging over and above normal channel maintenance will be required to support these vessels. The boats will discharge heated cooling water and non-oily bilge water. Most vessel trips will be from the Fourchon service base and most helicopter trips will originate from the Venice service base.

Diesel fuel will also be carried by the crewboats (maximum of 476 bbl) and supply vessels (7,142 bbl) and there will be weekly transfers of diesel (3,582 bbl) from Fourchon to the Holstein facilities. Other vessels carrying varying amounts of fuel and materials also may transit from shore to the Holstein Project area periodically during development activities. Accidents with these vessels could affect inshore water quality if an incident occurred near shore. The potential for oil spills from these sources is discussed further in Appendix A.

Conclusion

Inshore vessel traffic associated with the Holstein development will interact with coastal water and may negligibly affect water quality due to prop wash, accidental waste release, and other activities. Routine offshore activities associated with the Holstein development during both the production and decommissioning phases will not adversely affect coastal water quality because of the distance of the proposed action from the coast.

4.1.1.2. Offshore

Offshore activities, discharges, and spills will affect offshore water quality to varying degrees. Accidental hydrocarbon spills are addressed in Appendix A. Routine development activities that have the potential to affect water quality offshore include discharge of drill mud and cuttings; discharges of well treatment, completion, and workover fluids; installation of anchor systems, pipelines and other subsea infrastructure; and discharge of sanitary and domestic waste. The primary effects of these activities will be localized increases in total suspended solids (TSS) or turbidity. Sanitary and domestic waste discharges are expected to increase nutrient input and biological oxygen demand (BOD) slightly, but this is not normally a concern in open oceanic waters. All discharges will adhere to existing regulatory discharge criteria designed to mitigate significant environmental effects.

A large oil spill or blowout, a very rare event that would be an exception, is examined in detail in Appendix A. The effects on offshore water quality from an offshore spill or blowout will depend on type of accident (e.g., subsurface or surface blowout, surface spill, etc.), the type and volume of hydrocarbons released, the environmental conditions during the event, and the type and volume of dispersant that might be used, if any. The potential behaviors of oil originating from a deepwater, subsurface blowout or pipeline rupture are not well known, but it is likely that at least some of the oil will surface to form a slick (Appendix A).

Routine production activities that will affect water quality include produced water, cooling water, and sanitary and domestic waste discharges. Decommissioning effects would presumably be similar in scope and magnitude with offshore construction and installation operations.

Sources of turbidity from offshore operations are mostly associated with the development phase for this proposal. They include

- discharge of drilling muds and cuttings,
- installation/removal of subsea infrastructure,
- installation of mooring anchors, and
- pipelaying and trenching activities.

Suspension of fine fractions from the drilling mud and cuttings in the water column results in increased localized turbidity. Unless the TSS from the drilling discharges are very high and chronic and unless they impinge on sensitive benthic communities, increased localized turbidity is not normally considered to have a significant effect on the marine water column. Discharge of drilling muds and cuttings is discussed in more detail in Chapter 4.2.2.3, Impacts on Deepwater Benthos and Sediment Communities.

The first 620 m (2,032 ft) or so of each well will be jetted or drilled without the use of drilling fluids, and thus cuttings [worst-case estimate of 1,813 bbl (BP, 2001, page 5-5)] will be the only source contributing to increased turbidity at the beginning of operations. Surface sediments [at least the upper 91 m (300 ft)] at the Holstein Project are known to be very fine clays (Fugro-McClelland Geosciences, Inc., 2001; BP, 2001), which when disturbed may stay in suspension for some time. The very fine fraction of the jetted or drilled material, including some of the very fine surface sediments, may create near-bottom turbidity that will be transported away from the drill site by the bottom currents (range of speed means are 6.6 to 17.4 cm/s measured near the Sigsbee Escarpment; Table 4-1 below) before dispersing and settling out. The current meter data suggest that most of the transport will be to the southwest [bottom currents at Sigsbee current meter moorings I-1, I-2, and J-1 flow to the SW quadrant (180-270 degrees) most of the time (55-73%)].

Table 4-1
Near Bottom Current Speeds at Sigsbee Escarpment Measured Over One Year

Mooring	Current Meter Depth (m)	Water Depth (m)	Mean (cm/s)	Minimum (cm/s)	Maximum (cm/s)
I-1 (MMS/SAIC)	1,946	1,951	9.55	0.00	46.04
I-2 (MMS/SAIC)	1,989	2,000	17.39	0.55	90.08
J-1 (BP/SAIC)	1,360	1,375	6.64	3.00	49.52

The remaining portion of the bore holes will be drilled using synthetic-based fluids (SBF's). Following treatment for SBF recovery, the deepest proposed well will discharge a maximum of 1,530 bbl of mud, adhering to 2,309 bbl of cuttings (total discharge of 3,839 bbl). The resulting discharges should create little turbidity in the area except near the discharge point, as SBF's tend to consolidate the cuttings, causing them to drop rather quickly to the seabed (USDOI, MMS, 2000; USEPA, 2001). Furthermore, because the drill muds and cuttings will be discharged near the surface, much of the associated turbidity will be dispersed before reaching the deepwater seabed. Discharged materials will probably distribute to the southwest of the drill site as currents measured in the water column flow mostly in that direction (68-73% of the time as measured at 1,170 m depth and near bottom at J-1).

BP has requested coverage under the USEPA's NPDES General Permit (GMG290000) and therefore must adhere to the volume discharge rate as stipulated under Part I.B.1(b), "Limitations" of the permit. The maximum discharge rate of 1,000 bbl/hour will not be exceeded. BP will also comply with the modifications of this permit proposed on April 27, 2001, if the modifications are in effect at the time BP begins its drilling operations.

Some seafloor disturbance may be required during the installation of the proposed subsea infrastructure. If so, these disturbances on the soft seabed will create elevated turbidity levels over limited areas and are expected to be for relatively short durations. The emplacement of anchors and mooring systems will result in seabed disturbance of the soft sediments. There are no documented areas of hard substrate within the Holstein development area near the anchors and mooring systems. Installation of the spar will be aided by a dynamically-positioned derrick barge that does not require anchors.

In summary, turbidity per se will create little impact on the water quality in the grid area and hence on its benthic communities because the inputs will be limited in amount, and the discharges will be spread out over time. Light limitation (one of the effects of high turbidity) in deepwater areas is not an issue. Surface sediments in the deepwater GOM are relatively pristine so that any turbidity created by bottom disturbances will not decrease water quality other than for the expected TSS increase. Any effects from elevated turbidity will be short term, localized, and reversible. However, the material causing the turbidity, especially drilling muds and cuttings, may have an effect when settling to the bottom. This issue is discussed in detail in Chapter 4.2.2.3, Deepwater Benthos and Sediment Communities.

Major discharges estimated for the proposed Holstein Project are shown in BP's DOCD. Of the discharges listed in the plan, produced water is the most likely to affect offshore water quality to any degree because it may contain elevated levels of hydrocarbons and metals, and because it will be discharged more or less continuously in fairly large amounts (25,000 bbl/day) throughout the production phase. BP intends to mitigate any potential effects from produced-water discharges by re-injecting as much of the produced water as is possible into underground strata and to treat any discharged water to specification equal to or lower than the USEPA's regulated levels of 29 mg/l monthly average and 42 mg/l upset limit (BP, 2001). Any produced water that has been treated and discharged is expected to disperse rapidly into the open oceanic environment. Table 4-3 gives selected discharge requirements under the current USEPA's NPDES General Permit (GMG290000).

Table 4-2

Selected Discharge Requirements under the Current NPDES General Permit

Regulated Discharge Parameter	Discharge Limitation/ Prohibition	Monitoring and Reporting Requirement: Frequency	Monitoring Requirement: Methodology
Oil and grease	42 mg/l daily maximum	Once/month	Grab sample at effluent port
	29 mg/l monthly average	Record daily maximum and monthly average	
Flow rate (bbl/month)	Monitor	Estimate and record monthly average	Once/month
Free oil	No free oil	Once/day and record number of days a sheen is observed	Visual sheen
Toxicity	7-day minimum NOEC* and monthly average minimum NOEC*	Record lowest NOEC on test run once per calendar quarter for discharge rates above 4,600 bbl/day	Grab sample at effluent port

Note: *NOEC means "no observable effect concentration."

Most reported sublethal and community effects have occurred in areas where a large quantity of produced water was discharged in a very shallow water environment (Osenberg et al., 1992; Rabalais et al., 1992; Raimondi et al., 1992; Mulino et al., 1996; Neff and Sauer, 1996). Produced-water discharges in Grid 10 will disperse in the water column before they reach the bottom and thus will not interact with the benthic environment.

Conclusion

Near-bottom water quality, primarily TSS, will be affected during the period of development drilling and installation of subsea infrastructure, including the moorings and anchors. However, these activities are not expected to create a significant impact because they will be relatively short term, not geographically extensive, and the near-bottom TSS will likely be within the natural range encountered during episodic events of high current velocities. Routine discharges from development activities such as deck drainage, excess cement, other well fluids, sanitary and domestic wastes, and cooling water will affect water quality (e.g., TSS, nutrients, chlorine, BOD) within tens of meters of the discharge.

Treated produced-water discharge will occur at varying volumes (up to 25,000 bbl/day) throughout the production phase and will affect local water quality, primarily increases in metals and hydrocarbons levels, proximate to the spar. The plume behavior and shape will be variable depending upon prevailing environmental conditions but, in total, will affect a relatively small area of oceanic water and will be rapidly diluted. Overall, there will be no significant effects to the water quality.

Effects to water quality during decommissioning operations will be similar or less than those that occur during development and thus are not considered significant.

Offshore effects from an accidental discharge of oil will affect water quality immediately under the slick (top few meters of the water column). Operator-initiated activities to contain and clean up an oil spill would begin as soon as possible after an event. However, the remaining portion of the discharged oil would weather, disperse, and biodegrade within a short period of time so that no significant long-term effects on offshore water quality are expected to occur. Appendix A provides additional detail on spills.

4.1.2. Impacts on Air Quality

There will be a limited degree of degradation of air quality in the vicinity of the proposed operations for the period of estimated production activities. The air emissions are expected to increase until 2003 Table 3-1 in Chapter 3, then gradually reduce to lower levels in 2007 through 2024.

Air quality would be affected in the event of a blowout or oil spill. The volative organic compounds (VOC's), which would escape, are precursors to photochemically produced ozone. A spike in VOC's could contribute to a corresponding spike in ozone, especially if the release were to occur on a hot, sunny day in a NO_2-rich environment. The corresponding onshore area for the project is in attainment for ozone. (USEPA, 2001). If a fire occurs, particulate and combustible emissions will be released in addition to the VOC's.

Conclusion

The proposed action is not expected to result in any significant impacts to air quality.

4.2. BIOLOGICAL RESOURCES

4.2.1. Impacts on Sensitive Coastal Environments

The following section describes potential impacts to coastal barrier beaches and associated dunes from oil spills that might occur as a result of proposed activities in Grid 10. Appendix A also describes the probability of an oil spill and the estimated dispersal characteristics should a spill occur. The Oilmap spill model used by Morris Environmental, Inc. (BP, 2001) also describes probabilities of spill movement around the GOM and projected potential contacts with the shore. Spill response and effectiveness is also discussed in Appendix A.

Contact between an oil slick and a beach primarily depends upon environmental conditions and the nature of the oil spilled. Morris Environmental, Inc. (BP, 2001) indicates that, if a spill was to occur in Launch Area 44 and if it were to persist for 10 days, there is a very low probability of that spill contacting land within that timeframe.

It is not very likely that severe adverse impacts would occur to dunes from a spill within Grid 10. For storm tides to carry oil from a spill across and over the dunes, strong southerly or easterly winds must persist for an extended period of time, prior to or immediately after the spill. The strong winds that would be required to raise the water level sufficiently to contact dunes would also result in oil slick dispersal, thereby reducing impact severity at a landfall site. In addition, a study in Texas showed that oil on vegetated sand dunes had no deleterious effects on the existing vegetation or on the recolonization of the oiled sand by plants (Webb, 1988).

Cleanup operations associated with large oil spills can affect the stability of barrier beaches more than the spill itself. If large quantities of sand were removed during spill cleanup operations, a new beach profile and sand configuration would be established in response to the reduced sand supply and volume. The net result of these changes could be accelerated rates of shoreline erosion at the contact site and down drift of that site. This situation would be accentuated in sand-starved or eroding barrier beaches, such as those found on the Louisiana coast. State governments around the Gulf have recognized these problems and have established policies to limit sand removal by cleanup operations.

Conclusion

The proposed action is not expected to adversely alter barrier beach or dune configurations significantly as a result of a related oil spill should one occur.

4.2.1.1. Wetlands

A description of a hypothetical oil spill associated with the proposed action is provided in Appendix A. The information below regarding potential impacts of oil spills on wetlands is based on analyses in the Final EIS for Central Gulf of Mexico Lease Sales 169, 172, 175, 178, and 182 (USDOI, MMS, 1997a).

Data in Appendix A indicate that a very low probability exists for an oil spill to occur from the Holstein development. As discussed in USDOI, MMS (1997a), distant offshore spills have even a further diminished probability of impacting inland wetland shorelines and seagrasses, largely due to the sheltered locations of these habitats.

An inland fuel-oil spill may occur at a shore base or as a result of a vessel collision. The probability of an inland, fuel-oil spill occurring in association with the proposed action is very small. However, should a spill occur inshore or in nearshore waters, it presents a much greater potential for adversely impacting wetlands and seagrasses than an offshore spill, due simply to their proximity to the spill. Oil could accumulate in sheens and thick layers in the marsh and in protected pools and embayments.

The works of several investigators (Webb et al., 1981 and 1985; Alexander and Webb, 1983, 1985, and 1987; Lytle, 1975; Delaune et al., 1979; Fischel et al., 1989) were used to evaluate impacts of potential spills to area wetlands. For wetlands along the central Louisiana area, the critical oil concentration is assumed to be 1.0 liter/ m^2 of marsh. Concentrations above this will result in longer-term impacts to wetland vegetation, including some plant mortality and loss of land. Concentrations less than this may cause diebacks for one growing season or less, depending upon the concentration and the season during which contact occurs.

Conclusion

It is highly unlikely that significant adverse impacts to wetlands would result from a spill associated with the proposed project. If a spill does occurs at the offshore site, oceanographic and meteorological conditions are very unlikely to move oil far enough in a short enough time to cause oil contacts with wetlands. If an unlikely, project-related fuel-oil spill occurs inshore, some wetlands in the spill vicinity may be adversely impacted. A spill's secondary impacts from cleanup activities present a greater impact potential.

4.2.1.2. Seagrasses

Seagrasses have generally experienced little or no damage from oil spills (Chan, 1977; Zieman et al., 1984). The relative low susceptibility of seagrasses in the northern GOM to oil-spill impacts is partly the result of their location, which is subtidal, generally landward of barrier islands and in a region with a small tidal range. Furthermore, it should be noted that seagrasses are much less common in Louisiana, the most likely landfall for a spill, than elsewhere in the Gulf, particularly Florida.

The lack of low-tide exposure protects seagrasses from direct contact with oil. The degree of impact depends on water depth, the nature of the oil, and the tidal and weather events in the affected area during the presence of the floating oil. Another reason for the low susceptibility of seagrass to oil spills is that a large percentage of their biomass is found in the buried root and rhizome, from which the leaves generate. An oil spill that moves over a seagrass area would not be expected to directly cause anything but slight damage to the vegetation. Some seagrass dieback for one growing season might occur, largely depending upon water currents and weather. No permanent loss of seagrass habitat is expected to result from such spills.

During extremely low water conditions such as wind-driven tidal events, seagrass beds might be exposed to the air and could potentially be impacted directly by an oil slick. Even then, their roots and rhizomes remain buried in the water bottom. Given the geography of the coastal area discussed, a strong wind that could lower the water that much generally would be a northerly or westerly wind, which would push water out of bays and estuaries and drive a slick away from the coast. In this situation, oil that was already in the bay or sound would be driven against the southern or eastern shores. Any seagrass beds that may be exposed there might be contacted.

The greatest oil-spill effect to seagrass communities has been to the diversity and populations of the epifaunal community found in the grass bed. Should water turbulence and turbidity increase sufficiently, some oil on the water surface may be emulsified. Suspended particles in the water column will adsorb oil from a sheen as well as from emulsified droplets, causing some particulates to clump together and decrease their suspendability. Typically, submerged vegetation reduces water velocity among the vegetation as well as for a short distance above it. Reduced flow velocity or turbulence further enhances sedimentation.

Minute oil droplets, whether emulsified or bound to suspended particulates, may adhere to vegetation or other marine life; they may be ingested by animals, particularly by filter and sedimentation feeders; or they may settle onto bottom sediments in or around a bed. In these situations, oil has a limited life because it will be degraded chemically and biologically (Zieman et al., 1984).

The potential danger to a seagrass community from an oil-spill event is a reduction for up to two years of the diversity or population of epifauna and benthic fauna found in grass beds. The degree of impact further depends on the time of year, water depth, currents, and weather in the affected area during the presence of a slick, as well as oil density, solubility, ability to emulsify, and toxicity.

A more damaging scenario would involve the secondary impacts of a slick that remains, for a period of time, over a submerged bed of vegetation in a protected embayment during typical fairweather conditions. This would reduce light levels in the bed. If light reduction continues for several days, chlorophyll content in the leaves will be reduced (Wolfe et al., 1988), causing the grasses to yellow, reducing their productivity. By itself, shading from an oil slick should not last long enough to cause mortality. This depends upon the slick thickness, currents, weather, efforts to clean up the slick, and the nature of the embayment.

Also, a slick that remains over a submerged vegetation bed in an embayment will reduce or eliminate oxygen exchange between the air and the water of the embayment. Currents may not flush adequately oxygenated water from the larger waterbody to the shallow embayment. Seagrasses and related epifauna might be stressed and perhaps suffocated if the biochemical oxygen demand is high, as would be expected for a shallow waterbody that contains submerged vegetation, with its usual detritus load, and an additional burden of spilled oil (Wolfe et al., 1988).

Clean up of slicks that come to rest in shallow or protected waters [0 to 1.5 m (0 to 5 ft) deep] may be performed using "john" boats, booms, anchors and skimmers mounted on boats or shore vehicles. Personnel assisting in oil-spill cleanup in water shallower than about 1m (3-4 ft) may readily wade through the water to complete their tasks. Foot traffic and equipment can easily damage the seagrass beds. Oil can also be worked more deeply into their sediments by these activities.

As described for wetlands, oil that penetrates or is buried into the water bottom is less available for dissolution, oxidation, or microbial degradation. Oil may then be detectable in the sediments for five years or more, depending upon circumstances.

Navigational vessels that vary their route from established navigational channels can directly scar shallow beds of submerged vegetation with their props, keels (or flat bottoms), and anchors (Durako et al., 1992).

Conclusion

It is highly unlikely that significant adverse impacts to seagrasses would result from a spill associated with the proposed project. If a spill does occurs at the offshore site, oceanographic and meteorological conditions are very unlikely to move oil far enough in a short enough time to cause oil contacts with seagrasses. If an unlikely, project-related fuel-oil spill occurs inshore, some wetlands in the spill vicinity may be adversely impacted; however, seagrasses are unlikely to be impacted directly. A spill's secondary impacts, including shading, suffocation, and cleanup activities present a greater impact potential.

4.2.2. Impacts on Deepwater Benthic Communities/Organisms

4.2.2.1. Chemosynthetic Communities

BP proposes to drill Well "B" with an anchored MODU (semisubmersible rig). An area that could support a dense chemsynthetic invertebrate community is possible approximately 122 m (400 ft) from the MODU's # 8 anchor location. BP is required to comply with the MMS's Mitigation 5.01 (see wording below). No other potential chemosynthetic community areas were identified within 152 m (500 ft) of the remaining MODU's anchor pattern or the proposed spar anchor locations. Mitigation 5.01 reads as follows:

In your plan, you have stated that your proposed activities are in the vicinity of areas that could support high-density chemosynthetic communities. Therefore, please be reminded that you will use a state-of-the-art positioning system (e.g., differential global positioning system) on your anchor handling vessel to ensure that any sea floor disturbance resulting from your use of anchors (including that caused by the anchors, anchor chains, and wire ropes) does not occur within 250 feet of such areas (see the enclosed map which depicts the areas). Additionally, you will submit plats, at a scale of 1 inch equals 1,000 feet with DGPS accuracy, to this office within 60 days after completion of operations which depict the "as placed" location of all anchors, anchor chains, and wire ropes and demonstrate that the features were not physically impacted by these anchoring activities.

Conclusion

The proposed Holstein Project will not have an impact on known chemosynthetic communities.

4.2.2.2. Coral Reefs

Coral reefs in the GOM are normally associated with topographic features. There are no known topographic highs in Grid 10; thus, there are no known shallow-water coral reefs in this area (Figure 3-1). Deepwater coral reefs are rare in the GOM, and there are no documented hard substrate areas that might support deepwater corals in Grid 10.

Conclusion

The proposed project will have no impact on any known coral reefs.

4.2.2.3. Deepwater Benthos and Sediment Communities

The deepwater benthos in the immediate vicinity of the proposed project will be impacted by the discharge of drilling mud and cuttings (and to a limited extent, other well completion fluids), placement of mooring lines and anchor pilings, well site locations, and construction of the associated pipelines. The most common adverse impact will be physical smothering by sediments and anoxia caused by rapid biodegradation at the seafloor. Invertebrates, many with some degree of mobility, typically dominate the megafaunal benthic communities at the 1,324 m (4,344 ft) water depth. This zone has less biomass and species of megafauna than are found in shallower water (Gallaway et al., 2001). The macrofauna is dominated by deposit feeding polychaete worms with varying degrees of mobility and tolerance to disturbance. The meiofauna, primarily composed of small nematode worms, is more abundant than macrofauna, and their numbers decline with depth. Little is known of the microbiota in deepwater, but it probably includes hydrocarbon-degrading forms. All of the benthic communities found in Green Canyon Blocks 644 and 645 are not unique to the area and appear to be widespread throughout the Gulf, where depths, substrates, and other environmental factors are suitable.

The effects of drilling muds and cuttings on the deepwater benthos will be limited for the following reasons:

- Low Toxicity. The SBF's are expensive and are recycled. Any unusable portion is sent to approved disposal sites onshore. The SBF cuttings will be treated to conform to regulatory guidelines. The SBF is essentially nontoxic, and the composite formulation of the discharged fluid adhering to the cuttings has a very low toxicity to aquatic organisms. Most of the SBF's in current use can easily pass the USEPA's 96-hour, LC_{50} criteria of 30,000 ppm (McKelvie and Ayers, 1999). Test results with four types of SBF's on algae—mysids, copepods, mussels, and amphipods—range from 277 to 1,000,000 ppm (McKelvie and Ayers, 1999). Dose response studies on fish by Payne et al. (2001a and b) demonstrated that sediments contaminated with Hibernia (Grand Banks, Newfoundland) source cuttings containing an aliphatic

38

hydrocarbon-based synthetic drilling fluid (IPAR) had a very low toxicity potential. Acute toxicity was not observed in juvenile flounder exposed for up to two months to sediment containing approximately 6,000 ppm of diesel-range (aliphatic) hydrocarbons.

- Limited Biological Effects. The only direct biological effect reported for SBF's and associated cuttings in the field environment has been smothering of benthic animals by physical and/or anoxic conditions. Anoxia is caused by the rapid biodegradation of the SBF's. Organic enrichment due to the introduction of carbon into a carbon-poor environment has also been noted (Pompano Study).

- Limited Affected Area. Cuttings from wells drilled with SBF's tend to clump together and are transported to the bottom relatively quickly. Thus, the affected area will be relatively small. The vast majority of historical literature (based on the more toxic oil-based muds or water-based muds (WBM's), which tend to disperse farther) indicates biological effects generally do not occur beyond 500 m (1,640 ft) from the source, although several papers have noted subtle effects beyond that range. Most relevant is the recent research in the North Sea (Jensen et al., 1999) that studied a number of platforms that used only SBF's. That study found no benthic effects (i.e., benthic effects as measured by subtle community changes) beyond 250 m (820 ft) in most cases, 500 m (1,640 ft) in a few cases. However, one must note that the North Sea is a shallower environment than the deepwater Gulf of Mexico.

The anchor system and mooring lines should have minimal effects on the benthos because they will be kept in a semi-taut mode using a specialized tensioning system. Installation of the anchors and activities at the proposed well sites will physically disturb the benthos in the immediate area. The proposed pipeline installations (a 24-in for crude oil and a 20-in for natural gas) have the potential to disturb the benthos along a narrow corridor until they reach an existing transfer platform in shallower water. Detailed routing has not been determined, but routing considerations will include avoidance of potential sensitive areas of topographic features and chemosynthetic communities. The benthos would also be affected in the unlikely event of a subsea blowout that caused disturbance and slumping of the surrounding seabed.

Conclusion

Structure emplacement (including anchor installations and moorings), well drilling and completion operations, and pipelining activities will disturb benthic communities by smothering and displacing them from patches within 500 m (1,640 ft) of the spar location and within a limited area of the anchors. Partial recovery of the community will occur within months of the disturbance probably followed by a more or less full recovery within 1-2 years. This will not result in a significant impact on the benthic communities because the duration and area extent of the proposed activities will be limited.

Routine production activities will not significantly impact the benthos. A subsea blowout would physically disturb the benthos within a small radius of the blowout, but most of the released fluids are expected to go to the surface and not interact with deepwater benthos.

Effects of decommissioning are not well characterized at this time because the detailed decommissioning scenario is not known due to uncertainties in future strategies and technologies. However, the overall effects is expected to be less than the initial installation and thus not significant to the benthos.

4.2.3. Impacts on Marine Mammals

Factors that could adversely affect cetaceans include increased vessel traffic, degradation of water quality from operational discharges, helicopter and vessel traffic noise, platform and drillship noise, structure removals, seismic surveys, oil spills, oil-spill-response activities, loss of debris from service vessels and OCS structures, commercial fishing, capture and removal, and pathogens. The cumulative impact on cetaceans is expected to result in a number of chronic and sporadic sublethal effects that may serve to stress and/or weaken individuals of a local group or population and make them more susceptible to infection from natural or anthropogenic sources. Few lethal effects are expected from oil spills, chance collisions with service vessels, ingestion of plastic material, fishing, and pathogens. Oil spills of any size are estimated to be aperiodic events that may contact cetaceans. Deaths as a result of structure removals are not expected to occur because of anticipated mitigation measures required by NMFS and MMS. Disturbance (e.g., noise) and/or exposure to sublethal levels of biotoxins and anthropogenic contaminants may stress animals, weaken their immune systems, and make them more vulnerable to parasites and diseases that normally would not be fatal.

Another factor of concern is the ability that cetaceans (more specifically, sperm whales) possess for detecting and avoiding the various flowlines, risers, umbilicals, and mooring lines associated with the Holstein spar. Sperm whales are known to get entangled in deep-sea cables (Heezen, 1957). The net result of any disturbance would depend on the size and percentage of the population affected, ecological importance of the disturbed area, environmental and biological parameters that influence an animal's sensitivity to disturbance and stress, and the accommodation time in response to prolonged disturbance (Geraci and St. Aubin, 1980). Collisions between cetaceans and ships could cause serious injury or death (Laist et al., 2001). Sperm whales are one of 11 whale species that are hit commonly by ships (Laist et al., 2001). Collisions between OCS vessels and cetaceans in the grid area are expected to be unusual events.

Conclusion

The incremental contribution of the proposed action and known prospects in the grid is minimal and is unlikely to have significant long-term adverse impacts on the size and productivity of any marine mammal species or population stock in the northern GOM.

4.2.4. Impacts on Sea Turtles

Routine development, production and decommissioning activities that could impact sea turtles include vessel traffic, noise, trash and debris, and water quality impacts.

Small numbers of turtles could be killed or injured by chance collision with service vessels or by eating indigestible trash, particularly plastic items, accidentally lost from drill rigs, production facilities, and service vessels. Deaths due to structure removals will be unlikely due to mitigation requirements of NMFS and MMS. Drilling rigs and project vessels produce noise that could disrupt normal behavior patterns and create some stress potentially making sea turtles more susceptible to disease. Discharge of cuttings and associated SBF's are not expected to interact with sea turtles.

Oil spills and oil-spill-response activities are potential threats that could have lethal effects on turtles. Contact with oil, consumption of oil particles, and oil-contaminated prey could seriously effect individual sea turtles. Oil-spill-response planning and the habitat protection requirements of the Oil Pollution Act of 1990 should mitigate these threats.

Conclusion

Most OCS-related impacts on sea turtles are expected to be sublethal. Chronic sublethal effects (e.g., stress) resulting in persistent physiological or behavioral changes and/or avoidance of effected areas could cause declines in survival or productivity, resulting in gradual population declines. The incremental contributions of the proposed action and the projected development within Grid 10 are minimal and they are, therefore, unlikely to have significant long-term adverse effects on the size and productivity of any sea turtle species or stock in the northern GOM.

4.2.5. Impacts on Coastal and Marine Birds

4.2.5.1. *Nonendangered and Nonthreatened Birds*

This section discusses the possible effects of the proposed action and future actions within the grid on coastal and marine birds of the GOM and its contiguous waters and wetlands. Air emissions, water quality degradation resulting from discharges, helicopter and service vessel traffic and noise, light attraction, and discarded trash and debris from service vessels and the drilling rig may affect coastal and marine birds. A blowout or spill at the spar site represents a large spill scenario that is equivalent to a day's maximum production and is an amount much larger than the amounts that will actually be stored on site. Associated spill-response activities may also impact coastal and marine birds. Any effects would be especially critical for intensively managed populations such as endangered and threatened species that need to maintain a viable reproductive population size or that depend upon a few key habitats. Species of special concern are often populations at the edge of their range. These populations may be more vulnerable to effects than populations of the same species living near the center of their range.

Emissions of pollutants into the atmosphere from the activities associated with the proposed action and known future developments are projected to have minimal effects on offshore air quality because of the prevailing atmospheric conditions, emission heights, and pollutant concentrations. Such emissions are projected to have negligible effects on onshore air quality because of the atmospheric regime, emission rates, and distance of these emissions from the coastline. These judgments are based on average steady state conditions; however, there will be days of low mixing heights and low wind speeds that could further decrease air quality. These conditions are characterized by fog formation, which in the Gulf occurs about 35 days a year, mostly during winter. Impacts from offshore sources are reduced in winter because the frequency of significant onshore winds decreases and the removal of pollutants by rain increases. The summer is more conducive to air quality effects as onshore winds occur more frequently.

Helicopter and service-vessel traffic related to the proposed and future actions could sporadically disturb feeding, resting or nesting behavior of birds or cause abandonment of preferred habitat. These impact-producing factors could contribute to indirect population loss through reproductive failure resulting from nest abandonment. The FAA (Advisory Circular 91-36C) and corporate helicopter policy state that, when flying over land, the specified minimum altitude is 610 m (2,000 ft) over populated areas and biologically sensitive areas such as wildlife refuges and national parks. However, pilots traditionally have taken great pride in not disturbing birds. It is expected that approximately 10 percent of helicopter trips would occur at altitudes somewhat below the minimums listed above as a result of inclement weather. Although these incidents are very short term in duration and sporadic in frequency, they can disrupt coastal bird behavior and, at worst, possibly result in habitat or nest abandonment.

Service vessels would use selected nearshore and coastal (inland) navigation waterways, or corridors, and adhere to protocol established by the USCG for reduced vessel speeds within these inland areas. Routine presence and low speeds of service vessels within these waterways would diminish the effects of disturbance from service vessels on nearshore and inland populations of coastal and marine birds. The effects of routine service-vessel traffic on birds offshore therefore would be negligible.

Seabirds (e.g., laughing gulls and petrels) may be attracted by the lights and/or structures and may remain and feed in the vicinity of the spar structure. These individuals could be affected by operational discharges or runoff in the offshore environment. Impacts may be both direct and indirect.

Coastal and marine birds are periodically observed entangled and snared in discarded trash and debris. In addition, many species readily ingest small plastic debris, either intentionally or incidentally. Such interactions can lead to serious injury and death. The MMS prohibits the disposal of equipment, containers, and other materials into offshore waters by lessees (30 CFR 250.300). Thus, it is expected that coastal and marine birds would seldom become entangled in or ingest OCS-related trash and debris. MARPOL (Annex V, Public Law 100-220; 101 Statute 1458; effective January 1989) prohibits the disposal of any plastics at sea or in coastal waters. Thus, due to the low potential for interaction between coastal and marine birds and project-related debris, any effects will be negligible.

The operator postulated a large worst-case blowout or spill scenario (Appendix A). While the potential for reaching any specific part of the Louisiana coast from the spar site within 28 days is relatively small (1-8%, Morris Environmental, Inc. in BP, 2001), it is possible that various birds along the coast could experience mortality and reproductive losses. Recovery would depend on subsequent influxes of birds from nearby feeding, roosting and nesting habitats.

Oil-spill cleanup methods often require heavy traffic on beaches and wetland areas. For example, operations such as the application of oil dispersant and bioremediation chemicals, and the distribution and collection of oil containment booms and absorbent material involve labor intensive activities. The presence of humans, along with boats, aircraft, and equipment, will also disturb coastal birds after a spill. Investigations have shown that oil dispersant mixtures pose a similar threat to that of oil in its effects on bird reproduction (Albers, 1979; Albers and Gay, 1982). The external exposure of adult birds to oil/dispersant emulsions may reduce chick survival more than exposure to oil alone; however, successful dispersal of a spill will generally reduce the probability of exposure of coastal and marine birds to oil (Butler et al., 1988). It is possible that changes in the size of a breeding population may also be a result of disturbance from increased human activity related to cleanup, monitoring, and research efforts (Maccarone and Brzorad, 1994). A growing number of studies indicate that current rehabilitation techniques are not effective in returning healthy birds to the wild (Anderson et al., 1996; Boersma, 1995; Sharp, 1995 and 1996). Deterrent or preventative methods, such as scaring birds from the path of an approaching oil slick or the use of booms to protect sensitive colonies, have extremely limited applicability.

4.2.5.2. Federally Endangered and Threatened Birds

Piping Plover

The effects from offshore activities discussed above for shorebirds not listed as endangered or threatened also apply to the piping plover. A slick from a large spill or blowout, should it reach the coast, could injure or kill birds foraging or roosting along the shoreline. However, the amount of shoreline affected would be relatively small compared to the extensive shoreline habitat available in the northern GOM.

Bald Eagle

The bald eagle feeds on fish, waterfowl, shorebirds, and carrion near water. This bird may come in contact with an oil spill by eating contaminated dead and dying prey. Bald eagles have narrow preferences for nesting habitat. Any oiling of aquatic feeding habitat resulting in nest site abandonment could lead to relocation of a nest to less preferred habitat. This event, in turn, could reduce population growth for this already threatened species. However, the bald eagle has high mobility and, when an oil slick enters the feeding habitat, may relocate feeding to unpolluted parts of the waterbodies. When relocating feeding far from the nest, the eagle would successfully home to its nest after feeding because it prefers to build the nest in a highly visible place above the forest canopy.

Brown Pelican

The brown pelican is a species of special concern in Louisiana and Mississippi, although it is no longer listed as endangered or threatened in Florida or Alabama (USDOI, FWS, 1998). It is known to nest on Guillard Island, Alabama, a dredge spoil island in Mobile Bay. There have been no reported nesting sites in Mississippi. Impacts to individual brown pelicans would be similar to those identified for the nonendangered and nonthreatened species discussed in preceding sections.

Conclusion

It is expected that the majority of effects from the potential impact-producing factors on coastal and marine birds would be sublethal (behavioral effects and nonfatal intakes of discarded debris), causing temporary disturbance and displacement of localized groups, mostly inshore. However, chronic stress such as digestive upset, partial digestive occlusion, sublethal ingestions, and behavioral changes are often difficult to detect. Such stresses can weaken individuals and make them more susceptible to infection and disease as well as making migratory species less fit for migration. A large spill or blowout and the associated spill response can cause mortality to a number of bird species including ones of special concern. Although their rarity will make them less likely to be affected, any reductions in numbers may threaten their existence as a population.

Coastal and marine birds may encounter periodic disturbance and temporary displacement of localized groups and individuals from the routine activities associated with the proposed action and future known prospects within the grid. Decreases in the numbers of adults and/or nests could occur as a result of a large spill or blowout, if spill-related coastal habitat loss or degradation occurs. The risk of a spill of this size occurring is very small, and the risk of impinging on any specific area of the Louisiana coast is between 1 and 8 percent. Species groups experiencing the loss of individuals could require up to several years to recover to preexisting states.

4.2.6. Impacts on Fish Resources

Development activities that have potential to affect fish and fish habitat include drilling and vessel noise, discharge of mud and cuttings, and construction effects on water quality. Decommissioning effects would be similar to those from construction and installation of facilities. Production activities that may affect fish are those primarily associated with the "artificial reef effect" and the discharge of produced water.

Responses to noise are extremely variable and dependent upon many factors such as species, life stage, sound characteristics, environmental conditions, water depth, bottom substrate, and timing, to name just a few. Some research has been done and suggests that fish will habituate to routine noise as evidenced by their attraction to offshore structures in both numbers of species and individuals (Gallaway and Lewbel, 1982; and Stanley and Wilson, 1997). Herring are known to be sensitive to sound and to be affected by it (Blaxter et al., 1981; Schwarz and Greer, 1984), but even this species appears to habituate. For example, seiners fishing for Pacific herring will allow newly-arrived schools of herring to adjust to boat noises for several days before commencing seining activity (Schwarz and Greer, 1984).

Vessel traffic for the proposed action will be less than a 1 percent incremental increase over existing passages of traffic in the northern GOM. Most fish will habituate to regular ship traffic, particularly if it is not overly noisy or 'stop and start.' Even in this latter case, effects would last no more than a few hours or days.

Drill cuttings with mud adhering to them will be discharged to the water column at the well sites and may contain some contaminant metals that are harmful to fish. However, contaminant levels will reach background levels about 1,000 m (3,281 ft) from discharge and be undetectable beyond 3,000 m (9,843 ft) from the site (USDOI, MMS, 2001b). The SBF's are virtually nontoxic, and cuttings with adherent SBF are expected to reach the seabed quickly in the form of clumps. Biological effects on the benthos are not expected beyond 500 m (1,640) (Jensen et al., 1999; USEPA, 2001).

The spar and associated lines and risers can be expected to attract fish seeking cover and food. Produced-water discharges may affect fish in the immediate area of discharge, but the plume should reach non-impact levels within a few tens of meters. Likewise, concentrations sufficient to cause sublethal effects should cover a small area.

Accidental oil spills or blowouts also have the potential to affect fish resources. Adult fish will, for the most part, avoid the oil (Malins et al., 1982; NRC, 1985; Baker et al., 1991; Farr et al., 1995; USDOI, MMS, 2001a and b). Furthermore, adult fish must become exposed to crude oil for some time, probably on the order of several months for doses and types of oil to be encountered in the field, to suffer serious biological damage (Payne et al., 1988). Adult fish also possess some capability for metabolizing oil (Spies et al., 1982).

On the other hand, invertebrate and fish eggs and larvae are known to be very sensitive to oil in water (Linden et al., 1979; Longwell, 1977; Baker et al., 1991). However, most fish species produce very large numbers of eggs and larvae spread over wide areas. In order for an oil spill to affect fish resources at the population level, it would have to be very large and cover a very large area that corresponded to an area of highly concentrated eggs and larvae. In addition, the oil would have to disperse deep enough into the water column at levels high enough to cause toxic effects. None of these events would seem likely, even in the low-risk, large-spill scenario. However, it should be noted that the use of dispersants, while potentially beneficial for surface-using birds, turtles and mammals, could increase the effects on water column organisms including ichthyoplankton. A worst case, in terms of location, would be a spill of fresh oil in a shallow, enclosed bay that contained eggs and larvae of important inshore species such as menhaden, shrimp, or blue crabs. Oil from the hypothetical offshore blowout would be well weathered before it hit shore, if in fact it did so. In addition, spawning areas of most species of marine fish are widespread enough to avoid catastrophic effects at the population level.

Conclusion

Fish will habituate to the routine noise associated with the Holstein development. Nonroutine noise may affect behavior in the short term if the sound is sudden and strong enough, but recovery will occur within hours or at most a few days. In fact, the structures will probably attract a variety of fish species. Produced water will influence water quality and hence, could potentially produce sublethal effects in fish over a limited area. Any effects will be local and not significant.

Impacts on demersal fish from drilling activities will be negligible. There are no commercially-valuable demersal fish species in the area and effects on bottom fish habitat from cuttings and adherent SBF's will likely be limited to within 500 m (1,640 ft) of the discharge.

Specific effects from oil spills will depend on several factors including timing, location, volume and type of oil, environmental conditions, countermeasures used. The areas affected by the potential spill or blowout scenario will be avoided by adult fish. Fish eggs and larvae of some species of invertebrates and fish will be affected by a spill and some will suffer mortality in areas where their numbers are concentrated in the upper few meters of water and where oil concentrations under the slick are high enough. However, oil and fish concentrations, exposure times, and area affected will not be great enough to cause significant impacts to northern GOM fish populations.

In summary, it is expected that marine environmental degradation from the proposed action and future known prospects in the grid would have little effect on fish resources or essential fish habitat. The level of marine environmental degradation from the Holstein development is expected to cause a small, undetectable decrease in fish populations and EFH.

4.2.7. Impacts on Gulf Sturgeon

Generally, the westernmost extent of the endangered Gulf sturgeon's river and estuarine system habitat is the Pearl River (the eastern border of St. Tammany Parish, LA); however, extant occurrences include the Mississippi River and Lake Pontchartrain, Louisiana (Patrick, personal communication, 1996). The Pearl River area is over 322 km (200 mi) from the Holstein development (Green Canyon, Blocks 644 and 645) and is behind barrier islands. The calculated spill risk to these organisms is in all cases < 0.5 percent, the lowest discernable limit of the OSRA model. No impacts to Gulf sturgeon are expected from the proposed Holstein development nor from other developmental activities in Grid 10.

4.3. IMPACTS ON SOCIOECONOMIC CONDITIONS AND OTHER CONCERNS

4.3.1. Effects on Economic and Demographic Conditions

In Chapter 3, MMS defined the potential impact region as that portion of the GOM coastal zone whose social and economic well-being (population, labor, and employment) is directly or indirectly affected by the OCS oil and gas industry. In this section, MMS projects how and where future changes will occur and whether they correlate with the proposed action and future development in the grid.

4.3.1.1. Population and Education

The impact region's population will continue to grow, but at a slower rate. Minimal effects on population are projected from activities associated with the proposed action. While some of the labor force is expected to be local to the Port Fourchon and Venice, Louisiana, areas, most of the additional employees associated with the proposed action are not expected to require local housing. Activities relating to the proposed operations are not expected to significantly affect the region's educational levels.

4.3.1.2. Infrastructure and Land Use

While OCS-related servicing should increase in Port Fourchon and Venice, Louisiana, no expansion of these physical facilities is expected to result from the proposed activities. Changes in land use throughout the region as a result of the proposed activities are expected to be contained and minimal. While land use in the impact area will change over time, the majority of this change is estimated as general regional growth.

4.3.1.3. *Navigation and Port Usage*

The proposed action will use the existing onshore support bases located in Port Fourchon and or in Venice, Louisiana, for completion, facility installation, commissioning, and production activities. The vessels to be used will be crewboats and supply boats. The table below depicts the number of these boat trips per week anticipated for each type of operation named above. Both the Port Fourchon and Venice shore bases are capable of providing the services necessary for the proposed activities; therefore, no onshore expansion or construction is anticipated with respect to the proposed action.

Table 4-3

Number of Anticipated Boat Trips per Week for Each Activity

Type of Vessel	Completions	Facility Installations	Commissioning	Production
Crewboat	3	7	7	2
Supply Boat	2	7	5	3

4.3.1.4. *Employment*

The importance of the oil and gas industry to the coastal communities of the GOM is significant, particularly in Louisiana, eastern Texas, and coastal Alabama. Dramatic changes in the level of OCS oil and gas activity over recent years have resulted in similar fluctuations in population, labor, and employment in the GOM region. This economic analysis focuses on the potential direct, indirect, and induced impacts of the OCS oil and gas industry on the population and employment of the counties and parishes in the impact region.

To improve regional economic impact assessments and to make them more consistent with each other, MMS recently developed a methodology for estimating changes to employment and other economic factors. The methodology developed to quantify these impacts on population and employment takes into account changes in OCS-related employment, along with population impacts resulting from these employment changes within each individual coastal subarea.

The model for the GOM region has two steps. Since there are no publicly available models that estimate the expenditures resulting from offshore oil and gas activities, the first step in the model estimates the expenditures resulting from BP's Initial DOCD (for the fabrication/installation of a truss spar and the drilling and completion of five development wells from a MODU and 10 development wells from a platform drilling rig and the re-entering and completion of an existing appraisal well) and assigns these expenditures to industrial sectors in the 10 MMS coastal subareas defined in Chapter 3. The second step in the model uses multipliers from the commercial input-output model IMPLAN (using 1998 data, the latest available data) to translate these expenditures into direct, indirect, and induced employment and other economic factors. Direct employment results from the first round of industry spending. It is the employment that results from the initial dollars spent by BP on the spar and development wells from their fabrication/installation or completion through their productive lives. Indirect employment results as the initial spending reverberates through the economy. First, the suppliers of the goods and services for the spar and wells spend the initial direct dollars from the industry. These dollars are then re-spent by other suppliers until the initial dollars have trickled throughout the economy. Labor income produces induced spending by the households receiving that income.

Both the level (the amount spent) and the sectoral (the industry in which it is spent) allocation of expenditures can vary considerably. Because local economies vary, a separate set of IMPLAN multipliers is used for each MMS coastal subarea to which expenditures are assigned. Each set of multipliers is based on the actual historical patterns of economic transactions in the area. Model results for employment are presented in number of jobs per year, where one job is defined as a year of employment. This does not necessarily mean only one person occupies the position through out the year. One job may be equal to two part-time positions occupied over the year or one person occupying a position for 6 months, while another person occupies it for the other 6 months.

Table F-7 in Appendix F shows total employment projections for activities resulting from the proposed action for the peak year of 2004. The projections are expressed as absolute numbers and as a percentage of the employment levels expected if no development occurs. Note that Subareas LA-1, LA-2, LA-3, and MA-1 constitute the Central Planning Area; TX-1 and TX-2 represent the Western Planning Area; and FL-1, FL-2, FL-3, and FL-4 comprise the Eastern Planning Area. The baseline projections of employment used in this analysis are described in Chapter 3.

Since these baseline projections assume the continuation of existing social, economic, and technological trends, they also include employment resulting from the continuation of current patterns in OCS Program activities. Based on model results, peak-year (year 2004) direct employment associated with the proposed action is estimated at 801 jobs. Indirect employment for the peak year is projected at 346 jobs, while induced employment is calculated to be 369 jobs. Although the majority of employment is expected to occur in coastal TX-2, employment is not expected to exceed 1 percent of the total employment in any given subarea. Additional completions of development wells will occur in the years 2005 and 2006, resulting in an estimated 275-280 direct, indirect, and induced jobs throughout all subareas. Again, this represents less than 1 percent of total employment in any subarea. Direct, indirect, and induced employment from 2007 through 2021 (that associated with operation and maintenance and workover activities) is expected at about 50 jobs throughout all subareas and is expected be less than 1 percent of total employment in any subarea.

The resource costs of cleaning up an oil spill, both onshore and offshore, were not included in the above analysis for two reasons. First, oil-spill cleanup activities reflect the spill's opportunity cost. In other words, some of the resources involved in the cleanup of an oil spill, in the absence of that spill, would have produced other goods and services (e.g., tourism activities). Secondly, the mere occurrence of a spill is not a certainty. Spills are random accidental events. Given that the spar is fabricated and installed and the development wells are completed as described in the initial DOCD, the timing, numbers, sizes, offshore locations of occurrence, and onshore locations of contact of potential spills occurring over the drilling and production life of the plan are all unknown variables. Appendix A discusses oil spills in general and also the expected sizes, number, and probability of a spill from the proposed action. Additionally, the cost involved in any given cleanup effort is influenced by a variety of factors, such as whether or not the oil comes ashore, the type of coastal environment contacted by the spill, weather conditions at the time of the incident, the type and quantity of oil spilled, and the extent and duration of the oiling. Nevertheless, the same two-step model used above to project employment for the proposed action was applied to project the opportunity cost employment associated with cleaning up an oil spill. In this case, the first step considered estimates of the expenditures resulting from oil-spill cleanup activities should a worst-case blowout scenario spill occur. The second step incorporated the IMPLAN regional model multipliers to translate those expenditures into direct, indirect, and induced employment associated with oil-spill cleanup activities. The size of a scenario spill (on which model results are based) is assumed to be as much as 100,000 bbl a day for 30 days (Appendix A, Spill Volume(s) to be Analyzed). Based on model results, should such a spill occur, it is projected to cost about 68,748-137,332 person-years of employment for cleanup and remediation depending on whether some of the oil contacts land. Table F-8 in Appendix F summarizes the direct, indirect, and induced opportunity cost employment (by subarea and planning area) for an oil-spill cleanup should such a spill occur. Substantial employment impacts (over 3% of total employment in some subareas) are expected should a spill of such magnitude occur. However, employment associated with oil-spill cleanup is expected to be of short duration (less than 6 months), aside from employment associated with the legal aspects of a spill.

4.3.2. Effects on Environmental Justice

Executive Order 12898, entitled Federal Actions to Address Environmental Justice in Minority Populations and Low-Income Populations, directs Federal agencies to assess whether their actions have disproportionate environmental effects on people of ethnic or racial minorities or with low incomes. Those environmental effects encompass human health, social, and economic consequences.

The siting of onshore facilities related to OCS activities is usually based on economics, logistical considerations, zoning restrictions, and permitting requirements. Because of the need for contiguous land and the attraction of lower land values, such facilities, with their concomitant environmental implications, are often near low-income or minority populations. Within the impact region, the individuals potentially affected by the proposed action are African-Americans living in all of the Gulf Coast States, Asian-Americans in Alabama, and low-income fishermen and timber harvesters in the Gulf Coast States. Native Americans are few and widely dispersed throughout the five states. The impact region is not physically, culturally, or economically homogenous. Communities range in size from small municipalities to the urban environment. The racial and ethnic composition of the counties/parishes varies widely as does the distribution of income. While people of these minority groups are scattered throughout the impact region, there are concentrations.

Disproportionate and negative effects should not occur in the development's impact areas because the facilities, land use, and jobs already exist. If these change, especially if they increase and cause disruptions of local neighborhoods, then the relevant regulatory agencies should pay particular attention to how these neighborhoods are affected.

Conclusion

Should BP complete the activities described in their Initial DOCD, there would be very little economic stimulus to the GOM coastal impact area. Minimal effects, if any, on population and education are projected from activities associated with the proposed action. While land use in the impact area will change over time, the majority of this change is estimated as general regional growth. Port Fourchon and Venice, Louisiana, the designated service bases, are capable of providing the services necessary for the proposed activities; therefore, no onshore expansion or construction is anticipated with respect to the proposed action. Less than 1 percent increase in employment in any impact subareas is expect as a result of the proposed action. The opportunity cost employment associated with oil-spill cleanup activities, which is estimated to be relatively high is expected to be temporary and of short duration apart from the legal aspects associated with spill cleanups.

4.3.3. Impacts on Commercial Fisheries

Little or no impact is expected on commercial fishers from routine project activities. Offshore operators do not normally require a large exclusion area although the U.S. Coast Guard could enforce one of 500 m (1,640 ft) or so from structures, if requested or required. BP's normal practice is to monitor all local boat and ship traffic and to contact them by radio.

In the event of a spill, commercial fishermen will actively avoid the area of a spill and the area where there are ongoing activities to control a blowout. Even if fish resources successfully avoid spills, tainting (oily-tasting fish), public perception of tainting, or the potential of tainting commercial catches from oil or dispersants will prevent fishermen (either voluntarily or imposed by regulation) from initiating activities in the spill area. This in turn could decrease landings and/or value of catches for several months. However, GOM species can be found in many adjacent locations; Gulf commercial fishermen do not fish in one locale and have responded to past petroleum spills without discernible loss of catch or income by moving elsewhere for a few months.

There are few, if any, new potential fisheries that could occur in the Holstein area. The most likely target species would be epipelagic species that are highly mobile and have the ability to avoid disturbed areas. This fishery is traditionally pursued using a highly mobile longliner fleet. This type of fishery is less vulnerable to disturbance or loss of fishing space than others such as trap or bottom trawling fisheries.

Conclusion

There will be some unavoidable loss of fishing space due to the physical presence of the development that could otherwise have been used for pelagic fishing such as longlining. This impact is not considered to be significant because the overall footprint of the development is not large compared to the total space available in the Gulf. A large oil spill might have commercial implications, but for the most part, the Gulf fishing fleets are highly mobile and cover a wide area. In addition, there are no commercially important demersal species at the water depth of this proposed action.

4.3.4. Impacts on Recreational Resources and Beach Use

The value of recreation and tourism in the GOM coastal zone from Texas through Florida has been estimated at almost $20 billion annually (USDOI, MMS, 1990 in USDOI, MMS, 2001b). A significant portion of these expenditures is made in coastal counties where major shoreline beaches are primary recreational attractions. In 1996, for example, well over one million people visited the beaches of Galveston Island and the Padre Island National Seashore, demonstrating the popularity of destination beach parks as recreational resources. However, most of the coastline of Louisiana is not well developed.

The primary impact-producing factors associated with offshore oil and gas development, and most widely recognized as major threats to the enjoyment and use of recreational beaches, are oil spills (Appendix A), trash, and debris. Additional factors such as noise from aircraft can adversely affect a beach-related recreational experience. All these factors, either individually or collectively, may adversely affect the number and value of recreational beach visits.

The major recreational activity occurring on the OCS is recreational fishing and diving. A substantial recreational fishery, including SCUBA diving, is directly associated with oil and gas production platforms and stems from the fact that platforms beneficially function as high profile, artificial reefs that attract fish. The vast majority of this activity occurs substantially inshore of the grid area and the proposed action.

Conclusion

The risk of a large oil spill occurring due to the proposed development operations in Green Canyon Blocks 644 and 645 is very small. In the event such a spill did occur, according to trajectory analysis by Morris Environmental, Inc., there is little chance that significant amounts of oil would contact specific segments of Louisiana within 28 days of a spill, particularly after natural weathering and countermeasures. Because of the low probability, the limited coverage by oil, and recovery and remediation capabilities for accessible sandy beaches, significant impacts of beach resources are not expected. Project aircraft will normally be flying high enough (610 m or more) to avoid disturbance to beach-goers.

BP has an established waste management plan for all of their offshore operations. Some very limited amount of accidental loss of solid wastes may occur from time to time. The degree to which they affect coastal waters and recreation areas depends on the currents, winds, and weather. It is expected to have a negligible impact on recreational resources.

Present use of the Holstein area by recreational fishermen is minimal and, because of its distance from shore, little activity is expected.

4.3.5. Impacts on Archaeological Resources

4.3.5.1. Prehistoric

The Grid 10 area is not located within either of the MMS's designated high-probability areas for the occurrence of prehistoric or historic archaeological resources. Lease blocks with a high probability for prehistoric archaeological resources are found landward of a line that roughly follows the 60-m (197-ft) bathymetric contour. As stated in Chapter 3 of this document, MMS recognizes both the 12,000 B.P. date and 60-m (197 ft) water depth as the seaward extant of prehistoric archaeological potential on the OCS. The water depth of the Grid 10 area, is deeper than 1,000 m (3281 ft). The proposed spar is located in approximately 1,324 m (4,344 ft) of water in Green Canyon Block 645. Based on the extreme water depth of the spar location and the Grid overall, there is simply no potential for prehistoric archaeological resources in this area. Therefore, any oil and gas development within the grid will not impact prehistoric archaeological resources.

Proposed Action Analysis

The proposed action includes the use of a mobile offshore drilling unit (MODU) and its associated anchors, and the emplacement of a truss spar production facility and its associated anchors. These systems will impact the seafloor. The proposed offshore development as described in this plan, however, will not result in an impact to any inundated prehistoric archaeological site. The proposal is located beyond where such resources might be expected.

The MMS recognizes both the 12,000 B.P. date and 60-m (197 ft) water depth as the seaward extant of prehistoric potential on the OCS. The water depth of the proposed development and the Grid is greater than 1,000 m (3,281 ft). Therefore, the water depth is approximately 940 m (3,084 ft) deeper than the earliest known prehistoric archaeological sites in the Gulf of Mexico.

Conclusion

Based on the extreme water depth of the Holstein Project and Grid 10 as a whole, the oil or gas development within the grid will not impact any prehistoric archaeological resources.

4.3.5.2. Historic

There are areas of the northern GOM that are considered to have a high probability for historic-period shipwrecks as defined by an MMS-funded study and shipwreck model (Garrison et al., 1989 in USDOI, MMS, 2001b). The study expanded the shipwreck database in the GOM from 1,500 to more than 4,000 wrecks. Statistical analysis of shipwreck location data identified two specific types of high-probability areas—the first within 10 km (6.2 mi) of the shoreline, and the second includes areas proximal to historic ports, barrier islands, and other loss traps. High-probability search polygons associated with individual shipwrecks were created to afford protection to wrecks located outside of the two aforementioned high-probability areas.

An archaeological resources stipulation was included in all GOM lease sales from 1974 through 1994. The stipulation was incorporated into the MMS's Operational Regulations on November 21, 1994. The language of the stipulation was incorporated into the operational regulations under 30 CFR 250.194 with few changes, and all protective measures offered in the stipulation have been adopted by the regulation.

The MMS's NTL 98-06, issued on August 10, 1998, supersedes all other archaeological NTL's and LTL's and makes minor technical amendments, updates cited regulatory authorities, and continues to mandate a 50-m (164-ft) remote-sensing survey line-spacing density for historic shipwreck surveys in water depths of 60 m (197 ft) or less. The NTL also requires submission of an increased amount of magnetometer data to facilitate the MMS analyses. Survey and report requirements for prehistoric sites have not been changed.

Several OCS-related, impact-producing factors may cause adverse impacts to unknown historic archaeological resources. Offshore development could result in a drilling rig, pipeline, or anchors associated with the truss spar and derrick barge activities impacting a historic shipwreck. Direct physical contact with a shipwreck site could destroy fragile ship remains, such as the hull and wooden or ceramic artifacts, and could disturb the site context. The result would be the loss of archaeological data on ship construction, cargo, and the social organization of the vessel's crew, and the concomitant loss of information on maritime culture for the time period from which the ship dates.

The emplacement of anchors and grounded mooring components associated with the MODU and truss spar production facility have the potential to cause physical impact to historic archaeological resources on the seafloor. Based on the plan submitted by the applicant, the truss spar will be moored by a 16-line permanent, semi-taut, steel spiral strand wire (with platform and anchor chains) mooring system held in position by suction installed anchors. The MODU will be held on location with a conventional eight-point mooring system.

Pipeline installations also have the potential to cause a physical impact to historic archaeological resources. In a recent pipeline installation in March 2001, an 8-inch pipeline was laid across a historic shipwreck in a water depth of approximately 808 m (2,651 ft).

Petroleum spills have the potential to affect historic archaeological resources. Impacts to historic resources would be limited to visual impacts, and possibly to physical impacts associated with spill cleanup operations. On the continental shelf of the Gulf, oil and gas development activities have generated tons of ferromagnetic structures and debris, all of which tend to mask magnetic signatures of significant historic archaeological resources during magnetometer surveys. The task of locating historic resources via an archaeological survey has, therefore, been made more difficult as a result of operational activities.

Proposed Action Analysis

The specific locations of archaeological site areas cannot be identified without first conducting a remote-sensing survey of the seabed and near-surface sediments. The MMS, by virtue of its operational regulations under 30 CFR 250.194, requires that an archaeological survey be conducted prior to development of leases within the high-probability zones for historic and prehistoric archaeological resources. The Grid 10 area does not fall within the described MMS's high-probability zone. A review of the geophysical report submitted by the applicant indicated that no seafloor features suggestive of historic shipwrecks were recorded during the lease blocks' side-scan sonar survey. The aforementioned survey reduces the potential for an impact to occur by an estimated 90 percent (USDOI, MMS, 2001b).

The proposed action includes drilling, installation of the subsea lease-term pipelines and umbilicals, installation of the truss spar mooring system, installation of the spar topside facilities, completion of hookup, pull in of risers/umbilicals for the subsea wells, and initiation of production from dry tree and subsea wells.

Ferromagnetic debris associated with exploration and production activities has the potential to mask the magnetic signatures of historic shipwrecks. It is expected that most ferromagnetic debris associated with the proposed action would be removed from the seafloor during the required postlease site clearance and verification procedures. However, site clearance takes place after the useful life of the structures is complete. Therefore, there remains the potential for masking the signatures of historic shipwrecks as a result of ferromagnetic debris from OCS oil and natural gas activities.

Onshore historic properties include sites, structures, and objects such as historic buildings, forts, lighthouses, homesteads, cemeteries, and battlefields. Sites already listed on the National Register of Historic Places and those considered eligible for the National Register have already been evaluated as being able to make a unique or significant contribution to science. At present, unidentified historic sites may contain unique historic information and would have to be assessed after discovery to determine the importance of the data.

Onshore development in support of the proposed action, such as construction of new onshore facilities or pipelines, could result in the direct physical impact to previously unidentified historic sites. This direct physical contact with a historic site could cause physical damage to, or complete destruction of, information on the history of the region and the Nation. Each facility constructed must receive approval from the pertinent Federal, State, county/parish, and/or community involved. Protection of archaeological resources in these cases is expected to be achieved through the various approval processes involved. The proposed development will use existing support facilities. There is, therefore, no expected impact to onshore historic sites from any onshore development in support of the proposed action.

Should an oil spill contact a coastal historic site, such as a fort or a lighthouse, the major impact would be visual from petroleum contamination of the site and its environmental impacts to coastal historic sites are expected to be temporary and reversible.

The greatest potential impact to a historic shipwreck as a result of the proposed action would result from the emplacement of MODU anchors and anchors for vessels that support the installation of the truss spar facility and associated pipelines. The remote-sensing survey and archaeological clearance of sites required prior to an operator beginning oil and gas activities on a lease are estimated to be 90 percent effective at identifying possible historic shipwreck sites. Since the survey and clearance provide a significant reduction in the potential for a damaging interaction between an impact-producing factor and a historic shipwreck, there is a very small possibility of the proposed OCS activities or from future developments impacting a historic site.

According to Garrison et al. (1989), the shipwreck database lists no shipwrecks that fall within the Grid 10 area. All of the blocks within the Grid 10 area fall within the MMS GOM Region's low-probability area for the occurrence of historic shipwrecks.

Most other activities associated with the proposed action are not expected to impact historic archaeological resources. Ferromagnetic debris has the potential to mask the magnetic signatures of historic shipwrecks. It is expected that onshore archaeological resources would be protected through the review and approval processes of the various Federal, State, and local agencies involved in permitting onshore activities. There is a small chance of contact from an oil spill associated with the proposed action. Furthermore, the major impact from a spill contact on a historic coastal site, such as a fort or lighthouse, would be visual contamination. These impacts would be temporary and reversible.

Conclusion

Oil and gas activities associated with proposed development of Grid 10 area could impact a shipwreck because of incomplete knowledge on the location of shipwrecks in the Gulf. Although this occurrence is not probable, such an event could result in the disturbance or destruction of important historic archaeological information. Other factors associated with the proposed action are not expected to affect historic archaeological resources.

4.4. CUMULATIVE EFFECTS

The MMS addressed the cumulative effects of OCS- and non-OCS-related activities for the Central Planning Area and the Gulf Coast region for the years 1996 through 2036 as part of the NEPA documentation completed for proposed multisale lease activities. The latest publication applicable to Grid 10 is the Final EIS for Central GOM Lease Sales 169, 172, 175, 178, and 182 (USDOI, MMS, 1997a). Specific OCS-related effects from the proposed activities related to the Holstein Project are addressed in Chapters 4.1-4.3.

The following chapters discuss cumulative effects of non-OCS-related activities for selected resources in the Central Planning Area of the GOM.

4.4.1. Water Quality

4.4.1.1. Coastal

Major sources expected to contribute to the contamination of the GOM's coastal waters include the petrochemical industry, agriculture, urban expansion, municipal and camp sewerage treatment processes, marinas, commercial fishing, maritime shipping, and hydromodification activities.

The coastal waters of the Gulf have been heavily used by people and are now showing some signs of environmental stress. Large areas are experiencing nutrient overenrichment, low-dissolved oxygen, toxin and pesticide contamination, shellfish ground closures, and loss of wetlands. Contaminant inputs to coastal waters bordering the GOM will continue as a result of the large volumes of water entering the Gulf of Mexico from rivers that drain over two-thirds of the contiguous U.S. and from both municipal and industrial point and nonpoint-source discharges.

Lesser sources of contamination are likely to be forestry, recreational boating, livestock farming, manufacturing industries, nuclear power plant operations, and pulp and paper mills. Runoff and wastewater discharges from these sources may impact water quality to the extent that a significant percentage of the GOM's coastal waters may not attain certain Federal water quality standards.

4.4.1.2. Offshore

Major sources expected to contribute to effects on the Gulf's offshore waters include marine transportation, commercial fishing, and hydrocarbon seeps. The Gulf of Mexico is a very active maritime province with both international and domestic waterborne commerce. Discharges and debris from these vessels will affect the offshore water quality of the GOM. Commercial fishing activities will disturb the GOM's sediments resulting in localized impacts to the offshore waters. Natural hydrocarbon seeps have been documented in the deepwater area of the GOM (Brooks et al., 1986 and 1990; USDOI, MMS, 1996). MacDonald et al. (1996) identified 63 oil slicks from one or more remote-sensing images. These seeps contribute soluble hydrocarbon components into the water column. Seepage of a selected area in the GOM was estimated from two images.

The data suggest that the natural seepage is on the order of 4.3×10^3 to 7.8×10^4 m^3 y^{-1} in the 8,200-km^2 image area and 1.1×10^4 to 4.8×10^5 m^3 y^{-1} in the 15,000-km^2 image area (USDOI, MMS, 1996).

4.4.2. Air Quality

Effects on air quality within the study area will come primarily from industrial, power generation, and urban emissions. The coastal areas nearest the study area are currently designated as "attainment" for all the National Ambient Air Quality Standards-regulated pollutants except ozone. The USEPA has designated several areas along the Gulf Coast as "nonattainment" for ground-level ozone—Houston-Galveston-Brazoria, and Beaumont-Port Arthur areas in Texas and Lafourche Parish in Louisiana (USEPA, 2001).

4.4.3. Sensitive Coastal Environments

4.4.3.1. Coastal Barrier Beaches and Associated Dunes

Coastal barrier beaches of the Chenier Plain have experienced severe erosion and landward retreat because of human activities and natural processes. These adverse effects on barrier and dunes have come from changes to the natural dynamics of water and sediment flow along beaches the coast. Examples of these activities include pipeline canals, channel stabilization structures, beach stabilization structures, recreational use of vehicles on dunes and beaches, recreational and commercial development, and removal of coastal vegetation. Human activities cause direct impacts as well as accelerate natural processes that deteriorate coastal barrier features. Natural processes that contribute to most effects include storms, subsidence, and sea-level rise acting upon shorelines with inadequate sand content and supply.

Deterioration of Gulf barrier beaches is expected to continue in the future. Federal, State, and parish governments have made efforts over the last 10 years to slow beach erosion.

4.4.3.2. Wetlands

In most areas that might be influenced by the proposed action and Grid 10 development, the conversion of wetlands to agricultural, residential, and commercial uses has generally been the major cause of wetland loss. Commercial uses include dredging for both waterfront developments and coastal oil and gas activities. In the Chenier Plain of Louisiana, natural and man-induced erosion and subsidence are also important causes of wetland loss. Wetland loss is projected to continue around the WPA and CPA of the Gulf.

4.4.3.3. Seagrasses

Seagrasses are adversely affected by several human activities. These activities include changes to water quality resulting from riverine input, stream channelization, urban runoff, and industrial discharges; physical removal of plants by various forms of dredging, anchoring, and grounding of vessels; and severe storms. These impacts and the general decline of seagrasses are expected to continue into the near future. Various local, State, and Federal programs are focused upon reversing this trend.

4.4.4. Deepwater Benthic Communities/Organisms

4.4.4.1. Chemosynthetic Communities

No impacts to chemosynthetic communities from non-OCS-related activities are expected. Normal fishing practices should not disturb these areas. Other bottom-disturbing activities such as trawling and anchoring are virtually nonexistent at water depths greater than 400 m.

4.4.4.2. Coral Reefs

All of the recognized topographic features in the CPA are protected by "no activity zones" and other operational zones to minimize effects on associated coral reefs. Uncontrolled anchoring remains a threat to these areas. Increasing pressure is being exerted on these features from both commercial and recreational sources.

4.4.4.3. Deepwater Benthos and Sediment Communities

The most serious impact-producing factor that may affect deepwater benthos and sediment communities is the physical disturbance of the sea bottom. Within anchoring depths, marine transportation vessels may affect localized areas. Hypoxic conditions at the seafloor may affect the deepwater benthos and associated communities.

4.4.5. Marine Mammals

Marine mammals could be adversely affected by vessel traffic, degradation of water quality, aircraft and vessel noise, loss of debris from vessels, commercial fishing (capture and removal), pathogens, and negative impacts to prey populations. The cumulative impacts to marine mammals are expected to result in a number of chronic and sporadic lethal and sublethal effects. Sublethal effects may stress and/or weaken individuals of a local group or population, thus making them more susceptible to infection from natural or anthropogenic sources.

4.4.6. Sea Turtles

Factors with the potential to effect sea turtles include dredging operations, water quality and habitat degradation, trash and debris, vessel traffic, natural catastrophes (e.g., hurricanes, unseasonably cold weather), commercial and recreational fishing, beach and other lighting, and entrainment in industrial intakes (e.g., electrical generation plants). Small numbers of turtles could be killed or injured from chance collisions with vessels or from eating indigestible trash or debris (particularly plastic items). Noise from vessels could disrupt normal behavioral patterns and physiologically stress turtles making them more susceptible to disease. Pollution could indirectly affect sea turtles through food-chain biomagnification.

4.4.7. Coastal and Marine Birds

Possible impacts to coastal and marine birds can come from air emissions, water quality degradation, habitat loss and modification resulting from coastal construction and development, collisions with aircraft or vessels, noise from aircraft and vessels, trash and debris, and lighting. Any effects could be especially critical to endangered or threatened species that must maintain a viable reproductive population size or that are dependent on a few key habitat factors. Aircraft or vessel traffic could sporadically disturb feeding, resting, or nesting behavior of birds or cause abandonment of preferred habitat. Birds could become entangled and snared in trash and debris. In addition, they may ingest small plastic debris that could lead to injury or death.

4.4.8. Fish Resources

Degradation of water quality, loss of essential habitat (including wetlands loss), pathogens, trash and debris, riverine influences, and overfishing could affect fish resources. Eggs and larvae are more susceptible than adults to environmental contaminants. Portions of the Gulf experience hypoxia during portions of the year (LATEX B; Murray, 1998). However, areas of hypoxia typically occur only on the continental shelf.

4.4.9. Economic and Demographic Conditions

The economic and demographic conditions evaluated in this PEA are limited to that portion of the GOM's coastal zone whose social and economic well-being (population, labor, and employment) is directly or indirectly affected by the OCS oil and gas industry. The energy industry has become increasingly more global. While the OCS program, in general, has played a significant role in the GOM region's economy and demography, the activities proposed in Grid 10 are expected to have minimal economic and demographic consequences to the region.

4.4.9.1. Population and Education

The impact area's population is expected to grow at an average annual rate of 1.5 to 1.0 percent over the next 40 years with that growth slowing over time. This population growth is based on the continuation of existing conditions including OCS energy development. Activities in Grid 10 are not expected to affect the population's growth rate. Education levels are expected to remain unchanged by activities within the grid.

4.4.9.2. Infrastructure and Land Use

Sufficient infrastructure is in place to support activities within Grid 10. Sufficient land is designated in commercial and industrial parks and adjacent to the existing ports to minimize potential disruption to current residential and business use patterns. While land use in the area will change over time, the majority of this change is expected to be general regional growth.

4.4.9.3. Navigation and Port Useage

There are approximately 50 shore bases that are traditionally used by the oil and gas industry to support activities on the Federal OCS. Certain companies favor some of these bases for their offshore operations. No new expansion or construction is expected at these existing shore bases to support offshore activities within Grid 10.

4.4.9.4. Employment

The oil and gas industry is very important to many of the coastal communities of the GOM, especially in Louisiana and eastern Texas. Changes in OCS oil and gas activities have significant employment implications to these communities, particularly in industries directly and indirectly related to oil and gas development. However, the energy industry has global markets (both for the supply of goods and services needed to produce energy and demand for energy products). While mergers, relocations, and consolidation of oil and gas companies' assets have affected employment in the GOM region in recent years, employment changes to the coastal communities as a result of activities in Grid 10 are expected to be negligible.

4.4.10. Environmental Justice

Federal agencies are directed by Executive Order 12898 to assess whether their actions will have a disproportionate environmental effect on people of ethnic or racial minorities or with low incomes. Since sufficient onshore facilities are available to support offshore activities in Grid 10, no effects to minorities or people with low incomes in the Gulf counties and parishes are expected.

4.4.11. Commercial Fisheries

Federal and State fishery management agencies will control the "take" of commercial fishes. The agencies' primary responsibility is to manage effectively the fishery stock to perpetuate commercially important species. Various management plans aimed at selected species have been and will continue to be prepared. The GOM will remain one of the Nation's most important commercial fisheries area.

4.4.12. Recreational Resources and Beach Use

Factors such as land development, civil works projects, and natural phenomena have affected, and will continue to affect, beach stabilization, which ultimately affects the recreational use of beaches. Many of the people in the adjacent coastal states live in the coastal zone. Pressure on the natural resources within the coastal zone is expected to continue or possibly increase.

Man-induced debris and litter derived from both offshore and onshore sources are likely to diminish the tourist potential of beaches and degrade the ambience of shoreline recreational beaches, thereby affecting the enjoyment of recreational beaches throughout the planning area. MARPOL Annex V and cooperation and support from offshore industries to reduce marine debris through the GOM Program's Marine Debris Action Plan should lead to a decline in the level of human-generated trash that may adversely affect recreational beaches throughout the Gulf.

Although trash from onshore sources will continue to adversely affect the ambience of recreational beaches, the level of chronic pollution should decline. Beach use at the regional level is unlikely to change.

4.4.13. Archaeological Resources

4.4.13.1. Prehistoric

Grid 10 is located in deep water (greater than 1,000 m or 3,281 ft). It is not located in one of the MMS's designated high-probability areas for prehistoric sites. No potential exists to affect prehistoric archaeological resources.

4.4.13.2. Historic

Seafloor-disturbing activities such as anchoring have the potential to affect shipwrecks, if present. In-place mitigating measures would eliminate or minimize potential impacts to these resources.

More than 4,000 shipwrecks in the northern Gulf of Mexico have been identified in the MMS database. At least 33 merchant vessels and one U-boat were sunk in the Gulf during WWII; 7 of which are believed to be in the Lund and Mississippi Canyon areas. No shipwrecks are known to be located within Grid 10, and no potential sites have been identified in surveys for geohazards in Green Canyon Blocks 644 and 645.

5. CONSULTATION AND COORDINATION

The State of Louisiana has an approved Coastal Zone Management (CZM) Program. Therefore, a Certificate of Coastal Zone Consistency from the State was required for the proposed activities. The MMS mailed the plan and other required and necessary information to the State's appropriate CZM agency on September 4, 2001. The plan was received by the agency on September 6, 2001. The plan was assigned Project Number C20010422. The State of Louisiana provided a letter of its concurrence with the CZM Program on October 19, 2001.

To provide the public with official notice of the proposed activities planned for the Holstein development, the MMS published a brief description of the BP proposal in The Times-Picayune newspaper (southeast Louisiana coverage).

6. BIBLIOGRAPHY

Albers, P.H. 1979. Effects of Corexit 9527 on the hatchability of mallard eggs. Bull. Environ. Contam. and Toxicol. 23:661-668.

Albers, P.H. and M.L. Gay. 1982. Effects of a chemical dispersant and crude oil on breeding ducks. Bull. Environ. Contam. and Toxicol. 9:138-139.

Alexander, S.K. and J.W. Webb. 1983. Effects of oil on growth and decomposition of Spartina alterniflora. In: Proceedings, 1983 Oil Spill Conference . . . February 28-March 3, 1983, San Antonio, TX. Washington, DC: American Petroleum Institute. Pp. 529-532.

Alexander, S.K. and J.W. Webb. 1985. Seasonal response of Spartina alterniflora to oil. In: Proceedings, 1985 Oil Spill Conference . . . February 25-28, 1985, Los Angeles, CA. Washington, DC: American Petroleum Institute. Pp. 355-357.

Alexander, S.K. and J.W. Webb. 1987. Relationship of Spartina alterniflora growth to sediment oil content following an oil spill. In: Proceedings, 1987 Oil Spill Conference. April 6-9, 1988, Baltimore, MD. Washington, DC: American Petroleum Institute. Pp. 445-450.

American Gas Foundation. 2001. Fueling the future: natural gas and new technology for a cleaner 21st century, 2001 update. http://www.fuelingthefuture.org/FTFUpdate01.pdf. P. 3.

Anderson, C.M. and R.P. LaBelle. 1990. Estimated occurrence rates for accidental oil spills on the U.S. Outer Continental Shelf. Oil and Chemical Pollution 6:21-35.

Anderson, C.M. and R.P. LaBelle. 1994. Comparative occurrence rates for offshore oil spills. Spill Science and Technology Bulletin 1(2):131-141.

Anderson, C.M. and R.P. LaBelle. 2000. Update of comparative occurrence rates for offshore oil spills. Spill Science & Technology Bulletin 6(5/6):303-321.

Anderson, D.W., F. Gress, and D.M. Fry. 1996. Survival and dispersal of oiled brown pelicans after rehabilitation and release. Mar. Poll. Bull. 32:711-718.

Angelovic, J.W. 1989. Written communication. Condition of the fisheries. St. Petersburg, FL: U.S. Dept. of Commerce, National Marine Fisheries Service, Southeast Fisheries Center, Internal Memorandum. 5 pp.

Anuskiewicz, R.J. 1989. A study of maritime and nautical sites associated with St. Catherines Island, Georgia. Ph.D. dissertation presented to the University of Tennessee, Knoxville, TN. 90 pp.

Aten, L.E. 1983. Indians of the upper Texas coast. New York, NY: Academic Press.

Baker, J.M., R.B. Clark, and P.F. Kingston. 1991. Two years after the spill: environmental recovery in Prince William Sound and the Gulf of Alaska. Institute of Offshore Engineering, Heriot-Watt University, Edinburgh, EH14 4AS, Scotland. 31 pp.

Bakus, R.H., J.E. Craddock, R.L. Haedrich, and B.H. Robison. 1977. Atlantic mesopelagic zoogeography. In: Gibbs, R.H., Jr., ed. Fishes of the Western North Atlantic. Pp. 266-287.

Baxter, V.K. 1990. Common themes of social institution impact and response. In: Proceedings; Eleventh Annual Information Transfer Meeting. Sponsored by the Minerals Management Service, Gulf of Mexico OCS Region, November 13-15, 1990, New Orleans, LA. OCS Study MMS 91-0040. Pp. 270-273.

Baumgartner, M.F. 1995. The distribution of select species of cetaceans in the northern Gulf of Mexico in relation to observed environmental variables. M.Sc. Thesis, University of Southern Mississippi.

Baumgartner, M.F. 1997. The distribution of Risso's dolphin (*Grampus griseus*) with respect to the physiography of the northern Gulf of Mexico. Mar. Mamm. Sci. 13:614-638.

Bergquist, D.C., F.M. Williams, and C.R. Fisher. 2000. Longevity record for deep-sea invertebrate. Nature 43:499-500.

Blake, J.A., B. Hecker, J.F. Grassle, N. Maciolik-Blake, B. Brown, M. Curran, B. Dade, S. Freitas, and R.E. Ruff. 1985. Study of the biological processes on the U.S. south Atlantic slope and rise. Phase 1. Benthic Characterization Study. Final report submitted to the U.S. Dept. of the Interior, Minerals Management Service, Restin, VA. Contract No. 14-12-0001-30064. 142 pp. + appendices.

Blaxter, J.H.S., A.B. Gray and E.J. Denton. 1981. Sound and startle responses in herring shoals. J. Mar. Biol. Assoc. U.K. 61: 851-869.

Boersma, P.D. 1995. Prevention is more important than rehabilitation: oil and penguins don't mix. In: Proceedings, The Effects of Oil on Wilidlife, 4th International Conference, April, Seattle, WA.

Booker, R. 1971. Some aspects of the biology and ecology of the deep-sea echinoid Phormosoma placenta Wyv. Thompson. M.S. Thesis, Texas A&M University, College Station, TX.

Boyle, E.A., D.F. Reid, S.S. Huested, and J. Hering. 1984. Trace metals and radium in the Gulf of Mexico: an evaluation of river and continental shelf sources. Earth Planet Science Letters 69:69-87.

BP Exploration and Production, Inc. 2001. Joint initial unit development operations coordination document: Holstein deepwater development, Green Canyon Block 644 Unit, Leases OCS-G 11080 and OCS-G 11081, Green Canyon Blocks 644 and 645. BP Exploration and Production Inc.

Bright, T. 1968. A survey of the deep-sea bottom fishes of the Gulf of Mexico below 350 meter. Ph.D. Dissertation. Dept. of Oceanography, Texas A&M University, College Station, TX.

Brooks, J.M., and C.P. Giammona, eds. 1990. Mississippi-Alabama marine ecosystem study annual report, year 2. Volume I: Technical narrative. U.S. Dept. of the Interior, Minerals Management Service, Gulf of Mexico OCS Region, New Orleans, LA. OCS Study MMS 89-0095. 348 pp.

Brooks, J.M., D.A. Weisenburg, C.R. Schwab, E.L. Estes, and R.F. Shokes. 1981. Surficial sediments and suspended particulate matter. In: Middleditch, B.S. ed. Environmental effects of offshore oil production. New York, NY: Plenum Press. Pp. 69-111.

Brooks, J.M., H.B. Cox, W.R. Bryant, M.C. Kennicutt II, R.G. Mann, and T.J. McDonald. 1986. Association of gas hydrates and oil seepage in the Gulf of Mexico. Org. Geochem. 10:221-234

Brooks, J.M., M.C. Kennicutt II, and R.R. Bidigare. 1986a. Final cruise report for Offshore Operators Committee study of chemosynthetic marine ecosystems in the Gulf of Mexico. Geophysical and Environmental Research Group, Department of Oceanography, Texas A&M University, College Station, TX. 102 pp.

Brooks, J.M., H.B. Cox, W.R. Bryant, M.C. Kennicutt II, R.G. Mann, and T.J. McDonald. 1986b. Association of gas hydrates and oil seepage in the Gulf of Mexico. Org. Geochem. 10:221-234.

Brower, W.A., J.M. Meserve, and R.G. Quayle. 1972. Environmental guide for the U.S. Gulf Coast. U.S. Dept. of Commerce, National Oceanic and Atmospheric Administration, Environmental Data Service, National Climatic Center, Asheville, NC.

Brown, H.M., E.H. Owens, and M. Green. 1998. Submerged and sunken oil: response options, feasibility and expectations. Proceedings of the Twenty-First Artic and Marine Oil Spill program (AMOP) Technical Seminar. Volume 1. Pp. 135-147.

Brown, S. 2000. Do rising oil prices threaten economic prosperity? Southwest Economy. Federal Reserve Bank of Dallas. http://www.dallasfed.org/htm/pubs/swe/11_12_00 html. Issue 6, November/December.

Bruland, K.W. 1983, Trace elements in sea water. In: Riley, J.P. and R. Chester, eds. Chemical oceanography. Volume 8. New York, NY: Academic Press.

Bryan, F. and S.N. Lingamallu. 1990. Hydrogen sulfide occurrence in Gulf of Mexico outer continental shelf operations. U.S. Dept. of the Interior, Minerals Management Service, Gulf of Mexico OCS Region, New Orleans, LA. 8 pp.

Butler, R.G., A. Harfenist, F.A. Leighton, and D.B. Peakall. 1988. Impact of sublethal oil and emulsion exposure on the reproductive success of Leach's storm-petrels: short- and long-term effects. Journal of Applied Ecology 25:125-143.

Carney, R. 1971. Some aspects of the ecology of Mesothuria lactea Theel, a common bathyal holothurian in the Gulf of Mexico. M.S. Thesis, Texas A&M University, College, TX.

Carney, R.S., R.L. Haedrich, and G. T. Rowe. 1983. Zonation of fauna in the deep sea. In: Rowe, G.T., ed. Deep Sea Biology. New York, NY: John Wiley & Sons. Pp. 371-398.

Chan, E.I. 1977. Oil pollution and tropical littoral communities: biological effects at Florida Keys oil spill. In: Proceedings, 1977 Oil Spill Conference . . . March 8-10, 1977, New Orleans, LA. Washington, DC: American Petroleum Institute. Pp. 539-542.

Christmas, J.Y., D.J. Etzold, L.B. Simpson, and S. Meyers. 1988. The menhaden fishery of the Gulf of Mexico United States: a regional management plan. Gulf States Marine Fisheries Commission, Ocean Springs, MS. 139 pp.

Clark, R.B. 1978. Oiled seabird rescue and conservation Journal of the Fisheries Research Board of Canada 35:675-678.

Clark, R.B. 1984. Impact of oil pollution on seabirds. Environ. Pollut. Ser. A. 33:1-22.

Coastal Environments, Inc. (CEI). 1977. Cultural resources evaluation of the Northern Gulf of Mexico Continental Shelf. Prepared for Interagency Archaeological Services, Office of Archaeology and Historic Preservation, National Park Service, U.S. Dept. of the Interior. Baton Rouge, LA.

Coastal Environments, Inc. (CEI). 1982. Sedimentary studies of prehistoric archaeological sites. Prepared for the Division of State Plans and Grants, National Park Service. U.S. Dept. of the Interior, Minerals Management Service, New Orleans, LA.

Coastal Environments, Inc. (CEI). 1986. Prehistoric site evaluation on the Northern Gulf of Mexico Outer Continental Shelf: Ground truth testing of the predictive model. Prepared for the U.S. Dept. of the Interior, Minerals Management Service, New Orleans, LA.

Cochrane, J.D. and F.J. Kelly. 1986. Low-frequency circulation on the Texas-Louisiana continental shelf. Journal of Geophysical Research 91(C9):10,645-10,659.

Collard, S.B. 1990. Leatherback turtles feeding near a warmwater mass boundary in the eastern Gulf of Mexico. Marine Turtle Newsletter 50:12-14.

Continental Shelf Associates, Inc. 2000. Deepwater Gulf of Mexico environmental and socioeconomic data search and literature synthesis. Volume I: Narrative report. U.S. Dept. of the Interior, Minerals Management Service, Gulf of Mexico OCS Region, New Orleans, LA. OCS Study MMS 2000-049. 340 pp.

Corliss, J.B., J. Dymond, L.I. Gordon, J.M. Edmond, R.P. von Herzen, R.D. Ballard, K. Green, D. Williams, A. Bainbridge, K. Crane, and T.H. van Andel. 1979. Submarine thermal springs on the Galapagos Rift. Science 203:1073-1083.

Coull, B.C., R.L. Ellison, J.W. Fleeger, R.P. Higgins, W.D. Hope, W.D. Hummon, R.M. Rieger, W.E. Sterrer, H. Thiel, and J.H. Tietjen. 1977. Quantitative estimates of the meiofauna from the deep sea off North Carolina, U.S.A. Marine Biology 39:233-240.

Crocker, P.A. and P.C. Koska. 1996. Trends in water and sediment quality for the Houston Ship Channel. Texas Journal of Science 48(4):267-282.

Cruz-Kaegi, M.E. 1998. Latitudinal variations in biomass and metabolism of benthic infaunal communities. Ph.D. Dissertation, Texas A&M University, College Station, TX.

Cummings, W.C. 1985. Bryde's whale — Balaenoptera edeni. In: Ridgway, S.H. and R. Harrison, eds. Handbook of marine mammals. Vol. 3: The Sirenians and baleen whales. Academic Press, Inc. Pp. 137-154.

Darnell, R.M. 1988. Marine biology. In: Phillips, N.W. and B.M. James, eds. Offshore Texas and Louisiana marine ecosystems data synthesis. Volume II. Draft final report to the U.S. Dept. of the Interior, Minerals

Management Service, Gulf of Mexico OCS Region, New Orleans, LA. Contract No. 14-12-0001-30380. Pp. 203-338.

Darnell, R.M. and T.M. Soniat. 1979. The estuary/continental shelf as an interactive system. In: Livingston, R.J., ed. Ecological processes in coastal and marine systems. New York, NY: Plenum Press. 39 pp.

Davis, R.W. and G.S. Fargion, eds. 1996. Distribution and abundance of cetaceans in the north-central and western Gulf of Mexico, final report. Volume II: Technical report. U.S. Dept. of the Interior, Minerals Management Service, Gulf of Mexico OCS Region, New Orleans, LA. OCS Study MMS 96-0027. 357 pp.

Davis, R.W., G.S. Fargion, N. May, T.D. Leming, M. Baumgartner, W.E. Evans, L.J. Hansen, and K. Mullin. 1998. Physical habitat of cetaceans along the continental slope in the north-central and western Gulf of Mexico. Mar. Mamm. Sci. 14: 490-507.

Davis, R.W., W.E. Evans, and B. Würsig. 2000. Cetaceans, sea turtles and seabirds in the northern Gulf of Mexico: Distribution, abundance and habitat associations. Volume II: Technical report. Prepared by Texas A&M University at Galveston and the National Marine Fisheries Service. U.S. Dept. of the Interior, Geological Survey, Biological Resources Division, USGS/BRD/CR-1999-0006 and Minerals Management Service, Gulf of Mexico OCS Region, New Orleans, LA. OCS Study MMS 2000-003. 346 pp.

Delaune, R.D., W.H. Patrick, and R.J. Bureh. 1979. Effect of crude oil on a Louisiana *Spartina alterniflora* salt marsh. Environ. Poll. 20:21-31.

Deming, J. and J. Baross. 1993. The early diagenesis of organic matter: Bacterial activity. In: Engel, M. and S. Macko, eds. Organic Geochemistry. New York, NY: Plenum. Pp. 119-144.

Dodd, C.K., Jr. 1988. Synopsis of the biological data on the loggerhead sea turtle Caretta caretta (Linnaeus 1758). U.S. Dept. of the Interior, Fish and Wildlife Service. Biological Report 88(14). Gainesville, FL: National Ecology Research Center. 119 pp. Available from NTIS: PB89-109565.

Dowgiallo, M.J., ed. 1994. Coastal oceanographic effects of summer 1993 Mississippi River flooding. Special NOAA Report. NOAA Coastal Ocean Office/National Weather Service, Silver Spring, MD. 76 pp.

Durako, M.J., M.O. Hall, F. Sargent, and S. Peck. 1992. Propeller scars in sea grass beds: an assessment and experimental study of recolonization in Weedon Island State Preserve, Florida. Pp 42-53 in Web, F., ed. Proceedings from the 19th annual Conference of Wetland Restoration and Creation. Hillsborough Community College, Tampa, FL.

Ernst, C.H., R.W. Barbour, and J.E. Lovich. 1994. Turtles of the United States and Canada. Washington, DC: Smithsonian Institution Press. 578 pp.

Evans, D.R. and S.D. Rice. 1974. Effects of oil on marine ecosystems: a review for administrators and policy makers. Fishery Bull. 72(3):625-637.

Farr, A.J., C.C. Chabot, and D.H. Taylor. 1995. Behavioral avoidance of flurothene by flathead minnows (*Pimephales promelas*). Neurotoxicology and Teratology 17(3):265-271.

Federal Register. 1983. Proposed reclassification of the peregrine falcon in North America. 48 FR 41.

Federal Register. 1985. Endangered and threatened wildlife and plants; removal of the brown pelican in the southeastern United States from the list of endangered and threatened wildlife. 50 FR 23.

Federal Register. 1995. Incidental take of marine mammals; bottlenose dolphins and spotted dolphins. 50 FR 228.

Firth, R. 1971. A study of the deep-sea lobsters of the families Polychelidae and Nephropidae (Crustacea, Decapoda). Ph.D. Dissertation, Texas A&M University, College Station, TX.

Fischel, M., W. Grip, and I.A. Mendelssohn. 1989. Study to determine the recovery of a Louisiana marsh from an oil spill. In: Proceedings, 1989 Oil Spill Conference, February 13-16, 1989, San Antonio, TX. Washington, DC: American Petroleum Institute.

Fisher, C.R. 1990. Chemoautotrophic and methanotrophic symbioses in marine invertebrates: Reviews in Aquatic Sciences. 2:399-436.

Fritts, T.H., W. Hoffman, and M.A. McGehee. 1983a. The distribution and abundance of marine turtles in the Gulf of Mexico and nearby Atlantic waters. Journal of Herpetology 17:327-344.

Fritts, T.H., A.B. Irvine, R.D. Jennings, L.A. Collum, W. Hoffman, and M.A. McGehee. 1983b. Turtles, birds, and mammals in the northern Gulf of Mexico and nearby Atlantic waters. U.S. Dept. of the Interior, Fish and Wildlife Service, Division of Biological Services, Washington, DC: FWS/OBS82/65. 455 pp.

Fu, B. and P. Aharon. 1998. Sources of hydrocarbon-rich fluids advecting on the seafloor in the northern Gulf of Mexico. Gulf Coast Association of Geological Societies Transactions 48:73-81.

Fugro-McClelland Geosciences, Inc. 2001. Geotechnical investigation Holstein Prospect Boring HSB-1 and PCPTS HCPT-1/1a, HCPT-2/2a, HCPT-3 and HCPT-4/4a, Blocks 644 and 645, Green Canyon area. Volume 1: Field Report. Field Report No. 0201-4339. BP Corporation, Houston, Texas. 8 p. + Plates.

Gallaway, B. J. and G. S. Lewbel. 1982. The ecology of petroleum platforms in the northwestern Gulf of Mexico: a community profile. U.S. Fish and Wildlife Service, Office of Biological Services, Washington, D.C. FWS/OBS-82/27. Bureau of Land management, Gulf of Mexico OCS Regional Office, Open File Report 82-03. 92 p.

Gallaway, B.J., ed. 1988a. Northern Gulf of Mexico continental Slope Study, Final Report: Year 4. Vol.I. Executive Summary. Final report to the Minerals Management Service, New Orleans, LA. Contract No. 14-120001-30212. OCS Study/MMS 88-0052. 69 pp.

Gallaway, B.J., ed. 1988b. Northern Gulf of Mexico continental slope study, final report; year 4. Vol. II: Synthesis report. U. S. Dept. of the Interior, Minerals Management Service, Gulf of Mexico OCS Region, New Orleans, LA. OCS Study MMS 88-0053. 701 pp.

Gallaway, B.J., ed. 1988c. Northern Gulf of Mexico continental slope study, final report; year 4. Vol. III: Appendices. Final report to the Minerals Management Service, New Orleans, LA. Contract No. 14-120001-30212. OCS Study/MMS 88-0054. 378 pp.

Gallaway, B.J. and M.C. Kennicut II. 1988. Chapter 2. The characterization of benthic habitats of the northern Gulf of Mexico. p. 2-1 to 2-45. In: B.J. Gallaway (ed.). Northern Gulf of Mexico Continental Slope Study, Final Report: Year 4. Vol. III: Appendices. Final Report submitted to Minerals Management Service, New Orleans. Contract No. 14-12-0001-30212. OCS Study/MMS 88-0054. 378 p.

Gallaway, B.J., L.R. Martin, and R.L. Howard, eds. 1988. Northern Gulf of Mexico continental slope study: annual report, year 3. Volume I: Executive summary. U.S. Dept. of the Interior, Minerals Management Service, Gulf of Mexico OCS Region, New Orleans, LA. OCS Study MMS 87-0059. 154 pp.

Gallaway, B.J., J.G. Cole, and L.R. Martin. 2000. The deep sea Gulf of Mexico: an overview and guide. U.S. Dept. of the Interior, Minerals Management Service, Gulf of Mexico OCS Region, New Orleans, LA. OCS Study MMS 2000-000. 27 p.

Gallaway, B. J., J. G. Cole, and R. G. Fechhelm. 2001. Selected aspects of the ecology of the continental slope fauna of the Gulf of Mexico: a synopsis of the northern Gulf of Mexico Continental Slope Study, 1983-1988. [Draft] OCS Study MMS 0000-000. U.S. Dept. of the Interior, Minerals Management Service, Gulf of Mexico OCS Region, New Orleans. 37 p. + App.

Gambell, R. 1985. Sei whale — *Balaenoptera borealis*. In: Ridgway, S.H. and R. Harrison, eds. Handbook of marine mammals. Vol. 3: The sirenians and baleen whales. San Diego, CA: Academic Press. Pp. 155-170.

Garrison, E.G., C.P. Giammona, F.J. Kelly, A.R. Tripp, and G.A. Wolf. 1989. Historic shipwrecks and magnetic anomalies of the northern Gulf of Mexico: Reevaluation of archaeological resource management zone 1. U.S. Dept. of the Interior, Minerals Management Service, Gulf of Mexico OCS Region, New Orleans, LA OCS Study MMS 89-0024. 241 pp.

Gartner, J.V., Jr. 1993. Patterns of reproduction on the dominant lanternfish species (Pisces: Myctophidae) of the eastern Gulf of Mexico, with a review of reproduction among tropical-subtropical Myctophidae. Bull. Mar. Sci. 52(2):721-750.

Gartner, J.V., Jr., T.L. Hopkins, R.C. Baird, and D.M. Milliken. 1987. The lanternfishes of the eastern Gulf of Mexico. Fish. Bull. 85(1):81-98.

Geochemical and Environmental Research Group (GERG). 2000. Deepwater program: Northern Gulf of Mexico continental slope habitats and benthic ecology (DGoMB): Interim planning meeting report.

Geraci, J.R. and D.J. St. Aubin. 1980. Offshore petroleum resource development and marine mammals: a review and research recommendations. Marine Fisheries Review 42:1-12.

Global Marine's SCORE reflects strong recovery; dayrates poised for further advances. 2001. http://www.oilandgasonline.com/content/news/article.asp?DocID={27CEDA52-EC08-11D4-A76F-00D0B7694F32}. 17 January 2001.

Gray, W.M. 1992. Written communication. Updated forecast of Atlantic seasonal activity for 1992.

Greenberg, J. 2001. OSV day rates. Workboat. Volume 58, Number 9, September. P. 16.

Gulf of Mexico Weekly Rig Locator. 2001. http://www.oneoffshore.com/ ViewPublication?PUBID=23. Edition 010907, 7 September. gomdr.xis

Gulf States Marine Fisheries Commission. 1988. Thirty-eighth annual report (1986-1987) to the Congress of the United States and to the governors and legislators of Alabama, Florida, Louisiana, Mississippi, and Texas. Ocean Springs, MS. 90 pp.

Haig, S.M. and J.H. Plissner. 1993. Distribution and abundance of piping plovers: results and implications of the 1991 International Census. The Condor 95:145-156.

Hamilton, P., J. Singer, R. Wayland, and E. Waddel. 1989. The Loop Current and warm eddies in the Central and Western Gulf. Chapman Conference on the Physics of the Gulf of Mexico, FL.

Handley, L. R. 1995. Seagrass distribution in the northern Gulf of Mexico. p. 273-275. In: E. T. LaRoe, G.S. Farris, C.E. Puckett, P.D. Doran, and M.J. Mac (eds.). Our Living Resources. A Report to the Nation on the Distribution, Abundance, and Health of U.S. Plants, Animals, and Ecosystems. U.S. Dept. of the Interior, National Biological Service, Washington, D.C.

Heezen, B.C. 1957. Whales entangled in deep sea cables. Deep-sea Research 4:105-115.

Henry, J.A., K.M. Portier, and J. Coyne. 1994. The climate and weather of Florida. Sarasota, FL: Pineapple press, Inc.

Hess, N.A, and C.A Ribic. 2000. Seabird ecology. Chapter 8 in R.W. Davis, W.E. Evans, and B Würsig (eds.) Cetaceans, sea turtles and seabirds in the northern Gulf of Mexico, volume II: technical report: Prepared by Texas A&M University at Galveston and the National Marine Fisheries Service for the U.S. Department of the Interior, Geological Survey, Biological Resources Division, USCG/BRD/CR-1999-0006 and Minerals Management Service, Gulf of Mexico OCS Region, New Orleans, LA. OCS Study MMS 2000-003. 346 pp.

Hildebrand, H.H. 1995. A historical review of the status of sea turtle populations in the western Gulf of Mexico. In: Bjorndal, K.A., ed. Biology and conservation of sea turtles, second edition, Washington, DC: Smithsonian Institution Press. Pp. 447-453.

Hirth, H.F. 1997. Synopsis of the biological data on the green turtle *Chelonia mydas* (Linnaeus 1758). U.S. Dept. of the Interior, Fish and Wildlife Service. Biological Report 97(1).

Hopkins, T.L. and R.C. Baird. 1985. Feeding ecology of four hatchetfishes (Sternoptychidae) in the eastern Gulf of Mexico. Bull. Mar. Sci. 36(2):260-277.

Hsu, S.A. 1996. Analysis of ambient pollutant concentrations and meteorological conditions affecting EPA Class I and II areas in southeastern Louisiana. Volume II: Appendices. U.S. Dept. of the Interior, Minerals Management Service, Gulf of Mexico OCS Region, New Orleans, LA. OCS Study MMS 96-0063. 364 pp.

Irion, J.B., and R.J. Anuskiewicz. 1999. MMS seafloor monitoring project: The first annual technical report, 1997 field season. U.S. Dept. of the Interior, Minerals Management Service, Gulf of Mexico Region, New Orleans, LA. OCS Report MMS 99-0014.

James, B. 1972. Systematics and biology of the deep-water Palaeotaxodonata (Mollusca: Bivalvia) from the Gulf of Mexico. Ph.D. Dissertation, Texas A&M University, College Station, TX

Jefferson, T.A. 1995. Distribution, abundance, and some aspects of the biology of cetaceans in the offshore Gulf of Mexico. Ph.D. Thesis, Texas A&M University, College Station, TX. 232 pp.

Jefferson, T.A. and A.J. Schiro. 1997. Distribution of cetaceans in the offshore Gulf of Mexico. Mammal Review 27:27-50

Jefferson, T.A., S. Leatherwood, L.K.M. Shoda, and R.L. Pitman. 1992. Marine mammals of the Gulf of Mexico: A field guide for aerial and shipboard observers. College Station, TX: Texas A&M University Printing Center. 92 pp.

Jefferson, T.A., S. Leatherwood, and M.A. Webber. 1993. FAO species identification guide. Marine Mammals of the World. Food and Agriculture Organization, Rome. 320 pp.

Jensen, T., R. Palerud, F. Olsgard, and S. M. Bakke. 1999. Dispersion and effects of synthetic drilling fluids on the environment. Norwegian Ministry of Oil and Energy Technical Report No. 99-3507 Prepared by Olsgård Consulting, Akvaplan-niva, and Det Norske Veritas. 66 p.

Johnsgard, P.A. 1975. Waterfowl of North America. Bloomington and London: Indiana University Press.

Johnston, J.B., M.C. Watzin, J.A. Barras, and L.R. Handley. 1995. Gulf of Mexico coastal wetlands: case studies of loss trends. p. 269-272. In: E. T. LaRoe, G.S. Farris, C.E. Puckett, P.D. Doran, and M.J. Mac (eds.). Our Living Resources. A Report to the Nation on the Distribution, Abundance, and Health of U.S. Plants, Animals, and Ecosystems. U.S. Dept. of the Interior, National Biological Service, Washington, D.C.

Kennedy, E.A., Jr. 1976. A distribution study of deep-sea macrobenthos collected from the western Gulf of Mexico. Ph.D. Dissertation, Texas A&M University, College Station, TX.

Kennicutt M.C., J.M. Brooks, R.R. Bidigare, R.R. Fay, T.L. Wade, and T.J. McDonald. 1985. Vent-type taxa in a hydrocarbon seep region on the Louisiana slope. Nature 317:351-353.

Kennicutt, M.C., J. Sericano, T. Wade, F. Alcazar, and J.M. Rooks. 1987. High-molecular weight hydrocarbons in the Gulf of Mexico continental slope sediment: Deep-Sea Research, 34:403-424.

Kennicutt, M.C., J.M. Brooks, E.L. Atlas, and C.S. Giam. 1988. Organic compounds of environmental concern in the Gulf of Mexico: a review. Aquatic Toxicology 11:191-212.

Kerr-McGee Oil and Gas Corporation. 2001. Development operations coordination document: Nansen Project, East Breaks 602 (OCS-G 14205) and East Breaks 646 (OCS-G 20725). WJP Enterprises.

Kiff, L.F. 1988. Changes in the status of the peregrine falcon in North America: an overview. In: Cade, T.J., J.H. Enderson, C.G. Thelander, and C.M. White, eds. Peregrine falcon populations: their management and recovery. Boise, ID: The Peregrine Fund, Inc. Pp. 123-139.

Laist, D.W., A.R. Knowlton, J.G. Mead, A.S. Collet, and M. Podesta. 2001. Collisions between ships and whales. Mar. Mamm. Sci. 17:35-75.

Lanfear, K.J. and D.E. Amstutz. 1993. A reexamination of occurrence rates for accidental oil spills on the U.S. Outer Continental Shelf. Proceeedings of the Eighth Conference on the Prevention, Behavior, Control and Cleanup of Oil Spills, San Antonio, TX, February 28-March 3, 1983. Pp. 355-359.

Lang, W. H. Personal communication. 2001.

Leatherwood, S. and R.R. Reeves. 1983. Abundance of bottlenose dolphins in Corpus Christi Bay and coastal southern Texas. Contributions in Marine Science 26:179-199.

Leatherwood, S., T.A. Jefferson, J.C. Norris, W.E. Stevens, L.J. Hansen, and K.D. Mullin. 1993. Occurrence and sounds of Fraser's dolphins (*Lagenodelphis hosei*) in the Gulf of Mexico. Tex. J. Sci. 45:349-354.

Lee, R.F. 1977. Fate of Oil in the Sea. In: Fore, P.L., ed. Proceedings of the 1977 Oil Spill Response Workshop. U.S. Dept. of the Interior, Fish and Wildlife Service, Washington, D.C. Biological Services Program, FWS/OBS/77-24. Pp 43-54.

Lohoefener, R., W. Hoggard, K. Mullin, C. Roden, and C. Rogers. 1990. Association of sea turtles with petroleum platforms in the north-central Gulf of Mexico. U.S. Dept. of the Interior, Minerals Management Service, Gulf of Mexico OCS Region, New Orleans, LA. OCS Study MMS 90-0025. 90 pp.

Linden, O., J.R. Sharp, R. Laughlin, Jr., and J.M. Neff. 1979. Interactive effects of salinity, temperature, and chronic exposure to oil on the survival and development rate of embryos of the estuarine killfish *Fundulus heteroclitus*. Mar. Biol. 51:101-109.

Longwell, A.C. 1977. A genetic look at fish eggs and oil. Oceanus 20(4):46-58.

Lutcavage, M.E., P. Plotkin, B. Witherington, and P.L. Lutz. 1997. Human impacts on sea turtle survival. In: Lutz, P.L. and J.A. Musick, eds. The biology of sea turtles. Boca Raton, FL: CRC Press. Pp. 387-409.

Lytle, J.S. 1975. Fate and effects of crude oil on an estuarine pond. Proceedings of the Conference on Prevention and Control of Oil Pollution, San Francisco, CA. Pp. 595-600.

Maccarone, A.D. and J.N. Brzorad. 1994. Gulf and waterfowl populations in the Arthur Kill. In: Burger, J., ed. Before and after an oil spill: The Arthur Kill. New Brunswick, NJ: Rutgers University Press. Pp. 595-600.

MacDonald, I.R., ed. 1992. Chemosynthetic ecosystems study literature review and data synthesis: Volumes I-III. U.S. Dept. of the Interior, Minerals Management Service, Gulf of Mexico OCS Region, New Orleans, LA. OCS Study MMS 92-0033 through 92-0035.

MacDonald, I.R., N.L. Guinasso, Jr., J.F. Reilly, J.M. Brooks, W.R. Callender, and S.G. Gabrielle. 1990. Gulf of Mexico hydrocarbon seep communities: VI. Patterns in community structure and habitat. Geo-Marine Letters 10:244-252.

MacDonald, I.R., J.F. Reiley, Jr., S.E. Best, R. Sassen, N.L. Guinasso, Jr., and J. Amos. 1996. Remote sensing inventory of active oil seeps and chemosynthetic communities in the northern Gulf of Mexico. In: Schumacher, D. and M.A. Abrams, eds. Hydrocarbon migration and its near-surface expression. AAPG Memoir 66. Pp. 27-37.

Maciolik, N., B. Hecker, C. Rutman, J.F. Grassle, W. Dade, P. Boehm, W. Steinhaur, V. Starcyk, E. Baptiste, R. Ruff, and B. Brown. 1986. Study of biological processes on the U.S. north Atlantic slope and rise. Interim report submitted to the U.S. Dept. of the Interior, Minerals Management Service, Restin, VA. Contract No. 14-12-0001-30064. 201 pp. + appendices.

Maechtle, T.L. 1992. Padre Island peregrine falcon survey — spring and autumn 1991. Unpublished report.

Mager, A. and R. Ruebsamen. 1988. National Marine Fisheries Service habitat conservation efforts in the coastal southeastern United States. Mar. Fish. Rev. 50(3):43-50.

Malins, D.C., S. Chan, H.O. Hodgins, U. Varanasi, D.D. Weber, and D.W. Brown. 1982. The nature and biological effects of weathered petroleum. Environmental Conservation Division, Northwest and Alaska Fisheries Center, National Marine Fisheries Service, Seattle, WA. 43 pp.

Marks, S. 1996. Written communication. Meteorological file. Observations from rig during drilling of Destin Dome 57 #1 well. DD 57 drilling rigs. 300 pp.

Marks, S. 1997. Written communication. Compilation of meteorological data from actual observations in the Destin Dome Unit. 271 pp.

Marquez-M. ,R. 1990. FAO Species Catalogue. Volume 11: Sea turtles of the world. An annotated and illustrated catalogue of sea turtle species known to date. FAO Fisheries Synopsis. FAO, Rome.

Martin, R.P. 1991. Regional overview of wading birds in Louisiana, Mississippi, and Alabama. In: Proceedings of the Coastal Nongame Workshop. U.S. Dept. of the Interior, Fish and Wildlife Service, Region 4 and the Florida Game and Fresh Water Fish Commission. Pp. 22-33.

Martin, R.P. and G.D. Lester. 1991. Atlas and census of wading bird and seabird nesting colonies in Louisiana: 1990. Special Publication No. 3, Louisiana Dept. of Wildlife and Fisheries, Louisiana Natural Heritage Program.

McCarroll, J. 1998. Personal communication. U.S. Dept. of the Interior, Minerals Management Service, New Orleans District Office, New Orleans, LA.

McKelvie, S. and R. C. Ayers, Jr. 1999. Environmental effects of cuttings from synthetic based drilling fluids. A literature review. Draft Report by Robert Ayers & Associates Inc. and Rudall Blanchard Associates for the American Petroleum Institute. 33 p.

Menzies, R., R. George, and G. Rowe. 1973. Abyssal Environment and Ecology of the World Oceans. Wiley and Sons, New York.

Meylan, A., B. Schroeder, and A. Mosier. 1995. Sea turtle nesting activity in the State of Florida 1979-1992. Florida Marine Research Publications, Florida Marine Research Institute, No. 52.

Morrison, J.M., W.J. Merrell, Jr., R.M. Key, and T.L. Key. 1983. property distribution and deep chemical measurements within the western Gulf of Mexico. Journal Geophysical Research 88(C4):2,601-2,608.

Mullin, K.D., T.A. Jefferson, L.J. Hansen, and W. Hoggard. 1994a. First sightings of melon-headed whales (*Peponocephala electra*) in the Gulf of Mexico. Mar. Mamm. Sci. 10:342-348.

Mullin, K.D., L.V. Higgins, T.A. Jefferson, and L.J. Hansen. 1994b. Sightings of the Clymene dolphin (*Stenella clymene*) in the Gulf of Mexico. Mar. Mamm. Sci. 10:464-470.

Mullin, K.D., and W. Hoggard. 2000. Visual surveys of cetaceans and sea turtles from aricraft and ships. Chapter 4 in R.W. Davis, W.E. Evans, and B Würsig, eds. Cetaceans, sea turtles and seabirds in the northern Gulf of Mexico, volume II: technical report: Prepared by Texas A&M University at Galveston and the National Marine Fisheries Service for the U.S. Dept. of the Interior, Geological Survey, Biological Resources Division, USCG/BRD/CR-1999-0006 and Minerals Management Service, Gulf of Mexico OCS Region, New Orleans, LA. OCS Study MMS 2000-003, 346 p.

Mullin, K.D., W. Hoggard, C.L. Roden, R.R. Lohoefener, C.M. Rogers, and B. Taggart. 1994c. Cetaceans on the upper continental slope in the north-central Gulf of Mexico. U.S. Fish. Bull. 92:773-786.

Mullino, M.M., M.F. Rayle, J.C. Francis and M.A. Poirrier. 1996. Delineation of benthic impact and recovery at two produced water discharge sites in inshore Louisiana. p. 177-194. In: M. Reed and S. Johnsen (eds.). Produced Water 2 Environmental Issues and Mitigation Technologies. Plenum Press, New York.

Murray, S.P. 1998. An observational study of the Mississippi-Atchafalaya coastal plume: Final report. U.S. Dept. of the Interior, Minerals Management Service, Gulf of Mexico OCS Region, New Orleans, LA. OCS Study MMS 98-0040. 513 pp.

Musick, J. A. and C.J. Limpus. 1997. Habitat utilization and migration in juvenile sea turtles. In: Lutz, P.L. and J.A. Musick, eds. The biology of sea turtles. Boca Raton, FL: CRC Press. Pp. 137-164.

Nakassis, A. 1982. Has offshore oil production become safer? U.S. Geological Survey Open File Report 82-232. Reston, VA: U.S. Dept. of the Interior, Geological Survey. 27 pp

National Research Council (NRC). 1985. Oil in the sea: inputs, fates, and effects. Washington, DC: National Academy Press. 601 pp.

Native American Data Center. 1999. http://ww.indiandata.com/eastern.htm (31 October 1999).

Neff, J.M. and T.C. Sauer. 1996. Aromatic hydrocarbons in produced water: bioaccumulation and trophic transfer in marine food webs. p. 163-176. In: M. Reed and S. Johnsen (eds.). Produced Water 2 Environmental Issues and Mitigation Technologies. Plenum Press, New York.

Nelson, H.F. and E.E. Bray. 1970. Stratigraphy and history of the Holocene sediments in the Sabine-High Island Area, Gulf of Mexico. In: Morgam, J.P., ed. Deltaic Sedimentation; Modern and Ancient. Special Publn. No. 15. Tulsa, OK: SEPM.

Nowlin, W.D., Jr. 1972. Winter circulation patterns and property distributions. In: Capurra, L.R.A. and J.L. Reid, eds. Contributions on the Physical Oceanography of the Gulf of Mexico. Houston, TX: Gulf Publishing Company. Pp. 3-51.

Nowlin, W.D., Jr., A.E. Jochens, R.O. Reid, and S.F. DiMarco. 1998. Texas-Louisiana shelf circulation and transport processes study: Synthesis report. Volumes I and II. U.S. Dept. of the Interior, Minerals Management Service, Gulf of Mexico OCS Region, New Orleans, LA. OCS Study MMS 98-0036 and 98-0036. 502 and 288 pp., respectively.

O'Connor, T.P. 1990. Coastal environmental quality in the United States, 1990: Chemical contamination in sediment and tissues. A Special NOAA 20th Anniversary Report. U.S. Dept. of Commerce, National Oceanic and Atmospheric Administration, National Status and Trends Program, Rockville, MD. 34 pp.

O'Connor, T.P. and B. Beliaeff. 1995. Recent trends in coastal environmental quality: Results from the mussel watch project (National Status and Trends Program, Marine Environmental Quality). U.S. Dept. of Commerce, National Oceanic and Atmospheric Administration, National Ocean Service, Silver Spring, MD. 40 pp.

Osenberg, C.W., R.J. Schmitt, S.J. Holbrook and D. Canestro. 1992. Spatial scale of biological effects associated with an open coast discharge of produced water. Pp. 387-402. In: J.P. Ray and F.R. Engelhardt (eds.). Produced water: technological/environmental issues and solutions. Environmental Science Research,. Vol. 46. Plenum Press, New York.

O'Shea, T.J., B.B. Ackerman, and H.F. Percival, eds. 1995. Population biology of the Florida manatee. National Biological Service, Information and Technology Report 1.

O'Sullivan, S. and K.D. Mullin. 1997. Killer whales (Orcinus orca) in the northern Gulf of Mexico. Mar. Mamm. Sci. 13:141-147.

Parker, R.D., J.M. Morrison, and W.D. Nowlin, Jr. 1979. Surface drifter data from the Caribbean Sea and Gulf of Mexico, 1975-1978. Dept. of Oceanography, Texas A&M University, Reference 79-8-T. 169 pp.

Payne, J.F., J. Kiceniuk, L.L. Fancey, U. Williams, G.L. Fletcher, A. Rahimtula, and B. Fowler. 1988. What is a safe level of polycyclic aromatic hydrocarbons for fish: Subchronic toxicity study on winter flounder (*Pseudopleuronectes americanus*). Can. J. Fish. Aquat. Sci. 45:1983-1993.

Payne, J., C. Andrews, S. Whiteway and K. Lee. 2001a. Definition of sediment toxicity zones around oil development sites: does response relationships for the monitoring surrogates Microtox® and amphipods exposed to Hibernia source cuttings containing a synthetic base oil. Canadian Manuscript Report of Fisheries and Aquatic Sciences No. 2577. 10 p.

Payne, J., L. Fancey, C. Andrews, J. Meade, F. Power, K. Lee, G. Veinott and A. Cook. 2001b. Laboratory exposures of invertebrate and vertebrate species to concentrations of IA-35 (Petro-Canada) drill mud fluid, production water, and Hibernia drill mud cuttings. Canadian Manuscript Report of Fisheries and Aquatic Sciences No. 2560. 27 p.

Pequegnat, L. 1970. A study of deep-sea caridean shrimps (Crustacea: Decapoda: Natantia) of the Gulf of Mexico. Ph.D. Dissertation, Texas A&M University, College Station, TX.

Pequegnat, W.E. 1983. The ecological communities of the continental slope and adjacent regimes of the northern Gulf of Mexico. Final report to the U.S. Dept. of the Interior, Minerals Management Service, Gulf of Mexico OCS Region, New Orleans, LA. Contract No. AA851-CT1-12).

Pequegnat, W.E., B.J. Gallaway, and L. Pequegnat. 1990. Aspects of the ecology of the deepwater fauna of the Gulf of Mexico. American Zoologist 30: 45-64.

Power, J.H. and L.N. May, Jr. 1991. Satellite observed sea-surface temperatures and yellowfin tuna catch and effort in the Gulf of Mexico. Fish. Bull. 89:429-439

Price, J.M., C.F. Marshall, and E.M. Lear. 1999. Supplement to Oil-Spill Risk Analysis: Gulf of Mexico OCS Central and Western Lease Sales, 1998-2002, and Gulfwide OCS Program, 1998-2036. U.S. Dept. of the Interior, Minerals Management Service, Environmental Division, Herndon, VA. OCS Report MMS 99-0010. Available via http://www mms.gov/itd/pubs/1999/99-0010.pdf.

Pritchard, P.C.H. 1997. Evolution, phylogeny, and current status. In: Lutz, P.L. and J.A. Musick, eds. The biology of sea turtles. Boca Raton, FL: CRC Press. Pp. 1-28.

Rabalais, N.N. 1992. An updated summary of status and trends in indicators of nutrient enrichment in the Gulf of Mexico. Report to the Gulf of Mexico Program, Nutrient Enrichment Subcommittee. Stennis Space Center, MS. U.S. Environmental Protection Agency, Office of Water, Gulf of Mexico Program. EPA/800-R-92-004. 421 pp.

Rabalais, N.N., B.A. McKee, D.J. Reed and J.C. Means. 1992. Fate and effects of produced water discharges in coastal Louisiana, Gulf of Mexico. Pp. 355-369. In: J.P. Ray and F.R. Engelhardt (eds.). Produced water: technological/environmental issues and solutions. Environmental Science Research,. Vol. 46. Plenum Press, New York.

Raimondi, P.T. and R.J. Schmitt. 1992. Effects of produced water on settlement of larvae: Field tests using Red Abalone. Pp. 415-430. In: J.P. Ray and F.R. Engelhardt (eds.), Produced Water: Technological/Environmental Issues and Solutions. Environmental Science Research, Vol. 46. New York: Plenum Press.

Reeves, R.R., B.S. Stewart, and S. Leatherwood. 1992. The Sierra Club handbook of seals and sirenians. San Francisco, CA: Sierra Club Books.

Regg, J. 1998. Personal communication. U.S. Dept. of the Interior, Minerals Management Service, New Orleans District Office, New Orleans, LA.

Reggio, V.C., Jr., comp. 1989. Petroleum structures as artificial reefs: A compendium. U.S. Dept. of the Interior, Minerals Management Service, Gulf of Mexico OCS Region, New Orleans, LA. OCS Study MMS 89-0021. 176 pp.

Rice, D.W. 1989. Sperm whale — *Physeter macrocephalus* (Linnaeus, 1758). In: Ridgway, S.H. and R. Harrison, eds. Handbook of marine mammals. Vol. 4: River dolphins and the larger toothed whales. London: Academic Press, Inc. Pp. 177-234.

Richards, W.J., T. Leming, M.F. McGowan, J.T. Lamkin, and S. Kelley-Farga. 1989. Distribution of fish larvae in relation to hydrographic features of the Loop Current boundary in the Gulf of Mexico. Rapp. P.-v. Reun. Cons. Int. Explor. Mer. 191:169-176.

Rike, J.L. 2000. Downsizing the operation instead of the company. In: McKay, M. and J. Nides, eds. Proceedings, Eighteenth Annual Gulf of Mexico Information Transfer Meeting, December 1998. U.S. Dept. of the Interior, Minerals Management Service, Gulf of Mexico OCS Region, New Orleans, LA. OCS Study MMS 2000-030. Pp. 469-475.

Roberts, H.H., P. Aharon, R. Carney, J. Larkin, and R. Sassen. 1990. Sea floor responses to hydrocarbon seeps, Louisiana continental slope. Geo-Marine Letter 10(4):232-243.

Roberts, H.H., and R.S. Carney. 1997. Evidence of episodic fluid, gas, and sediment venting on the northern Gulf of Mexico continental slope: Economic Geology. 92:863-879.

Roberts, T. 1970. A preliminary study of the family Penaeidae and their distribution in the deep water of the Gulf of Mexico. M.S. Thesis, Texas A&M University, College Station, TX.

Roberts, T. 1977. An analysis of deep-sea benthic communities in the northeast Gulf of Mexico. Ph.D. Dissertation, Texas A&M University, College Station, TX.

Robinson, M.K. 1973. Atlas of monthly mean sea surface and subsurface temperature and depth of the top of the thermocline Gulf of Mexico and Caribbean Sea. Scripps Institution of Oceanography, Reference 73-8. 12 pp. + 93 figures.

Rowe, G.T. and D.W. Menzel. 1971. Quantitative benthic samples from the deep Gulf of Mexico with some comments on the measurement of deep-sea biomass. Bull. Mar. Sci. 21(2):556-566.

Rowe, G., M. Sibuet, J. Deming. A. Khripounoff, J. Tietjen, S. Macko, and R. Theroux. 1991. "Total" sediment biomass and preliminary estimates of organic carbon residence time in the deep-sea benthos. Marine Ecology Progress Series 79:99-114.

Rye, H. and P.J. Brandvik. 1997. Verification of subsurface oil spill models. In: Proceedings, 1997 International Oil Spill Conference, April 7-10, 1997, Fort Lauderdale, FL. American Petroleum Institute Publication No. 4651. Pp. 551-557.

Sassen, R., J.M. Brooks, M.C. Kennucutt, II, I.R. MacDonald, and N.L. Guinasso, Jr. 1993. How oil seeps, discoveries relate in deepwater Gulf of Mexico. Oil and Gas Journal 91(16):64-69.

Schwarz, A. L. and G.L. Greer. 1984. Responses of Pacific herring, *Clupea harengus pallasi*, to some underwater sounds. Can. J. Fish. Aquat. Sci. 41: 1183-1192.

Sharp, B.E. 1995. Does the cleaning and treatment of oiled seabirds mean that they are rehabilitated — what about post-release survival? In: Proceedings, The Effects of Oil on Wildlife, 4th International Conference, April 1995, Seattle, WA.

Sharp, B.E. 1996. Post-release survival of oiled, cleaned seabirds in North America. Ibis 138:222-228.

Simmons, M.R. 2000. Outlook for Natural Gas: is a train wreck pending? http://www.simmonsco-intl.com/research/docview.asp?viewnews=true&newstype=2&viewdoc=true&dv=true&doc=100. 6 December.

S.L. Ross Environmental Research Ltd. 1997. Fate and behavior of deepwater subsea oil well blowouts in the Gulf of Mexico. Internal report. U.S. Dept. of the Interior, Minerals Management Service, Gulf of Mexico OCS Region, New Orleans, LA.

Smith, M. 1996. Written communication. Notes on GRI Offshore Gas Processing Workshop, February 13, 1996, New Orleans, LA. 10 pp. + appendices.

Sparks, T.D., J.C. Norris, R. Benson, and W.E. Evans. 1996. Distributions of sperm whales in the northwestern Gulf of Mexico as determined from an acoustic survey. In: Proceedings of the 11th Biennial Conference on the Biology of Marine Mammals, 14-18 December 1995, Orlando, FL. 108 pp.

Spies, R.B., J.S. Felton, and L. Dillard. 1982. Hepatic mixed-function oxidases in California flatfishes are increased in contaminated environments and by oil and PCB ingestion. Mar. Biol. 70:117-127.

Stanley, D.R. and C.A. Wilson. 1997. Seasonal and spatial variation in the abundance and size distribution of fishes associated with a petroleum platform in the northern Gulf of Mexico. Can. J. Fish. Aquat. Sci. 54: 1166-1176.

Stauffer, K. 1998. Personal communication. U.S. Dept. of the Interior, Minerals Management Service, New Orleans District Office, New Orleans, LA.

Stewart, B.S. and S. Leatherwood. 1985. Minke whale — *Balaenoptera acutorostrata*. In: Ridgway, S.H. and R. Harrison, eds. Handbook of marine mammals. Vol. 3: The Sirenians and baleen whales. Academic Press, Inc. Pp. 91-136.

Terres, J.K. 1991. The Audubon Society Encyclopedia of North American Birds. New York: Wing Books. 1,109 pp.

Texas General Land Office. 1996. An environmental economic opportunity report. EnviroNomics (Summer 1996). Austin, TX. Pp. 5 and 8.

Texas Parks and Wildlife Department. 1990. Texas colonial waterbird census summary. Texas Parks and Wildlife Dept. and the Texas Colonial Waterbird Society, Special Administrative Report.

Thiel, H. 1983. Meiobenthos and nanobenthos of the deep sea. In: Rowe, G.T., ed. Deep-Sea Biology: Chapter 5. New York, NY: John Wiley & Sons. Pp. 167-230.

Thorpe, H. 1996. Oil and water. Texas Monthly 24(2):88-93 and 140-145.

Tietjen, J.H. 1971. Ecology and distribution of deep-sea meiobenthos off North Carolina. Deep-Sea Res. 18:941-954.

Trefry J.H. 1981. A review of existing knowledge on trace metals in the Gulf of Mexico. In: Proceedings of a Symposium on Environmental Research Needs in the Gulf of Mexico (GOMEX): Vol. II-B. U.S. Dept. of Commerce, National Oceanic and Atmospheric Administration, Environmental Research Lab. Pp. 225-259.

U.S. Dept. of Commerce. 1967. United States coast pilot 5. Atlantic Coast, Gulf of Mexico, Puerto Rico and Virgin Islands, 6th ed. Washington, DC: U.S. Coast and Geodetic Survey, Environmental Science Services Administration. 301 pp.

U.S. Dept. of Commerce. National Marine Fisheries Service. 1997. Fisheries of the United States, 1997. Current Fisheries Statistics. U.S. Dept. of Commerce, National Marine Fisheries, Service, Washington, DC.

U.S. Dept. of Commerce. National Marine Fisheries Service. 2001. Information and databases on fisheries landings. Internet site: http://www.st nmfs.gov/st1/commercial/landings/annual_landings html.

U.S. Dept. of Commerce, National Marine Fisheries Service and U.S. Dept. of the Interior, Fish and Wildlife Service. 1991a. Recovery plan for U.S. population of Atlantic green turtle. U.S. Dept. of Commerce, National Marine Fisheries Service, Washington, DC. 52 pp.

U.S. Dept. of Commerce, National Marine Fisheries Service and U.S. Dept. of the Interior, Fish and Wildlife Service. 1991b. Recovery plan for U.S. populations of loggerhead turtle. U.S. Dept. of Commerce, National Marine Fisheries Service, Washington, DC. 64 pp.

U.S. Dept. of Commerce, National Marine Fisheries Service and U.S. Dept. of the Interior, Fish and Wildlife Service. 1992a. Recovery plan for the Kemp's ridley sea turtle (*Lepidochelys kempii*). U.S. Dept. of Commerce, National Marine Fisheries Service, St. Petersburg, FL. 40 pp.

U.S. Dept. of Commerce, National Marine Fisheries Service and U.S. Dept. of the Interior, Fish and Wildlife Service. 1992b. Recovery plan for leatherback turtles in the U.S. Caribbean, Atlantic, and Gulf of Mexico. U.S. Dept. Commerce National Marine Fisheries Service, Washington, DC. 65 pp.

U.S. Dept. of Commerce, National Marine Fisheries Service and U.S. Dept. of the Interior, Fish and Wildlife Service. 1993. Recovery plan for hawksbill turtles in the U.S. Caribbean Sea, Atlantic Ocean, and Gulf of Mexico. U.S. Dept. of Commerce, National Marine Fisheries Service, St. Petersburg, FL. 52 pp.

U.S. Dept. of Commerce. National Marine Fisheries Service. 1999a. Final Fishery Management Plan for Atlantic tunas, swordfish, and sharks. Volumes 1-3. U.S. Dept. of Commerce, Marine Fisheries Service, Highly Migratory Species Division. April 1999.

U.S. Dept. of Commerce. National Marine Fisheries Service. 1999b. Amendment 1 to the Atlantic billfish fishery management plan. U.S. Dept. of Commerce, National Marine Fisheries Service, Highly Migratory Species Division. April 1999.

U.S. Dept. of Commerce. National Oceanic and Atmospheric Administration. 1991. Our living oceans. The first annual report on the status of U.S. living marine resources. NOAA Tech. Memo. NMFS-F/SPO-1. 123 pp.

U.S. Dept. of Commerce. National Oceanic and Atmospheric Administration. 1992a. Agricultural pesticide use in coastal areas: a national summary. September 1992. 111 pp.

U.S. Dept. of Commerce. National Oceanic and Atmospheric Administration. 1992b. Report to the Congress on ocean pollution, monitoring, and research. U.S. Dept. of Commerce, National Oceanic and Atmospheric Administration, National Ocean Service. November 1990. 56 pp.

U.S. Dept. of Commerce. National Oceanic and Atmospheric Administration. 1992c. The National Status and Trends Program for marine environmental quality. U.S. Dept. of Commerce, National Oceanic and Atmospheric Administration, National Ocean Service. March 1992. 18 pp.

U.S. Dept. of the Interior, Bureau of Indian Affairs, Geographic Data Service Center. 1998. http://www.gdsc.bia.gov/pdf/usa.pdf (December 1998).

U.S. Dept. of the Interior. Fish and Wildlife Service. 1984. Southeastern states bald eagle recover plan. U.S. Dept. of the Interior, Fish and Wildlife Service, Southeast Region, Atlanta, GA.

U.S. Dept. of the Interior. Fish and Wildlife Service. 1994. Whooping crane recovery plan. U.S. Dept. of the Interior, Fish and Wildlife Service, Southeast Region, Atlanta, GA. 92 pp.

U.S. Dept. of the Interior. Fish and Wildlife Service. 1998. Division of Endangered Species. Species Accounts. Internet site: http://www fws.gov/r9endspp/i/b/sab2s html.

U.S. Dept. of the Interior. Minerals Management Service. 1988. Meteorological database and synthesis for the Gulf of Mexico. Prepared by Florida A&M University for the Minerals Management Service, Gulf of Mexico OCS Region, New Orleans, LA. OCS Study MMS 88-0064. 486 pp.

U.S. Dept. of the Interior. Minerals Management Service. 1996. Outer continental shelf oil and gas leasing program: 1997-2000—final environmental impact statement; Volumes I-III. U.S. Dept. of the Interior, Minerals Management Service, Washington, DC. OCS EIS/EA MMS 96-0043.

U.S. Dept. of the Interior. Minerals Management Service. 1997a. Gulf of Mexico OCS oil and gas lease sales 169, 172, 175, 178 and 182: Central Planning Area, final environmental impact statement. U.S. Dept. of the Interior, Minerals Management Service, Gulf of Mexico OCS Region, New Orleans, LA. OCS EIS/EA MMS 97-0033. Available from NTIS, Springfield, VA: PB98-116916.

U.S. Dept. of the Interior. Minerals Management Service. 1997b. Federal offshore statistics: 1995. Leasing, exploration, production, and revenue as of December 31, 1995. U.S. Dept. of the Interior, Minerals Management Service, Operations and Safety Management, Herndon, VA. OCS Report MMS 97-0007. 103 pp.

U.S. Dept. of the Interior. Minerals Management Service. 1998. Gulf of Mexico OCS oil and gas lease sales 171, 174, 177, and 180: Western Planning Area, final environmental impact statement. U.S. Dept. of the Interior, Minerals Management Service, Gulf of Mexico OCS Region, New Orleans, LA. OCS EIS/EA MMS 98-0008. Available from NTIS, Springfield, VA.

U.S. Dept. of the Interior. Minerals Management Service. 2001a. Proposed OCS lease sale 180, Western Gulf of Mexico — environmental assessment. U.S. Dept. of the Interior, Minerals Management Service, Gulf of Mexico OCS Region, New Orleans, LA. OCS EIS/EA MMS 2001-034.

U.S. Dept. of the Interior. Minerals Management Service. 2001b. Gulf of Mexico OCS oil and gas lease sale 181: Eastern Planning Area, final environmental impact statement. U.S. Dept. of the Interior, Minerals Management Service, Gulf of Mexico OCS Region, New Orleans, LA. OCS EIS/EA MMS 2001-051.

U.S. Dept. of the Interior. Minerals Management Service. 2001c. Offshore stats: An update of OCS-related natural gas and oil information (updated January 25, 2001). U.S. Dept. of the Interior, Minerals Management Service, Engineering & Operations Division, Operations Analysis Branch, Herndon, VA.

U.S. Environmental Protection Agency. 1999. Effluent limitations guidelines and new source performance standards for synthetic-based and other non-aqueous drilling fluids in the oil and gas extraction point source category; proposed rule. February 3, 1999. 64(22):5,488-5,554.

U.S. Environmental Protection Agency. 2001. Green book, non-attainment areas for criteria pollutants. http://www.epa.gov/oar/oaqps/greenbk/.

Wallace, D.W. 1980. Distribution of Mississippi River water under high flow conditions in the Gulf of Mexico. Florida Marine Research Publications, Florida Dept. of Natural Resources, Marine Research Laboratory. 40 pp.

Waring, G.T., D.L. Palka, K.D. Mullin, J.H.W. Hain, L.J. Hansen, and K.D. Bisack. 1997. U.S. Atlantic and Gulf of Mexico marine mammal stock assessments — 1996. NOAA Tech. Memo. NMFS-NE-114.

Webb, J.W. 1988. Establishment of vegetation on oil-contaminated dunes. Shore and Beach, October. Pp. 20-23.

Webb, J.W., G.T. Tanner, and B.H. Koerth. 1981. Oil spill effects on smooth cordgrass in Galveston Bay, Texas. Contributions in Marine Science 24:107-114.

Webb, J.W., S.K. Alexander, and J.K. Winters. 1985. Effects of autumn application of oil on Spartina alterniflora in a Texas salt marsh. Environ. Poll., Series A. 8(4):321-337.

Weber, M., R.T. Townsend, and R. Bierce. 1992. Environmental quality in the Gulf of Mexico: A citizen's guide. Center for Marine Conservation. 2nd edition, June 1992. 130 pp.

Wigley, R.L. and A.D. McIntyre. 1964. Some quantitative comparisons of offshore meiobenthos and macrobenthos south of Martha's Vineyard. Limno. Oceanogr. 9:485-493.

Winn, H.E. and N.E. Reichley. 1985. Humpback whale — *Megaptera novaeangliae*. In: Ridgway, S.H. and R. Harrison, eds. Handbook of marine mammals. Vol. 3: The sirenians and baleen whales. London: Academic Press, Inc. Pp. 241-274.

Wolfe, S.H., J.A. Reidenauer, and D.B. Means. 1988. An ecological characterization of the Florida Panhandle. U.S. Dept. of the Interior, Minerals Management Service, Gulf of Mexico OCS Region, New Orleans, LA. Fish Wildlife Service Biological Report 88(12) and Minerals Management Service OCS Study MMS 88-0063. 277 pp.

Würsig, B., T.A. Jefferson, and D.J. Schmidly. 2000. The marine mammals of the Gulf of Mexico. College Station, TX: Texas A&M University Press. 232 pp.

Yochem, P.K. and S. Leatherwood. 1985. Blue whale — *Balaenoptera musculus*. In: Ridgway, S.H. and R. Harrison, eds. Handbook of marine mammals. Vol. 3: The sirenians and baleen whales. London: Academic Press, Inc. Pp. 193-240.

Zieman, J.C., R. Orth, R.C. Phillips, G. Thayer, and A. Thornhaug. 1984. The effects of oil on seagrass ecosystems. In: Cairns, J. and A. Buikema, eds. Recovery and restoration of marine ecosystems. Stoneham, MA: Butterworth Publications. Pp. 37-64.

7. APPENDICES

APPENDIX A
Accidental Hydrocarbon Discharge Analysis

APPENDIX A

ACCIDENTAL HYDROCARBON DISCHARGE ANALYSIS

Analysis of the Potential for an Accidental Oil Spill and Potential for Impacts from Production Activities in Green Canyon Blocks 644 and 645, Holstein Project (N-7216)

Introduction

The National Environmental Policy Act, as amended, (NEPA) requires Federal agencies to consider potential environmental impacts (direct, indirect, and cumulative) of proposed actions as part of agency planning and decisionmaking processes. The NEPA analyses address many issues relating to potential effects, including issues that may have a very low probability of occurrence but which the public considers important or for which the environmental consequences could be significant.

The past several decades of spill data show that accidental oil spills associated with oil and gas exploration and development are low-probability events on the Federal Outer Continental Shelf (OCS) of the Gulf of Mexico (GOM), yet the effects from oil spills is of concern to the public. This appendix summarizes key information about the low probability of accidental spills from offshore oil and gas activities in the GOM.

Spill Prevention

The MMS has comprehensive, pollution-prevention requirements that include numerous redundant levels of safety devices, as well as inspection and testing requirements to confirm that these devices work properly. Many of these requirements have been in place since about 1980. Spill trends analysis for the GOM OCS show that spills from facilities have decreased over time, indicating that the MMS's engineering and safety requirements have minimized the potential for spill occurrence and associated impacts. Details regarding the MMS's engineering and safety requirements can be found in 30 CFR 250.800, Subpart H.

Historic OCS Spills

This summary of past OCS spills uses data for the 1985-1999 interval. This time period was selected because it reflects more modern engineering and regulatory requirements. For the period 1985-1999, there were no spills >1,000 barrels (bbl) from OCS platforms, eight spills > 1,000 bbl from OCS pipelines, and no spills > 1,000 bbl from OCS blowouts (Table A-1—for pipelines only). It is considered a conservative assumption that a spill would need to be at least 1,000 bbl or greater in order for it to stay together as a slick long enough to significantly affect shorelines and associated resources. It should be noted that past OCS spills, some of which are considerably larger than 1,000 bbl, have not resulted in any documented significant impacts to shorelines or other resources. The most recent Final Environmental Impact Statements (EIS's) for Central Gulf Lease Sales 169, 172, 175, 178, and 182, and Eastern Gulf Lease Sale 181 provide additional information on past OCS spills and their potential effects.

Estimating Future Potential Spills

The MMS estimates the risk of future potential spills by multiplying variables to result in a numerical expression of risk. These variables include the potential of a spill occurring based on historical OCS spill rates and a variable for the potential for a spill to be transported to environmental resources based on trajectory modeling. The following subsections describe the spill occurrence and transport variables used to estimate risk and the risk calculations for the proposed action.

Spill-Occurrence Variable (SOV) -- Represents the Potential for a Spill

The spill-occurrence variable (SOV) is derived from past OCS spill frequency, i.e., data from past OCS spills are used to estimate future potential OCS spills. The MMS has estimated spill rates for spills from the following sources: facilities, pipelines, and blowouts.

Spill rates for facilities and pipelines have been developed for several time periods and an analysis of trends for spills is presented in Update of Comparative Occurrence Rates for Offshore Oil Spills (Anderson and LaBelle, 2000). Spill rates for the most recent period analyzed, 1985-1999, are presented here. Data for this recent period should reflect more modern spill-prevention equipment and requirements.

Spill rates for facilities and pipelines are based on the number of spills per volume of oil handled. Spill rates for blowouts are based on the number of blowouts with a release of oil per number of wells drilled. Spill rates for the period 1985-1999 are shown in Table A-2. It should be noted that there were no platform or blowout spills > 1,000 bbl for the period 1985-1999. The use of "zero" spills in estimation calculations would result in a zero spill rate. To allow for conservative future predictions of spill occurrence, a spill number of one was "assigned" to provide a non-zero spill rate for blowouts. The spill period was expanded to 1980 to include a spill for facilities. While there were no blowouts or facility spills during the 1985-1999 period, spills could occur in the future. In fact, a pipeline spill of > 1,000 bbl was reported subsequent to this period, so it is reasonable to include "a spill" to provide a non-zero calculation rate.

Spill rates are combined with site-specific data on production or pipeline volumes or number of wells drilled to result in a site-specific SOV.

Transport Variable (TV) -- Represents the Potential for a Spill to be Transported to Important Environmental Resources

The transport variable (TV) is derived using an oil-spill trajectory model. This model predicts the direction that winds and currents would transport spills. The model uses an extensive database of observed and theoretically computed ocean currents and fields that represent a statistical estimate of winds and currents that would occur over the life of an oil and gas project, which may span several decades. This model produces the TV that can be combined with other variables, such as the SOV, to estimate the risk of future potential spills and impacts.

Risk Calculation for the Proposed Action

The proposed action includes the drilling, completion, and production of 15 wells (Wells E-S); the reentering, completion, and production of the Green Canyon Block 645 Well No.1; and the installation of a truss spar in Green Canyon Blocks 644 and 645 in approximately 1,324 m (4,344 ft) of water. Table A-3 presents an estimate of spill risk to resources. The risk estimate was calculated using the spill rate of 0.13 spills per billion barrels of oil produced, the estimated production for the proposed action, and oil spill trajectory calculations.

The coastline and associated environmental resources are presented in Table A-3. The final column in Table A-3 presents the result of combining the SOV and the TV. It should be noted that the estimated risk is essentially below the lower mathematical limits of the calculations. In other words, the risk of a spill from the facility could be considered to be so low as to be near zero.

Given the low risk that a spill may occur and spill-prevention and response requirements, significant impacts to environmental resources are unlikely. The most recent Final EIS's for Central Gulf Lease Sales 169, 172, 175, 178, and 182, and Eastern Gulf Lease Sale 181 provide additional information on spills and potential impacts. The following section provides additional information regarding the spill-response preparedness requirements of MMS.

Spill Response

The MMS has extensive requirements for (1) the prevention of a spill and (2) preparedness to respond to an accidental spill. The MMS spill-prevention requirements and the low incidence of historic OCS spills were addressed earlier in this document. This section presents information on MMS's requirements for spill-response preparedness.

MMS Spill-Response Program

The MMS's Oil Spill Program oversees the review of oil-spill response plans, coordinates inspection of oil-spill response equipment, and conducts unannounced oil-spill drills. This program also supports continuing research to foster improvements in spill prevention and response. Studies funded by MMS address issues such as improvements in spill prevention and response, in-situ burning, and dispersant use.

In addition, MMS works closely with the U.S. Coast Guard and other members of the multi-agency National Response System and their National Strike Force to further improve spill-response capability in the GOM. The Gulf Strike Force includes 38 members and associated response expertise and equipment. The combined resources of these groups and the resources of commercially contracted oil-spill response organizations result in extensive equipment availability and properly trained personnel for spill response in the GOM.

Spill Response for This Project

BP has an oil-spill response plan on file with MMS and has current contracts with offshore oil-spill response organizations.

Potential spill sources for this project include a spill during the life of the facility, an accidental blowout during drilling, or a spill of diesel fuel stored on the facility. The operator has addressed these spill sources in their oil-spill response plan and has demonstrated spill-response preparedness for accidental releases from these sources.

The MMS will continue to verify the operator's capability to respond to oil spills via the MMS Oil Spill Program. The operator is required to keep their oil-spill response plan up-to-date in accordance with MMS's regulations. The operator must also conduct an annual drill to test the adequacy of their spill-response preparedness. The MMS also conducts unannounced drills to further verify the adequacy of an operator's spill-response preparedness; such a drill could be conducted for this proposed action.

Table A-1

Historical Record of OCS Spills > 1,000 Barrels from OCS Pipelines, 1985-1999

Spill Date	Area and Block (water depth and distance from shore)	Volume Spilled (bbl)	Cause of Spill
February 7, 1988	South Pass 60 (75 ft, 3.4 mi)	15,576	Service vessel's anchor damaged pipeline
January 24, 1990	Ship Shoal 281 (197 ft, 60 mi)	14,423*	Anchor drag -- flange and valve broke off
May 6, 1990	Eugene Island 314 (230 ft, 78 mi)	4,569	Trawl drag pulled off valve
August 31, 1992	South Pelto 8 (30 ft, 6 mi)	2,000	Hurricane Andrew -- loose drilling rig's anchor drag damaged pipeline
November 22, 1994	Ship Shoal 281 (197 ft, 60 mi)	4,533*	Trawl drag
January 26, 1998	East Cameron 334 (264 ft, 105 mi)	1,211*	Service vessel's anchor drag damaged pipeline during rescue operation
September 29, 1998	South Pass 38 (110 ft, 6 mi)	8,212	Hurricane Georges -- mudslide parted pipeline
July 23, 1999	Ship Shoal 241 (133 ft, 50 mi)	3,189	Jack-up barge sat on pipeline

*condensate rather than oil

Table A-2

Spill Rates Used to Estimate the Potential for Future Spills

Spill Source	Volume of Oil Handled (billions of barrels)	Number of Wells Drilled	No. of Spills >1,000 Barrels	Risk of Spill from Facilities or Pipelines per Billion Barrels	Risk of Spill from Drilling Blowout per Well
Facilities	7.41	Not Applicable	1a	>0 to <0.13c	Not Applicable
Pipelines	5.81	Not Applicable	8	1.38	Not Applicable
Drilling	Not Applicable	14,067	1b	Not Applicable	>0 to <0.00007c

[a] There were actually zero spills of > 1,000 bbl from facilities during the period 1985-1999. The data shown represent the 1980-1999 interval. The spill period for facility spills was expanded to 1980 to include a spill for facilities to allow for a non-zero risk.

[b] There were no spills of > 1,000 bbl from blowouts during the period 1985-1999. One spill was "assigned" to provide a non-zero spill rate for calculations.

[c] There were no facility or blowout spills of > 1,000 bbl for the period 1985-1999. However, a non-zero spill rate was calculated by expanding the facility period to 1980 and by "assigning" a blowout spill. Therefore, the spill rates for these categories are presented as greater than zero, but below the rates calculated by expanding the data period and assigning a spill.

Table A-3
Spill Risk Estimate

Environmental Resource	Spill Occurrence Variable1 (%)	Transport Variable2 within 30 Days (%)	Spill Risk3 within 30 Days (%)
County/Parish, State			
Calhoun, TX	4	<0.5	<0.5
Matagorda, TX	4	<0.5	<0.5
Brazoria, TX	4	<0.5	<0.5
Chambers, TX	4	1	<0.5
Jefferson, TX	4	<0.5	<0.5
Cameron, LA	4	4	<0.5
Vermilion, LA	4	3	<0.5
Iberia, LA	4	1	<0.5
St. Mary, LA	4	1	<0.5
Terrebonne, LA	4	6	<0.5
LaFourche, LA	4	2	<0.5
Jefferson, LA	4	<0.5	<0.5
Plaquemines, LA	4	1	<0.5
Orleans, LA	4	<0.5	<0.5
St. Charles, LA	4	<0.5	<0.5
St. Bernard, LA	4	<0.5	<0.5
St.Tammany, LA	4	<0.5	<0.5
Hancock, MS	4	<0.5	<0.5
Mobile, AL	4	<0.5	<0.5
Baldwin, AL	4	<0.5	<0.5
Escambia, FL	4	<0.5	<0.5
Santa Rosa, FL	4	<0.5	<0.5
Okaloosa, FL	4	<0.5	<0.5
Walton, FL	4	<0.5	<0.5
Bay, FL	4	<0.5	<0.5
Gulf, FL	4	<0.5	<0.5
Franklin, FL	4	<0.5	<0.5
Lee, FL	4	<0.5	<0.5
Monroe, FL	4	<0.5	<0.5
Dade, FL	4	<0.5	<0.5
Other Resources			
Florida Keys National Marine Sanctuary	4	1	<0.5
Flower Garden Banks NMS	4	1	<0.5
TX Offshore State Waters	4	2	<0.5
LA Offshore State Waters	4	21	1

[1] The percent chance of a spill event occurring from the proposed action.

[2] The percent chance that winds and currents will move a point projected onto the surface of the Gulf beginning within the area of Green Canyon Blocks 644 and 645 and ending at specified shoreline segments or environmental resources. These results are the results of a numerical model that calculates the trajectory of a drifting point projected onto the surface of the water using temporally and spatially varying winds and ocean current fields (Price et al., 1997). These probabilities do not factor in the risk of spill occurrence, consideration of the spill size, any spill response or cleanup actions, or any dispersion and weathering of the slick with time.

[3] The probability of a spill occurring and contacting identified environmental features represents the weighted risk that accounts for both the risk that a large spill will occur and the risk that it will contact locations where the resources occur, given the assumptions already described in footnotes 1 and 2.

[4] <0.5 equals less than 0.5%, which is the lower limit of the model's predictive range.

APPENDIX B
Meteorological Conditions

APPENDIX B

METEOROLOGICAL CONDITIONS

General Description

The Gulf of Mexico (GOM) is influenced by a maritime subtropical climate controlled mainly by the clockwise circulation around the semi-permanent area of high barometric pressure commonly known as the Bermuda High. The Bermuda High is a high-pressure cell. The center of the high is usually located at the Atlantic Ocean or sometimes near the Azores Islands off the coast of Spain (Henry et al., 1994). The GOM is located to the southwest of this center of circulation. This proximity to the high-pressure system results in a predominantly east to southeasterly flow in the GOM region. Two important classes of cyclonic storms are occasionally superimposed on this circulation pattern. During the winter months of December through March, cold fronts associated with cold continental air masses influence mainly the northern coastal areas of the GOM. Behind the fronts, strong north winds bring drier air into the region. During the summer and fall months of June through October, tropical cyclones may develop or migrate into the GOM. These storms may affect any area of the GOM and substantially alter the local wind circulation around them. In coastal areas, the sea breeze effect may become the primary circulation feature during the summer months of May through October. In general, however, the maritime subtropical climate is the dominant feature in driving all aspects of the weather in this region; as a result, the climate shows relatively small diurnal variation in summer.

Two types of air masses primarily govern the climatology of the GOM region. One type of air mass is the warm and moist, maritime tropical air; the other type is very cold and dry, continental polar air. During summer months, the mid-latitude polar jet retreats northward, allowing maritime air to dominate through the GOM. In the southeastern region of the GOM, the climate is dominated by the warm and moist, maritime tropical air year round.

Pressure, Temperature, and Relative Humidity

The western extension of the Bermuda High into the GOM dominates the circulation throughout the year; the high-pressure center is weakening in winter and strengthening in summer. The average monthly pressure shows a west to east gradient during the summer. In the winter, the monthly pressure is more uniform. The minimum average monthly pressure occurs during the summer. The maximum pressure occurs during the winter as a result of the pressure and influence of transitional continental cold air.

At coastal locations, the average air temperature vary with latitude and exposure. Winter temperatures depend on the frequency and intensity of penetration by polar air masses from the north. Air temperature over the open Gulf exhibit much smaller variation on a daily and seasonal basis due to the moderating effect of the large body of water.

The relative humidity over the GOM region is high throughout the year. Minimum humidities occur during the late fall and winter when cold, continental air masses bring dry air into the northern Gulf. Maximum humidities occur during the spring and summer. Due to the presence of the warm, moist, maritime tropical air mass in the southern GOM, the relative humidity in this region is high for the whole year.

Surface Winds

Winds are more variable near the coast than over open waters because coastal winds are more directly influenced by the moving cyclonic storms that are characteristic of the continent and because of the land and sea breeze regime. During the relatively constant summer conditions, the southerly positions of the Bermuda High generates predominantly southeasterly winds in the northern Gulf and easterly winds in the southern parts of the Gulf. Winter winds usually blow from northeasterly directions and become more easterly in the southern parts of the Gulf.

Precipitation and Visibility

Precipitation is frequent and abundant throughout the year but does show distinct seasonal variation. The highest precipitation rates occur during the warmer months of the year. The warmer months usually have convective cloud systems that produce showers and thunderstorms; however, these thunderstorms rarely cause any damage or have attendant hail (USDOC, 1967; Brower et al., 1972). Hail can occur when water droplets freeze in the strong updraft of a convective cloud system. Winter rains are associated with the frequent passage of frontal systems through the area. Rainfalls are generally slow, steady, and relatively continuous, often lasting several days. In the northern parts of the Gulf, snowfalls are rare, and when frozen precipitation does occur, it usually melts upon contact with the ground. Incidence of frozen precipitation decreases with distance offshore and rapidly reaches zero. The annual average precipitation in Lake Charles, Louisiana, is 1.35 m (53 in). In the southern portions of the GOM, because of warm climate, the frozen precipitation is unlikely to occur.

Warm, moist Gulf air blowing slowly over chilled land or water surfaces brings about the formation of fog. Fog occurrence decreases seaward, but visibility has been less than 800 m (less than ½ mile) due to offshore fog in the coastal area. Coastal fogs generally last 3 or 4 hours, although particularly dense sea fogs may persist for several days. The poorest visibility conditions occur during winter and early spring. The period from November through April has the most days with low visibility. Industrial pollution and agricultural burning also impact visibility.

Atmospheric Stability and Mixing Height

Mixing height is very important because it determines the volume of air available for dispersing pollutants. Mixing height is directly related to vertical mixing in the atmosphere. A mixed layer is expected to occur under neutral and unstable atmospheric conditions. Vertical mixing is most vigorous during unstable conditions. Vertical motion is suppressed during stable conditions. The mixing height tends to be lower in winter, and daily variations are smaller than in summer.

Not all of the Pasquill-Gifford stability classes are found offshore in the GOM. Specifically, the F stability class seldom occurs and the G stability class is markedly absent. The G stability class is the extremely stable condition that only develops at night over land with rapid radiative cooling. This large body of water is simply incapable of losing enough heat overnight to set up a strong radiative inversion. Likewise, A stability class is rarely present but could be encountered during cold air outbreaks in the wintertime, particularly over warmer waters. Category A is the extremely unstable condition that requires a very rapid warming of the lower layer of the atmosphere, along with cold air aloft. This is normally brought about when cold air is advected aloft, and in strong insolation rapidly warms the earth's surface, which, in turn, warms the lowest layer of the atmosphere. Once again, the ocean surface is incapable of warming rapidly;

therefore, you would not expect to find stability class A over the ocean. For the most part, the stability is neutral to slightly unstable.

In this area, the over-water stability is predominantly unstable, with neutral conditions making up the bulk of the remainder of the time (Hsu, 1996; Marks, written communication, 1996 and 1997; Nowlin et al., 1998). Stable conditions do occur, although infrequently.

The mixing heights offshore are quite shallow, 900 m or less (Hsu, 1996; Nowlin et al., 1998). The exception to this is close to shore, where the influence of the land penetrates out over the water for a short distance. Transient cold fronts also have an impact on the mixing heights; some of the lowest heights can be expected to occur with frontal passages and on the cold-air side of the fronts. This effect is caused by the frontal inversion.

Severe Storms

The GOM is part of the Atlantic tropical cyclone basin. Tropical cyclones generally occur in summer and fall seasons; however, the Gulf also experiences winter storms or extratropical storms. These winter storms generally originate in middle and high latitudes and have winds that can attain speeds of 15-26 m/sec (11.2-58.2 mph). The Gulf is an area of cyclone development during cooler months due to the contrast of the warm air over the Gulf and the cold continental air over North America. Cyclogenesis, or the formation of extratropical cyclones, in the GOM is associated with frontal overrunning (Hsu, 1992). The most severe extratropical storms in the Gulf originate when a cold front encounters the subtropical jetstream over the warm waters of the Gulf. Statistics of 100-year data of extratropical cyclones reveal that most activity occurs above 25°N. in the Western GOM. The mean number of these storms ranges from 0.9 storms per year near the southern tip of Florida to 4.2 over central Louisiana (USDOI, MMS, 1988).

The frequency of cold fronts in the Gulf exhibits similar synoptic weather patterns during the four-month period of December through March. During this time the area of frontal influence reaches south to 10°N. Frontal frequency is about nine fronts per month in February (1 front every 3 days on the average) and about seven fronts per month in March (1 front every 4-5 days on the average). By May, the frequency decreases to about four fronts per month (1 front every 7-8 days), and the region of frontal influence retreats to about 15°N. During June through August frontal activity decreases to almost zero and fronts seldom reach below 25°N. (USDOI, MMS, 1988).

Tropical cyclones affecting the Gulf originate over the equatorial portions of the Atlantic Ocean, the Caribbean Sea, and the GOM. Tropical cyclones occur most frequently between June and November. Based on 42 years of data, there are about 9.9 storms per year with about 5.5 of those becoming major hurricanes in the Atlantic Ocean (Gray, written communication, 1992). Data from 1886 to 1986 show that 44.5 percent of these storms, or 3.7 storms per year, will affect the GOM (USDOI, MMS, 1988). The Yucatan Channel is the main entrance of Atlantic storms into the GOM, and a reduced translation speed over Gulf waters leads to longer residence times in this basin. The probability of occurrence for a tropical storm in Louisiana and Mississippi is on average about 15 percent.

There is a high probability that tropical storms will cause damage to physical, economic, biological, and social systems in the Gulf. Tropical storms also affect OCS operations and activities; platform design needs to consider the storm surge, waves, and currents generated by tropical storms. Most of the damage is caused by storm surge, waves, and high winds. Storm surge depends on local factors, such as bottom topography, coastline configuration, and storm intensity. Water depth and storm intensity control wave height during hurricane conditions. Sustained winds for major hurricanes (Saffir-Simpson Category 3 and above) are higher than 49 m/sec (109.6 mph).

APPENDIX C
Geology

APPENDIX C

GEOLOGY

General Description

The present day Gulf of Mexico (GOM) is a small ocean basin with an area of more than 1.5 million km^2; its greatest water depth is approximately 3,700 m. It is almost completely surrounded by land, opening to the Atlantic Ocean through the Straits of Florida and to the Caribbean Sea through the Yucatan Channel. Underlying the present GOM and the adjacent coast is the larger geologic basin that began forming in Triassic time. Over the last 20 million years, clastic sediments (sands and silts) have poured into the GOM Basin from the north and west. The centers of sediment deposition shifted progressively eastward and southward in response to changes in the source of sediment supply. Sediments more than 15 km in thickness have been deposited. Each sediment layer is different, reflecting the source of the material and the geologic processes occurring during deposition. In places where the Gulf was shallow and intermittently dry, evaporitic deposits such as salt were formed. Where gradual subsidence and shallow seas persisted overtime, marine plants and animals created reefs. Where marine life was abundant, the deposition of limestone was dominant.

The physiographic provinces in the GOM — shelf, slope, rise, and abyssal plain — reflect the underlying geology. In the Gulf, the continental shelf extends seaward from the shoreline to about the 200-m (656 ft) water depth and is characterized by a gentle slope of less than one degree. The shelf is wide off Texas, but it is narrower or absent where the Mississippi River delta has extended across the entire shelf. The continental slope extends from the shelf edge to the continental rise, usually at about the 2,000-m (6,562 ft) water depth. The topography of the slope in the Gulf is uneven and is broken by canyons, troughs, and escarpments. The gradient on the slope is characteristically 3-6 degrees, but it may exceed 20 degrees in some places, particularly along escarpments. The continental rise is the apron of sediment accumulated at the base of the slope. It is a gentle incline, with slopes of less than one degree, to the abyssal plain. The abyssal plain is the flat region of the basin floor at the base of the continental rise.

The Western Gulf, which includes both the Western and Central Planning Areas, is a clastic province. Many wells have been drilled in the Western Gulf, and the geology has been studied in detail for the identification and development of natural gas and oil resources.

Sedimentary features, such as deltas, fans, canyons, and sediment flow forms, are formed by the erosion of land and deposition of sediments. Structural features, such as faults, folds, and ridges, are produced by displacement and deformation of rocks. The regional dip of sediments in the GOM is interrupted by salt diapirs, shale diapirs, and growth faults. Deformation has been primarily in response to heavy sediment loading.

The most significant factor controlling the hydrocarbon potential in the northern GOM is the environment of deposition. Sediments deposited on the outer shelf and upper slope have the greatest potential for hydrocarbon accumulation because it is the optimum zone for encountering the three factors necessary for the successful formation and accumulation of oil and gas: source material, reservoir space, and geologic traps. The massive shale beds with high organic content are excellent source beds. The thick sands and sandstones with good porosity (pore space between the sand grains where oil and gas can exist) and permeability (connections between the pore spaces through which oil and gas can flow) provide reservoir space. Impermeable shales, salt dome caprocks, and faults serve as seals, trapping oil and gas in the pore spaces of the reservoir rocks.

The geologic horizons with the greatest potential for hydrocarbon accumulation on the continental shelf of the northern GOM, Pliocene, and Pleistocene in age. Producing horizons become progressively younger in a seaward direction. Recent developments in high-energy, 3D seismic technology has allowed industry to "see" below the regional salt layers and identify potential "subsalt plays" or hydrocarbon traps. Exploration and development in the GOM have resulted in the identification of more than 1,000 fields.

The presence of hydrogen sulfide (H2S) within formation fluids occurs sporadically throughout the GOM OCS. H2S -rich oil and gas is called "sour." Approximately 65 operations have encountered H2S -bearing zones on the GOM OCS to date. Occurrences of H2S offshore Texas are in Miocene Age rocks and occur principally within a geographically narrow band. There is some debate as to the origin of H2S in these wells offshore Texas, as they were reported mostly from deep, high-temperature drilling wells using a ligno-sulfonate mud component, which is widely believed to break down under high wellbore temperature to generate H2S. The occurrences of H2S offshore Louisiana are mostly on or near piercement domes with caprock and are associated with salt and gypsum deposits. The H2S from a caprock environment is generally thought to be a reaction product of sulfates and hydrocarbons in the presence of sulfate-reducing microbes. In some areas offshore Louisiana, H2S -rich hydrocarbons are produced from lower Cretaceous Age limestone deposits not associated with piercement domes. Generally speaking, formations of Lower Cretaceous Age or older (which are deeply buried in the Gulf) are prone to contain H2S in association with hydrocarbons (cf. Bryan and Lingamallu, 1990). There has also been some evidence that petroleum from deepwater plays contain significant amounts of sulfur (cf. Smith, written communication, 1996; Thorpe, 1996).

The concentrations of H2S found in conjunction with hydrocarbons vary extensively. The examination of in-house data suggest that H2S concentrations vary from as low as fractional parts per million (ppm) to as high as 650,000 ppm in one isolated case (the next highest concentrations of H2S reported are about 55,000 and 19,000 ppm). The concentrations of H2S found to date are generally greatest in the eastern portion of the CPA.

Geologic Hazards

The major geologic hazards that may affect oil and gas activities within the GOM north of 26°N. latitude can be generally grouped into the following categories: (1) slope instability and mass transport of sediments; (2) gas hydrates; (3) sediment types and characteristics; and (4) tectonics.

Geologic conditions that promote seafloor instability are variable sediment types, steep slopes, high-sedimentation rates, gas hydrates at or near the seafloor, interstitial gas, faulting, areas of lithified and mounded carbonates, salt and shale mobilization, and mudflows. Some features that may indicate a possible unstable condition include step faulting, deformed bedding, detached blocks, detached masses, displaced lithologies, acoustically transparent layers, anomalously thick accumulations of sediment, and shallow faulting and fissures. These features can be identified on seismic survey profiles or through coring samples.

Mass movement of sediments includes landslides, slumps, and creeps. Sediment types, accumulation rates, sediment accumulation over features with seafloor relief, and internal composition and structure of the sedimentary layers are all factors that affect seafloor stability. Rapidly accumulated sediments that have not had the opportunity to dewater properly are underconsolidated. These underconsolidated sediments can be interbedded with normal or overconsolidated sediments and may act as slide zones causing mass movement or collapse. A slope of less than one degree can be sufficient to cause sliding or slumping when high sedimentation rates have resulted in underconsolidation or high pore-pressure conditions in the sediments.

In the deepwater areas of the Gulf, slope stability and soil properties are of great concern in the design of oil and gas operations. Slopes steep enough to create conditions conducive to mass transport are found regionally on the continental slope. Steeper slopes are found locally along the walls of canyons and channels, adjacent to salt structures, and at fault scarps.

Gas hydrates occur in the upper sediments and are of biogenic in origin rather than petrogenic. Methane is the major and often the only component. Gas hydrates are more prevalent in deeper waters than on the shelf because of the lower temperature and high pressures at greater depths. The effect of gas pressure, distribution of gas in pores, solution-dissolution potential, and upward dispersal characteristics are factors considered in the engineering design of production facilities.

Overpressured salt, shale, and mud have a tendency to become plasticized and mobile. Movements of overpressured salts and shales could form mounds and diapirs. Large diapirs formed by the upward movement of shale or salt originates from a greater depth and do not form an environmental geologic hazard by itself. These features have associated faulting and sometimes collapse structures. Their upward movement causes slope steepening and consequently slumping. Movement of overpressured mud could form mud volcanoes. Soft mud diapirs resulting from delta front muds are excellent indicators of an unstable sediment at shallow depths.

Evidence of geologic hazards includes hydrocarbon seeps, deformed bedding, detached blocks or masses, anomalously thick accumulations of sediments, shallow faulting and fissures, diapirs, sediment dikes or mud lumps, displaced lithologies, internal chaotic masses, hummocky topography, en echelon faulting, and horst and graben blocks. Evidence of geologic hazards can be obtained or seen by using core sampling techniques, high-resolution seismic surveying, and side-scan sonar. Geologic hazards pose engineering, structural design, and operational constraints that can usually be effectively mitigated through existing or new technologies and designs.

APPENDIX D

Physical Oceanography

APPENDIX D

PHYSICAL OCEANOGRAPHY

The Gulf of Mexico is a semi-enclosed, subtropical sea with an area of approximately 1.5 million km^2. The main physiographic regions of the Gulf Basin are the continental shelf (including the Campeche, Mexican, and U.S. shelves), continental slopes and associated canyons, abyssal plains, the Yucatan Channel, and Florida Straits.

The continental shelf width along the Gulf coastline varies from about 350 km offshore West Florida to 16 km off the Mississippi River, then to 156 km off Galveston, Texas, and finally decreasing to 88 km off Port Isabel near the Mexican border. The depth of the central abyss ranges to approximately 3,700 m. The water volume of the Gulf, assuming a mean water depth of 2 km, is 2 million km^3. The shelf's volume, assuming a mean water depth of 50 m, is 25,000 km^3. The Gulf is unique among the world's mediterranean seas, having two entrances: the Yucatan Channel and the Straits of Florida. Both straits restrain communication from the deep Atlantic waters because of the limited sill depths—1,600 m in the Yucatan Channel and about 1,000 m in the Straits of Florida. A portion of the Gulf Stream system, the parent Loop Current, whose presence and influence are described below, is present in the Gulf. Along the 24,800-km Gulf coastline, 21 major estuaries are found on the U.S. coast. The amount of freshwater input to the Gulf Basin from precipitation and a number of rivers—dominated by the Mississippi and Atchafalaya Rivers—is enough to influence the hydrography of most of its northern shelves. The basin's freshwater budget shows a net deficit, however, due to the high rate of evaporation.

Sea-surface temperatures in the Gulf range from nearly isothermal (29-30°C) in August to a sharp horizontal gradient in January, ranging from 25°C in the Loop core to 14-15°C along the shallow northern coastal estuaries. August temperatures at 150-m water depth show a warm Loop Current and an anticyclonic feature in the Western Gulf (both about 18-19°C) grading into surrounding waters of 15-16°C along the slope. The entire pattern is maintained during winter, but warmer by about 1°C. At 1,000 m water depth, the temperature remains close to 5°C year-round. Intimately related with the vertical distribution of temperature is the thermocline, defined as the depth at which the temperature gradient is at maximum. During January, the thermocline depth is about 91-107 m in the Western and Central Gulf and about 30-61 m in the Eastern Gulf. In May, the thermocline depth is about 46 m throughout the entire Gulf (Robinson, 1973). This depth is important because it demarcates the bottom of the mixed layer and acts as a barrier to the vertical transfer of materials and momentum.

Surface salinities along the northern Gulf display seasonal variations because of the seasonality of the freshwater input. During months of low freshwater input, deep Gulf water penetrates into the shelf, and salinities near the coastline range between 29 and 32 parts per thousand (ppt). High, freshwater-input conditions (spring-summer months) are characterized by strong horizontal gradients and inner-shelf salinity values of less than 20 ppt (Wallace, 1980; Cochrane and Kelly, 1986).

Sharp discontinuities of temperature and/or salinity at the sea surface, such as fronts associated with eddies or river plumes or the Loop Current front, are dynamic features that may act to concentrate buoyant material such as spilled oil, detritus, or plankton. These materials are not transported by the front's movements such as the slow westward drift of eddies or Loop Current incursion. The motion consists mainly of lateral movement along the front instead of motion across the front. In addition to open ocean fronts, a coastal front, which separates turbid, lower salinity water from the open-shelf regime, is probably a permanent feature of the northern Gulf shelf. This front lies about 30-50 km offshore. It is not known how strongly this front might affect buoyant material transport.

The Loop Current, a highly variable current feature, enters the Gulf through the Yucatan Channel and exits through the Straits of Florida (as the Gulf Stream) after tracing an arc that may intrude as far north as the Mississippi-Alabama shelf. The Loop consists of ascending and descending 30-km-wide bands of rapidly moving water enclosing a relatively quiescent inner region; the entire feature may be clearly seen in hydrographic sections down to about 1,000 m. Below that level, there is evidence of a countercurrent. The volumetric flux of the Loop has been estimated at 30 million m3/sec. This volume flow is enough to replace the water volume of the Gulf shelf in about 10 days.

Major Loop Current eddies move into the Western Gulf along various paths to a region between 25°-28°N. and 93°-96°W. Recent analysis of frontal-positions data indicates that the eddy-shedding period varies between 6.5 and 9.5 months with an average of 7.5 months (Hamilton et al., 1989). Major eddies have diameters on the order of 300-400 km and may clearly be seen in hydrographic data to a depth of about 1,000 m. The eddies move at speeds ranging from 2 to 5 km/day, decreasing in size as they mix with resident waters. The life of an individual eddy to its eventual assimilation by regional circulation patterns in the Western Gulf is about 1 year.

Eddy-shedding from the Loop Current is the principal mechanism coupling the circulation patterns of the eastern and western parts of the basin. The heat and salt budgets of the Gulf are dependent on this importation, balanced by seasonal cooling and river input, and probably also by internal, deeper currents that are poorly understood. The eddies are frequently observed to affect local current patterns along the Louisiana/Texas slope, hydrographic properties, and possibly the biota of fixed platforms or hard bottoms. There is some evidence that these large reservoirs of warm water play some role in strengthening tropical cyclones when their paths coincide.

Smaller anticyclonic eddies have been observed to be generated by the Loop Current, although it is not known if the process is merely a scaled-down version of the above cycle. They have diameters on the order of 100 km, but the few data available indicate a shallow hydrographic signature on the order of 200 m. Their observed movements indicate a tendency to translate westward along the Louisiana/Texas slope. Similar in size, cyclonic eddies are observed in the Eastern Gulf, are associated with the eddy-shedding cycle, and occur along the Louisiana/Texas slope. Their genesis and role in the overall Gulf circulation are not well studied. A major cyclonic eddy seems to be resident in the southern part of the Western Gulf, based on older data synthesis; however, some recent evidence points toward a more complex, less homogeneous structure.

Aside from the wind-driven surface layer, current regimes on the outer shelf and slope are the result of balance between the influence of open Gulf circulation features and the shelf circulation proper, which is dominated by long-term wind forcing. A western boundary current, driven both by prevailing winds and the semi-permanent anticyclonic eddy, occurs offshore northern Mexico and South Texas. A strong east-northeasterly current along the remaining Texas and Louisiana slope has been explained partly by the effects of the semi-permanent, anticyclonic eddy and a partner cyclonic eddy ("modon pair") and partly by the mass-balance requirements of eddy movement. When the Loop Current impinges onto the Florida slope and shelf, it has been observed that the current structure acts to upwell nutrient-rich water from deeper zones, a mechanism that may also take place as eddies move along the Louisiana/Texas slope, accounting for the increased productivity recognized in these areas. West of approximately Cameron, Louisiana (93°W.), current measurements clearly show a strong response of coastal current to the winds, setting up a large-scale, anticyclonic gyre. The inshore limb of the gyre is the westward or southwestward (downcoast) component that prevails along much of the coast, except in July-August. Because the coast is concave, the shoreward prevailing wind results in a convergence of coastal currents at a location where the winds are normal to the shore or at the downcoast extent of the gyre. A prevailing countercurrent toward the northeast along the shelf edge constitutes the outer limb of the gyre. The convergence at the southwestern end of the gyre migrates seasonally with the direction of the prevailing wind, ranging from a point south of the Rio Grande in the fall to the Cameron area by July. The gyre is normally absent in July but reappears in August-September when a downcoast wind component develops (Cochrane and Kelly, 1986). The Mississippi/Alabama shelf circulation is controlled by the Loop Current, winds, tides, and freshwater input. The West Florida shelf circulation is dominated by tides, winds, eddy-like perturbations, and the Loop Current.

Longshore currents, consisting of tidal, wind-driven, and density-gradient components, predominate over across-shelf components within a narrow band close to the coast (on the order of 10-20 km, referred to as the coastal boundary layer). Typical maximum tidal currents within this band would be about 15 cm/sec. These currents will cause a particle displacing, known as the tidal excursion, at 2-3 km. Currents, driven by synoptic-scale winds, range up to 25-50 cm/sec for conditions that are not extreme, with 10- to 100-km excursions expected for a typical 5-day "wind event." Longshore currents due to winter northers, tropical storms, and hurricanes may range up to hundreds of cm/sec, depending on local topography, fetch, and duration. Should an oil spill occur, deviations from results predicted by open-ocean models could happen at coastal fronts, where concentration and lateral translation could occur, and within the longshore-current zone, where significant transport away from the "expected" point of contact could occur, as determined by local tidal phase and predominant winds.

Studies of surface drifters are useful and illustrative in the study of oil movement because, hopefully, surface slicks will respond to currents in a similar way. A summary of drifter studies across the Gulf (Parker et al., 1979) indicated that the Texas coastline and the southern and eastern Florida coastlines receive the most landings. Other coastlines along the Gulf received very small numbers of landings. Strangely, during summer and fall, the Louisiana and Texas coastlines received sizable fractions of the landings. However, these results contain some bias because populated or frequently visited areas would show more landings than desolated areas.

Summer waves in the Western Gulf tend to be smaller than those in the Eastern Gulf. Waves in both regions intensify in winter, with the Western Gulf showing a clear mode at 2-3 m.

APPENDIX E

Other Information on Grid 10

Table E-1

Grid 10 -- Exploration Drilling Activities

Area/Block	Company	Well Name	Well Type	Bore Hole Status	Well Spud Date	Total Depth Date	Water Depth
GB 877	Kerr-McGee	1	E	AST			5,340
GB 877	Kerr-McGee	1	E	ST	6/07/2001	8/15/2001	5,325
GB 877	Kerr-McGee	1	E	DRL	8/24/2001		5,334
GB 920	Shell	1	E	PA	6/07/1999	7/04/1999	5,100
GC 286	Exxon-Mobil	1	E	PA	4/09/1991	6/29/1991	3,124
GC 460	Texaco	1	E	ST	3/20/1998	6/24/1998	4,019
GC 460	Texaco	1	E	ST	7/02/1998	7/14/1998	4,019
GC 460	Texaco	1	E	PA	7/25/1998	8/09/1998	4,019
GC 461	BP	1	E	ST	6/07/1998	7/20/1998	4,229
GC 461	BP	1	E	PA	7/23/1998	8/20/1998	4,240
GC 463	BP	1	E	ST	8/29/1998		4,032
GC 463	BP	1	E	PA		12/01/1998	4,032
GC 505	Texaco	1	E	PA	3/14/1997	7/12/1997	4,262
GC 505	Texaco	2	E	ST	10/09/1997	12/01/1997	4,262
GC 505	Texaco	2	E	PA		1/14/1998	4,262
GC 506	Texaco	1	E	PA		1/30/1995	4,243
GC 506	Texaco	3	E	ST	9/16/1998	11/01/1998	4,250
GC 506	Texaco	3	E	ST	11/04/1998		4,250
GC 506	Texaco	3	E	ST	12/02/1998	1/04/1999	4,250
GC 506	Texaco	3	E	PA	1/14/1999	1/16/1999	4,250
GC 509	Texaco	1	E	PA	5/23/1996	6/30/1996	4,380
GC 544	Shell	1	E	PA	6/07/1998	7/01/1998	4,190
GC 644	BP	1	E	ST		1/09/1999	4,292
GC 644	BP	1	E	TA	1/19/1999	2/11/1999	4,292
GC 645	BP	1	E	TA	9/28/1999		4,352
GC 680	Kerr-McGee	1	E	APD	N/A	N/A	5,089
GC 730	Conoco	1	E	DSI	7/25/2001	7/28/2001	4,445
GC 819	Conoco	1	E	CNL	N/A	N/A	5,255
GC 852	Conoco	1	D	APD	N/A	N/A	5,503
GC 854	Shell	1	E	PA	1/19/1999	1/21/1999	5,518
GC 854	Shell	2	E	PA	1/22/1999	3/02/1999	5,518
GC 908	Shell	1	E	PA	1/27/1990	1/29/1990	5,630
GC 908	Shell	2	E	PA	2/06/1990	4/20/1990	5,678
GC 942	Conoco	1	E	DRL	7/29/2001		6,637
WR 70	Texaco	1	E	PA	3/12/1999	3/02/2001	5,505
WR 313	Ocean Energy	1	E	APD	N/A	N/A	6,300

Remarks: APD = application for permit to drill   Notes: BG is Garden Banks
          CNL = cancelled   GC is Green Canyon
          DRL = drilling   WR is Walker Ridge
          DSI = drilling shut in
          PA = plugged and abandoned
          TA = temporarily abandoned

Table E-2

Grid 10 -- Approved Plans

Area/Block	Initial Plan Control Number	Plan Type	Company	Water Depth Range (feet)
GB 657	N-6730	EP	RME Petroleum	4,360
GB 788	N-3698	EP	Shell Offshore	5,081-5,281
GB 832	N-3698	EP	Shell Offshore	5,081-5134
GB 833	N-7059	EP	Kerr-McGee	5,335
GB 876	N-3698	EP	Shell Offshore	5,210-5,281
GB 877	N-7059	EP	Kerr-McGee	5,340-5,350
GB 920	N-6420	EP	Shell DW Dev.	5,062-5,150
GB 921	N-7281	EP	Kerr-McGee	5,315
GC 242	N-6431	EP	Shell DW Dev.	3,141-3,222
GC 286	N-3975	EP	Exxon Mobil	3,130
GC 379	N-7266	EP	Kerr-McGee	3,825-3,885
GC 416	N-5620	EP	Texaco	4,210
GC 459	N-6385	EP	Texaco	4,020-4,180
GC 460	N-5620	EP	Texaco	4,275
GC 461	N-6006	EP	BP	4,250
GC 463	N-6231	EP	BP	4,018-4,019
GC 505	N-5495	EP	Texaco	4,280
GC 506	N-5495	EP	Texaco	4,270
GC 507	N-7251	EP	Amerada Hess	3,870-4,014
GC 509	N-4485	EP	Texaco	4,380-4,450
GC 544	N-5910	EP	Shell DW Prod.	4,180-4,190
GC 601	N-7030	EP	BHP Petroleum	4,492-4,515
GC 640	N-7157	EP	Chevron	4,065-4,332
GC 644	N-6263	EP	BP	4,292
GC 645	N-6263	EP	BP	4,422
GC 645	N-7216	DOCD	BP	4,340-4,344
GC 680	N-7191	EP	Kerr-McGee	4,995-5,090
GC 730	N-7023	EP	Conoco	4,399-4,445
GC 775	N-6432	EP	Conoco	5,100-5,160
GC 808	N-6456	EP	Conoco	5,410-5,566
GC 810	N-3138	EP	Shell DW Dev.	
GC 819	N-6277	EP	Conoco	5,238-5,317
GC 844	N-6391	EP	Exxon Mobil	5,577
GC 845	N-6391	EP	Exxon Mobil	5,577-6,408
GC 852	N-6456	EP	Conoco	5,429-5,503
GC 854	N-3138	EP	Shell DW Dev.	
GC 863	N-3423	EP	Shell Offshore	5,117-5,245
GC 864	N-3423	EP	Shell Offshore	5,100-5,232
GC 907	N-3367	EP	Shell Offshore	5,518-5,636
GC 908	N-3367	EP	Shell Offshore	5,518-5,626
GC 942	N-6534	EP	Conoco	6,515-6,658
GC 950	N-7239	EP	Union Oil of CA	5,065-5,216
WR 24	N-7237	EP	Union Oil of CA	5,382-5,430
WR 25	N-7237	EP	Union Oil of CA	5,382-5,430
WR 26	N-6363	EP	Texaco	5,370
WR 29	N-7159	EP	Texaco	5,584-5,931
WR 70	N-6363	EP	Texaco	5,468-5,500
WR 313	N-7129	EP	Kerr-McGee	6,275-6,450

Notes: DOCD is Development Operations Coordination Document
EP is Exploration Plan
GB is Garden Banks
GC is Green Canyon
WR is Walker Ridge

Table E-3

Grid 10 – Lease Status

Area/Block	Lease Number	Company
GB 613	G15926	Mobil Producing Texas & New Mexico Inc.
GB 657	G19148	RME Petroleum Company
GB 700	G19154	RME Petroleum Company
GB 701	G19155	RME Petroleum Company
GB 744	G15946	Mobil Producing Texas & New Mexico Inc.
GB 833	G21406	Kerr-McGee Oil & Gas Corporation
GB 877	G21408	Kerr-McGee Oil & Gas Corporation
GB 921	G21409	Kerr-McGee Oil & Gas Corporation
GB 1008	G19242	Shell Offshore Inc.
GB 1009	G19243	Exxon Mobil Corporation
GC 203	G22937	Shell Offshore Inc.
GC 242	G21788	Vastar Resources, Inc.
GC 247	G15564	Shell Offshore Inc.
GC 285	G18353	Vastar Resources, Inc.
GC 286	G18354	Vastar Resources, Inc.
GC 291	G18358	EEX Corporation
GC 292	G18359	Shell Offshore Inc.
GC 325	G21203	BHP Petroleum (GOM) Inc.
GC 329	G22940	Nexen Petroleum Offshore U.S.A. Inc.
GC 330	G20060	Vastar Resources, Inc.
GC 335	G15577	BP Exploration & Production Inc.
GC 336	G22941	Murphy Exploration & Production Company
GC 337	G22942	Murphy Exploration & Production Company
GC 362	G18371	Ocean Energy, Inc.
GC 367	G20066	BHP Petroleum (GOM) Inc.
GC 376	G18373	Amerada Hess Corporation
GC 378	G22946	Kerr-McGee Oil & Gas Corporation
GC 379	G22947	Kerr-McGee Oil & Gas Corporation
GC 380	G22948	Murphy Exploration & Production Company
GC 381	G22949	Spinnaker Exploration Company, L.L.C.
GC 409	G16740	MOBIL OIL EXPLORATION & PRODUCING SOUTHEAST INC.
GC 410	G16741	Marathon Oil Company
GC 411	G16742	Shell Offshore Inc.
GC 412	G16743	Shell Offshore Inc.
GC 413	G21208	BHP Petroleum (GOM) Inc.
GC 416	G22954	Nexen Petroleum Offshore U.S.A. Inc.
GC 419	G15585	Amerada Hess Corporation
GC 420	G18383	Amerada Hess Corporation
GC 421	G21210	Amerada Hess Corporation
GC 422	G16744	Amoco Production Company
GC 423	G16745	Amoco Production Company
GC 424	G22955	Exxon Asset Management Company
GC 425	G22956	Spinnaker Exploration Company, L.L.C.
GC 446	G16747	MOBIL OIL EXPLORATION & PRODUCING SOUTHEAST INC.
GC 447	G22960	Texaco Exploration and Production Inc.
GC 448	G15587	Shell Offshore Inc.
GC 451	G18391	Chevron U.S.A. Inc.
GC 452	G15588	BHP Petroleum (GOM) Inc.
GC 453	G15589	BHP Petroleum (GOM) Inc.
GC 455	G16748	Shell Offshore Inc.
GC 456	G20069	BHP Petroleum (GOM) Inc.
GC 457	G16749	BHP Petroleum (GOM) Inc.
GC 458	G16750	BHP Petroleum (GOM) Inc.

Table E-3. Grid 10—Lease Status (continued).

Area/Block	Lease Number	Company
GC 460	G22961	Nexen Petroleum Offshore U.S.A. Inc.
GC 461	G21797	Vastar Resources, Inc.
GC 463	G22962	BP Exploration & Production Inc.
GC 464	G22963	BP Exploration & Production Inc.
GC 467	G22964	Nexen Petroleum Offshore U.S.A. Inc.
GC 486	G21799	Kerr-McGee Oil & Gas Corporation
GC 488	G20071	RME Petroleum Company
GC 490	G16751	MOBIL OIL EXPLORATION & PRODUCING SOUTHEAST INC.
GC 491	G22967	Texaco Exploration and Production Inc.
GC 492	G16752	Maxus (U.S.) Exploration Company
GC 496	G15591	BHP Petroleum (GOM) Inc.
GC 497	G15592	BHP Petroleum (GOM) Inc.
GC 499	G15593	Shell Offshore Inc.
GC 500	G15594	Shell Offshore Inc.
GC 504	G22968	Exxon Asset Management Company
GC 505	G22969	Mariner Energy, Inc.
GC 506	G21800	Vastar Resources, Inc.
GC 507	G22970	Amerada Hess Corporation
GC 511	G22971	Exxon Asset Management Company
GC 513	G22972	Dominion Exploration & Production, Inc.
GC 529	G20075	Kerr-McGee Oil & Gas Corporation
GC 530	G20076	MOBIL OIL EXPLORATION & PRODUCING SOUTHEAST INC.
GC 533	G22973	Kerr-McGee Oil & Gas Corporation
GC 534	G22974	Kerr-McGee Oil & Gas Corporation
GC 535	G13697	MOBIL OIL EXPLORATION & PRODUCING SOUTHEAST INC.
GC 536	G22975	Kerr-McGee Oil & Gas Corporation
GC 541	G15596	BHP Petroleum (GOM) Inc.
GC 545	G21215	BHP Petroleum (GOM) Inc.
GC 546	G21216	BHP Petroleum (GOM) Inc.
GC 548	G22976	Exxon Asset Management Company
GC 549	G22977	Exxon Asset Management Company
GC 551	G15599	Texaco Exploration and Production Inc.
GC 553	G13698	Texaco Exploration and Production Inc.
GC 554	G22978	BHP Petroleum (GOM) Inc.
GC 555	G22979	BHP Petroleum (GOM) Inc.
GC 557	G22980	Dominion Exploration & Production, Inc.
GC 575	G18400	MOBIL OIL EXPLORATION & PRODUCING SOUTHEAST INC.
GC 576	G18401	MOBIL OIL EXPLORATION & PRODUCING SOUTHEAST INC.
GC 577	G20078	MOBIL OIL EXPLORATION & PRODUCING SOUTHEAST INC.
GC 578	G13699	MOBIL OIL EXPLORATION & PRODUCING SOUTHEAST INC.
GC 579	G13700	MOBIL OIL EXPLORATION & PRODUCING SOUTHEAST INC.
GC 580	G16756	MOBIL OIL EXPLORATION & PRODUCING SOUTHEAST INC.
GC 581	G22983	Kerr-McGee Oil & Gas Corporation
GC 584	G16757	Chevron U.S.A. Inc.
GC 585	G15600	BHP Petroleum (GOM) Inc.
GC 589	G21217	BHP Petroleum (GOM) Inc.
GC 595	G16758	Texaco Exploration and Production Inc.
GC 596	G16759	Texaco Exploration and Production Inc.
GC 597	G16760	Texaco Exploration and Production Inc.
GC 598	G16761	Texaco Exploration and Production Inc.
GC 599	G16762	MOBIL OIL EXPLORATION & PRODUCING SOUTHEAST INC.
GC 600	G22984	BHP Petroleum (GOM) Inc.
GC 601	G21218	Marathon Oil Company
GC 617	G18404	MOBIL OIL EXPLORATION & PRODUCING SOUTHEAST INC.
GC 618	G18405	Shell Offshore Inc.
GC 619	G18406	MOBIL OIL EXPLORATION & PRODUCING SOUTHEAST INC.
GC 620	G18407	MOBIL OIL EXPLORATION & PRODUCING SOUTHEAST INC.
GC 621	G20079	MOBIL OIL EXPLORATION & PRODUCING SOUTHEAST INC.

Table E-3. Grid 10—Lease Status (continued).

Area/Block	Lease Number	Company
GC 622	G16766	MOBIL OIL EXPLORATION & PRODUCING SOUTHEAST INC.
GC 623	G16767	MOBIL OIL EXPLORATION & PRODUCING SOUTHEAST INC.
GC 624	G16768	MOBIL OIL EXPLORATION & PRODUCING SOUTHEAST INC.
GC 625	G16769	MOBIL OIL EXPLORATION & PRODUCING SOUTHEAST INC.
GC 626	G20080	Exxon Mobil Corporation
GC 629	G15601	BHP Petroleum (GOM) Inc.
GC 630	G15602	BHP Petroleum (GOM) Inc.
GC 633	G18408	Union Oil Company of California
GC 637	G18409	Union Oil Company of California
GC 638	G18410	Union Oil Company of California
GC 639	G20081	Agip Petroleum Co. Inc.
GC 640	G20082	Chevron U.S.A. Inc.
GC 641	G16770	Texaco Exploration and Production Inc.
GC 642	G16771	Texaco Exploration and Production Inc.
GC 643	G16772	MOBIL OIL EXPLORATION & PRODUCING SOUTHEAST INC.
GC 644*	G11080	BP Exploration & Production Inc.
GC 645*	G11081	BP Exploration & Production Inc.
GC 663	G18413	MOBIL OIL EXPLORATION & PRODUCING SOUTHEAST INC.
GC 664	G18414	MOBIL OIL EXPLORATION & PRODUCING SOUTHEAST INC.
GC 665	G22985	BHP Petroleum (GOM) Inc.
GC 666	G22986	BHP Petroleum (GOM) Inc.
GC 667	G18415	MOBIL OIL EXPLORATION & PRODUCING SOUTHEAST INC.
GC 668	G18416	MOBIL OIL EXPLORATION & PRODUCING SOUTHEAST INC.
GC 670	G20086	Exxon Mobil Corporation
GC 671	G18417	MOBIL OIL EXPLORATION & PRODUCING SOUTHEAST INC.
GC 672	G18418	MOBIL OIL EXPLORATION & PRODUCING SOUTHEAST INC.
GC 676	G18419	Union Oil Company of California
GC 679	G21811	Dominion Exploration & Production, Inc.
GC 680	G22987	Kerr-McGee Oil & Gas Corporation
GC 683	G18421	Shell Offshore Inc.
GC 684	G16776	Texaco Exploration and Production Inc.
GC 685	G16777	Texaco Exploration and Production Inc.
GC 686	G16778	Conoco Inc.
GC 687	G18422	Union Oil Company of California
GC 688	G18423	Marathon Oil Company
GC 689	G22988	Shell Offshore Inc.
GC 708	G18426	Union Oil Company of California
GC 711	G18427	MOBIL OIL EXPLORATION & PRODUCING SOUTHEAST INC.
GC 723	G21813	Samedan Oil Corporation
GC 724	G21814	Samedan Oil Corporation
GC 727	G16783	Texaco Exploration and Production Inc.
GC 728	G16784	Texaco Exploration and Production Inc.
GC 729	G16785	Texaco Exploration and Production Inc.
GC 730	G20088	Conoco Inc.
GC 731	G18430	Union Oil Company of California
GC 732	G18431	OXY USA Inc.
GC 733	G18432	OXY USA Inc.
GC 750	G22991	Dominion Exploration & Production, Inc.
GC 752	G22992	BHP Petroleum (GOM) Inc.
GC 753	G22993	BHP Petroleum (GOM) Inc.
GC 759	G18434	Exxon Mobil Corporation
GC 760	G18435	Exxon Mobil Corporation
GC 764	G16792	Conoco Inc.
GC 765	G16793	Conoco Inc.
GC 766	G22994	Kerr-McGee Oil & Gas Corporation
GC 768	G21817	Samedan Oil Corporation
GC 771	G16794	Texaco Exploration and Production Inc.
GC 772	G22995	Chevron U.S.A. Inc.

Table E-3. Grid 10—Lease Status (continued).

Area/Block	Lease Number	Company
GC 773	G16795	Texaco Exploration and Production Inc.
GC 774	G20089	Conoco Inc.
GC 775	G22996	Conoco Inc.
GC 795	G20093	MOBIL OIL EXPLORATION & PRODUCING SOUTHEAST INC.
GC 796	G20094	MOBIL OIL EXPLORATION & PRODUCING SOUTHEAST INC.
GC 797	G22997	BHP Petroleum (GOM) Inc.
GC 800	G16796	Exxon Mobil Corporation
GC 803	G22998	Amerada Hess Corporation
GC 805	G18440	Conoco Inc.
GC 806	G16798	Union Oil Company of California
GC 807	G16799	Conoco Inc.
GC 808	G16800	Conoco Inc.
GC 809	G16801	Conoco Inc.
GC 810	G22999	Kerr-McGee Oil & Gas Corporation
GC 812	G18441	Union Oil Company of California
GC 813	G18442	Union Oil Company of California
GC 814	G18443	Union Oil Company of California
GC 815	G18444	Union Oil Company of California
GC 817	G16802	Conoco Inc.
GC 818	G16803	Conoco Inc.
GC 819	G16804	Conoco Inc.
GC 820	G16805	Conoco Inc.
GC 821	G16806	BP Exploration & Production Inc.
GC 837	G20100	MOBIL OIL EXPLORATION & PRODUCING SOUTHEAST INC.
GC 838	G18445	MOBIL OIL EXPLORATION & PRODUCING SOUTHEAST INC.
GC 839	G18446	MOBIL OIL EXPLORATION & PRODUCING SOUTHEAST INC.
GC 847	G23000	Chevron U.S.A. Inc.
GC 849	G18448	Union Oil Company of California
GC 850	G16815	Conoco Inc.
GC 851	G16816	Union Oil Company of California
GC 852	G16817	Conoco Inc.
GC 853	G16818	Conoco Inc.
GC 858	G18449	Union Oil Company of California
GC 860	G23001	Exxon Asset Management Company
GC 861	G16819	Conoco Inc.
GC 862	G20101	Conoco Inc.
GC 865	G16820	Chevron U.S.A. Inc.
GC 881	G20105	MOBIL OIL EXPLORATION & PRODUCING SOUTHEAST INC.
GC 882	G20106	MOBIL OIL EXPLORATION & PRODUCING SOUTHEAST INC.
GC 889	G16827	Exxon Mobil Corporation
GC 890	G23002	Chevron U.S.A. Inc.
GC 891	G23003	Amerada Hess Corporation
GC 893	G18451	Conoco Inc.
GC 894	G18452	Conoco Inc.
GC 896	G16830	Conoco Inc.
GC 897	G16831	Conoco Inc.
GC 898	G16832	Conoco Inc.
GC 899	G21818	BP Exploration & Oil Inc.
GC 900	G21819	BP Exploration & Oil Inc.
GC 901	G18453	Union Oil Company of California
GC 902	G18454	BP Exploration & Production Inc.
GC 905	G23004	Union Oil Company of California
GC 906	G18455	Union Oil Company of California
GC 907	G18456	Union Oil Company of California
GC 908	G18457	Union Oil Company of California
GC 930	G20109	Exxon Mobil Corporation
GC 931	G20110	Exxon Mobil Corporation
GC 932	G20111	Exxon Mobil Corporation

Table E-3. Grid 10—Lease Status (continued).

Area/Block	Lease Number	Company
GC 933	G20112	Exxon Mobil Corporation
GC 937	G18458	Conoco Inc.
GC 938	G18459	Conoco Inc.
GC 939	G18460	Conoco Inc.
GC 941	G16837	Conoco Inc.
GC 942	G16838	Conoco Inc.
GC 943	G18461	Union Oil Company of California
GC 944	G18462	BP Exploration & Production Inc.
GC 945	G18463	BP Exploration & Production Inc.
GC 946	G18464	BP Exploration & Production Inc.
GC 949	G23005	Exxon Asset Management Company
GC 950	G18465	Union Oil Company of California
GC 951	G18466	Union Oil Company of California
GC 952	G18467	Texaco Exploration and Production Inc.
GC 953	G20113	BHP Petroleum (GOM) Inc.
GC 969	G16843	Exxon Mobil Corporation
GC 970	G16844	Exxon Mobil Corporation
GC 974	G20118	Exxon Mobil Corporation
GC 975	G20119	MOBIL OIL EXPLORATION & PRODUCING SOUTHEAST INC.
GC 976	G20120	MOBIL OIL EXPLORATION & PRODUCING SOUTHEAST INC.
GC 977	G20121	Exxon Mobil Corporation
GC 981	G18468	Conoco Inc.
GC 982	G18469	Conoco Inc.
GC 983	G18470	Conoco Inc.
GC 986	G18471	Exxon Mobil Corporation
GC 987	G18472	Exxon Mobil Corporation
GC 989	G18473	Exxon Mobil Corporation
GC 990	G18474	Union Oil Company of California
GC 993	G21227	Texaco Exploration and Production Inc.
GC 994	G18475	Texaco Exploration and Production Inc.
GC 995	G18476	Texaco Exploration and Production Inc.
GC 996	G16845	Texaco Exploration and Production Inc.
GC 997	G20122	Marathon Oil Company
KC 40	G19463	Shell Offshore Inc.
KC 41	G19464	Exxon Mobil Corporation
KC 128	G20899	Devon Energy Production Company, L.P.
WR 1	G16933	Exxon Mobil Corporation
WR 2	G16934	Exxon Mobil Corporation
WR 3	G20258	MOBIL OIL EXPLORATION & PRODUCING SOUTHEAST INC.
WR 4	G16935	Exxon Mobil Corporation
WR 5	G16936	Exxon Mobil Corporation
WR 6	G16937	Exxon Mobil Corporation
WR 7	G16938	Exxon Mobil Corporation
WR 8	G20259	Exxon Mobil Corporation
WR 9	G20260	Exxon Mobil Corporation
WR 19	G18625	Exxon Mobil Corporation
WR 21	G18626	Kerr-McGee Oil & Gas Corporation
WR 22	G18627	Kerr-McGee Oil & Gas Corporation
WR 23	G18628	Amoco Production Company
WR 24	G23028	Union Oil Company of California
WR 25	G18629	Union Oil Company of California
WR 26	G16939	Texaco Exploration and Production Inc.
WR 27	G16940	Texaco Exploration and Production Inc.
WR 28	G16941	Texaco Exploration and Production Inc.
WR 29	G16942	Texaco Exploration and Production Inc.
WR 45	G18632	Exxon Mobil Corporation
WR 46	G16944	Exxon Mobil Corporation
WR 47	G20265	MOBIL OIL EXPLORATION & PRODUCING SOUTHEAST INC.

Table E-3. Grid 10—Lease Status (continued).

Area/Block	Lease Number	Company
WR 48	G16945	Exxon Mobil Corporation
WR 49	G16946	MOBIL OIL EXPLORATION & PRODUCING SOUTHEAST INC.
WR 50	G16947	Vastar Resources, Inc.
WR 51	G16948	Exxon Mobil Corporation
WR 64	G18634	Exxon Mobil Corporation
WR 65	G18635	Kerr-McGee Oil & Gas Corporation
WR 66	G18636	Kerr-McGee Oil & Gas Corporation
WR 67	G18637	Union Oil Company of California
WR 68	G18638	Kerr-McGee Oil & Gas Corporation
WR 69	G18639	Texaco Exploration and Production Inc.
WR 70	G16949	Texaco Exploration and Production Inc.
WR 71	G16950	Texaco Exploration and Production Inc.
WR 72	G16951	Texaco Exploration and Production Inc.
WR 73	G20266	Marathon Oil Company
WR 89	G18641	Union Oil Company of California
WR 90	G20269	Exxon Mobil Corporation
WR 91	G20270	MOBIL OIL EXPLORATION & PRODUCING SOUTHEAST INC.
WR 92	G16952	Exxon Mobil Corporation
WR 93	G16953	MOBIL OIL EXPLORATION & PRODUCING SOUTHEAST INC.
WR 94	G16954	Exxon Mobil Corporation
WR 95	G16955	Exxon Mobil Corporation
WR 98	G21841	Union Oil Company of California
WR 99	G21842	Union Oil Company of California
WR 100	G23030	Union Oil Company of California
WR 101	G23031	Union Oil Company of California
WR 102	G23032	Chevron U.S.A. Inc.
WR 103	G23033	Chevron U.S.A. Inc.
WR 105	G20271	Kerr-McGee Oil & Gas Corporation
WR 108	G18642	Kerr-McGee Oil & Gas Corporation
WR 109	G18643	Kerr-McGee Oil & Gas Corporation
WR 111	G18644	Kerr-McGee Oil & Gas Corporation
WR 112	G18645	Kerr-McGee Oil & Gas Corporation
WR 113	G18646	Kerr-McGee Oil & Gas Corporation
WR 114	G21843	Kerr-McGee Oil & Gas Corporation
WR 115	G21844	Vastar Resources, Inc.
WR 116	G21845	Vastar Resources, Inc.
WR 117	G21846	Vastar Resources, Inc.
WR 133	G20277	Exxon Mobil Corporation
WR 134	G20278	Union Oil Company of California
WR 135	G20279	Exxon Mobil Corporation
WR 137	G16956	MOBIL OIL EXPLORATION & PRODUCING SOUTHEAST INC.
WR 138	G16957	Exxon Mobil Corporation
WR 139	G16958	Exxon Mobil Corporation
WR 142	G21848	Union Oil Company of California
WR 143	G21849	Union Oil Company of California
WR 144	G23034	Conoco Inc.
WR 145	G18648	Conoco Inc.
WR 148	G21850	BP Exploration & Oil Inc.
WR 155	G18649	Kerr-McGee Oil & Gas Corporation
WR 158	G21852	Vastar Resources, Inc.
WR 159	G21853	Vastar Resources, Inc.
WR 160	G21854	Vastar Resources, Inc.
WR 181	G16959	Exxon Mobil Corporation
WR 182	G16960	Exxon Mobil Corporation
WR 186	G20292	Shell Offshore Inc.
WR 187	G23036	Conoco Inc.
WR 188	G18654	Union Oil Company of California
WR 224	G18659	Union Oil Company of California

Table E-3. Grid 10—Lease Status (continued).

Area/Block	Lease Number	Company
WR 225	G18660	Kerr-McGee Oil & Gas Corporation
WR 269	G18672	Kerr-McGee Oil & Gas Corporation
WR 270	G21857	Kerr-McGee Oil & Gas Corporation
WR 271	G23042	Ocean Energy, Inc.
WR 313	G18683	Kerr-McGee Oil & Gas Corporation
WR 313	G18683	Ocean Energy, Inc.
WR 355	G20312	MOBIL OIL EXPLORATION & PRODUCING SOUTHEAST INC.
WR 356	G20313	MOBIL OIL EXPLORATION & PRODUCING SOUTHEAST INC.

Notes: GB is Garden Banks
GC is Green Canyon
KC is Keathley Canyon
WR is Walker Ridge
* Denotes a MMS Approved Unit

APPENDIX F

SOCIOECONOMIC CONDITIONS

Table F-1

Listing of Counties and Parishes of the Coastal Impact Area

LA-1	LA-2	LA-3	MA-1
Acadia, LA Calcasieu, LA Cameron, LA Iberia, LA Lafayette, LA St. Landry, LA St. Martin, LA Vermilion, LA	Ascension, LA Assumption, LA East Baton Rouge, LA Iberville, LA Lafourche, LA Livingston, LA St. Mary, LA Tangipahoa, LA Terrebonne, LA West Baton Rouge, LA	Jefferson, LA Orleans, LA Plaquemines, LA St. Bernard, LA St. Charles, LA St. James, LA St. John the Baptist, LA St. Tammany, LA	Baldwin, AL Hancock, MS Harrison, MS Jackson, MS Mobile, AL Stone, MS

TX-1	TX-2	FL-1	FL-3
Aransas, TX Calhoun, TX Cameron, TX Jackson, TX Kenedy, TX Kleberg, TX Nueces, TX Refugio, TX San Patricio, TX Victoria, TX Willacy, TX	Brazoria, TX Chambers, TX Fort Bend, TX Galveston, TX Hardin, TX Harris, TX Jefferson, TX Liberty, TX Matagorda, TX Montgomery, TX Orange, TX Waller, TX Wharton, TX	Bay, FL Escambia, FL Okaloosa, FL Santa Rosa, FL Walton, FL **FL-2** Dixie, FL Franklin, FL Gulf, FL Jefferson, FL Levy, FL Taylor, FL Wakulla, FL	Charlotte, FL Citrus, FL Collier, FL Hernando, FL Hillsborough, FL Lee, FL Manatee, FL Pasco, FL Pinellas, FL Sarasota, FL **FL-4** Miami-Dade, FL Monroe, FL

Table F-2

IMPLAN Industrial Sector Data by Coastal Subareas

(Numbers are percentages of expenditures by oil and gas industry to the respective onshore subareas where dollars are spent.)

SECTOR	DEFINITION	TX-1	TX-2	LA-1	LA-2	LA-3	MA-1	FL-1	FL-2	FL-3	FL-4	GULF-OTHER	US-OTHER
38	Oil & Gas Operations	0.00	0.34	0.09	0.06	0.15	0.00	0.00	0.00	0.00	0.00	0.23	0.12
50	New Gas Utility Facilities	0.07	0.38	0.05	0.10	0.10	0.10	0.00	0.00	0.00	0.00	0.11	0.07
53	Misc. Natural Resource Facility Construction	0.03	0.21	0.23	0.15	0.30	0.02	0.00	0.00	0.00	0.00	0.01	0.03
56	Maintenance and Repair, Other Facilities	0.06	0.31	0.04	0.08	0.09	0.08	0.00	0.00	0.00	0.00	0.21	0.11
57	Other Oil & Gas Field Services	0.00	0.30	0.26	0.12	0.16	0.00	0.00	0.00	0.00	0.00	0.07	0.05
160	Office Furniture and Equipment	0.15	0.54	0.00	0.00	0.08	0.23	0.00	0.00	0.00	0.00	0.00	0.00
178	Maps and Charts (Misc. Publishing)	0.12	0.59	0.02	0.06	0.11	0.10	0.00	0.00	0.00	0.00	0.01	0.00
206	Explosives	0.50	0.50	0.00	0.00	0.00	0.00	0.00	0.00	0.00	0.00	0.00	0.00
209	Chemicals, NEC	0.03	0.64	0.04	0.10	0.04	0.04	0.00	0.00	0.00	0.00	0.04	0.04
210	Petroleum Fuels	0.11	0.50	0.09	0.16	0.09	0.05	0.00	0.00	0.00	0.00	0.00	0.00
232	Hydraulic Cement	0.00	0.10	0.00	0.00	0.00	0.10	0.00	0.00	0.00	0.00	0.50	0.30
258	Steel Pipe and Tubes	0.00	0.50	0.31	0.05	0.07	0.00	0.00	0.00	0.00	0.00	0.08	0.04
284	Fabricated Plate Work	0.04	0.63	0.06	0.09	0.05	0.14	0.00	0.00	0.00	0.00	0.00	0.00
290	Iron and Steel Forgings	0.00	0.81	0.00	0.00	0.05	0.00	0.00	0.00	0.00	0.00	0.14	0.00
307	Turbines	0.05	0.65	0.00	0.10	0.20	0.00	0.00	0.00	0.00	0.00	0.00	0.00
311	Construction Machinery & Equipment	0.06	0.42	0.00	0.06	0.19	0.11	0.00	0.00	0.00	0.00	0.11	0.06
313	O&G Field Machinery & Equipment	0.03	0.18	0.27	0.18	0.22	0.00	0.00	0.00	0.00	0.00	0.05	0.04
331	Special Industrial Machinery	0.00	0.00	0.00	0.38	0.54	0.00	0.00	0.00	0.00	0.00	0.00	0.03
332	Pumps & Compressors	0.04	0.30	0.17	0.22	0.09	0.00	0.00	0.00	0.00	0.00	0.12	0.06
354	Industrial Machines, NEC	0.05	0.66	0.06	0.10	0.06	0.06	0.00	0.00	0.00	0.00	0.00	0.00
356	Switchgear	0.00	0.63	0.00	0.07	0.11	0.07	0.00	0.00	0.00	0.00	0.11	0.00
374	Communication Equipment, NEC	0.13	0.50	0.00	0.00	0.25	0.00	0.00	0.00	0.00	0.00	0.13	0.00
392	Shipbuilding and Ship Repair	0.09	0.24	0.05	0.24	0.18	0.19	0.00	0.00	0.00	0.00	0.00	0.00
399	Transportation Equipment, NEC	0.00	0.78	0.06	0.11	0.00	0.06	0.00	0.00	0.00	0.00	0.00	0.00
401	Lab Equipment	0.00	1.00	0.00	0.00	0.00	0.00	0.00	0.00	0.00	0.00	0.00	0.00
403	Instrumentation	0.01	0.13	0.39	0.27	0.08	0.00	0.00	0.00	0.00	0.00	0.08	0.04
435	Demurrage/Warehousing/Motor Freight	0.11	0.37	0.21	0.09	0.09	0.01	0.00	0.00	0.00	0.00	0.07	0.00
436	Water Transport	0.02	0.27	0.10	0.25	0.22	0.04	0.01	0.00	0.01	0.00	0.06	0.00
437	Air Transport	0.03	0.42	0.11	0.11	0.08	0.02	0.00	0.00	0.00	0.01	0.21	0.00

Table F-2 . IMPLAN Industrial Sector Data by Coastal Subareas (Numbers are percentages of expenditures by oil and gas industry to the respective onshore subareas where dollars are spent.) (continued).

SECTOR	DEFINITION	TX-1	TX-2	LA-1	LA-2	LA-3	MA-1	FL-1	FL-2	FL-3	FL-4	GULF-OTHER	US-OTHER
441	Communications	0.09	0.51	0.07	0.11	0.11	0.11	0.00	0.00	0.00	0.00	0.00	0.00
443	Electric Services	0.13	0.36	0.06	0.15	0.12	0.18	0.00	0.00	0.00	0.00	0.00	0.00
444	Gas Production/Distribution	0.10	0.54	0.08	0.07	0.05	0.03	0.00	0.00	0.00	0.00	0.05	0.04
445	Water Supply	0.08	0.43	0.08	0.12	0.05	0.11	0.00	0.00	0.00	0.00	0.01	0.01
446	Waste Treatment/Disposal	0.00	1.00	0.00	0.00	0.00	0.00	0.00	0.00	0.00	0.00	0.00	0.00
454	Eating/Drinking	0.00	0.24	0.28	0.08	0.40	0.00	0.00	0.00	0.00	0.00	0.00	0.00
455	Misc. Retail	0.09	0.48	0.06	0.10	0.15	0.11	0.00	0.00	0.00	0.00	0.00	0.00
459	Insurance	0.04	0.47	0.07	0.12	0.09	0.00	0.00	0.00	0.00	0.00	0.17	0.03
462	Real Estate	0.09	0.47	0.04	0.08	0.11	0.08	0.00	0.00	0.00	0.00	0.11	0.01
469	Advertisement	0.06	0.45	0.06	0.08	0.15	0.08	0.00	0.00	0.00	0.00	0.12	0.01
470	Other Business Services	0.00	0.60	0.11	0.09	0.06	0.00	0.00	0.00	0.00	0.00	0.09	0.05
473	Misc. Equipment Rental and Leasing	0.09	0.26	0.22	0.10	0.10	0.01	0.00	0.00	0.00	0.00	0.18	0.03
490	Doctors & Veterinarian Services	0.09	0.53	0.06	0.09	0.14	0.08	0.00	0.00	0.00	0.00	0.00	0.00
494	Legal Services	0.07	0.48	0.07	0.11	0.19	0.08	0.00	0.00	0.00	0.00	0.00	0.00
506	Environmental/Engineering Services	0.06	0.38	0.11	0.08	0.08	0.03	0.01	0.00	0.02	0.00	0.20	0.01
507	Acct/Misc. Business Services	0.06	0.46	0.05	0.09	0.13	0.07	0.00	0.00	0.00	0.00	0.11	0.01
508	Management/Consulting Services	0.04	0.54	0.04	0.09	0.11	0.05	0.00	0.00	0.00	0.00	0.11	0.01
509	Testing/Research Facilities	0.00	0.38	0.14	0.14	0.05	0.00	0.00	0.00	0.00	0.00	0.21	0.11

Table F-3

Population Forecast from 2000 to 2040 by Year and by Coastal Subarea

Year	LA-1	LA-2	LA-3	MA-1	TX-1	TX-2	FL-1	FL-2	FL-3	FL-4	CGOM	WGOM	EGOM	EPA	GOM	Planning Areas
2000	697.71	996.23	1310.80	912.11	923.09	5021.05	772.44	122.07	3742.86	2278.24	3916.85	5944.14	6915.61	894.51	16776.60	10755.50
2001	702.97	1009.46	1316.37	922.24	933.22	5094.84	785.47	124.05	3797.49	2301.37	3951.04	6028.06	7008.38	909.52	16987.48	10888.62
2002	708.32	1022.75	1321.96	932.40	943.46	5168.84	798.60	125.98	3852.31	2324.62	3985.43	6112.30	7101.51	924.58	17199.24	11022.31
2003	713.52	1035.84	1327.37	942.43	953.61	5242.00	811.55	127.92	3906.48	2347.62	4019.16	6195.61	7193.58	939.48	17408.35	11154.25
2004	718.76	1049.09	1332.81	952.57	963.88	5316.20	824.72	129.89	3961.41	2370.85	4053.22	6280.07	7286.88	954.61	17620.17	11287.91
2005	723.93	1062.05	1338.21	962.52	973.95	5388.52	837.50	131.81	4014.97	2393.69	4086.71	6362.47	7377.97	969.31	17827.15	11418.49
2006	729.06	1074.99	1341.68	972.41	984.06	5460.94	850.35	133.75	4068.57	2416.50	4118.14	6445.00	7469.17	984.11	18032.31	11547.25
2007	734.23	1088.09	1345.15	982.39	994.28	5534.33	863.41	135.72	4122.88	2439.52	4149.87	6528.61	7561.54	999.13	18240.01	11677.61
2008	739.44	1101.35	1348.64	992.49	1004.60	5608.70	876.66	137.73	4177.92	2462.57	4181.91	6613.31	7655.05	1014.38	18450.29	11809.60
2009	744.68	1114.78	1352.13	1002.68	1015.03	5684.08	890.12	139.76	4233.70	2486.23	4214.21	6699.11	7749.80	1029.87	18663.18	11943.25
2010	749.61	1126.80	1355.55	1011.98	1024.54	5750.80	901.81	141.53	4283.11	2507.79	4243.94	6775.34	7834.24	1043.34	18853.52	12062.62
2011	754.87	1139.92	1362.85	1022.05	1034.92	5824.07	914.79	143.48	4337.39	2531.16	4279.69	6858.99	7926.83	1058.28	19065.51	12196.96
2012	760.17	1153.19	1370.19	1032.23	1045.40	5898.28	927.97	145.46	4392.36	2554.75	4315.77	6943.68	8020.53	1073.43	19279.99	12332.88
2013	765.50	1166.62	1377.57	1042.50	1055.99	5973.43	941.33	147.46	4448.03	2578.55	4352.19	7029.42	8115.37	1088.79	19496.98	12470.40
2014	770.88	1180.20	1384.99	1052.88	1066.68	6049.54	954.88	149.50	4504.40	2602.58	4388.94	7116.22	8211.36	1104.38	19716.52	12609.54
2015	775.93	1192.43	1392.07	1062.37	1076.45	6117.37	966.77	151.29	4554.67	2624.70	4422.80	7193.82	8297.43	1118.06	19914.05	12734.68
2016	781.35	1205.73	1397.79	1072.59	1087.08	6191.57	979.91	153.27	4609.64	2648.60	4457.47	7278.65	8391.42	1133.18	20127.54	12869.30
2017	786.82	1219.17	1403.54	1082.91	1097.82	6266.66	993.24	155.27	4665.27	2672.72	4492.44	7364.49	8486.49	1148.50	20343.42	13005.43
2018	792.32	1232.77	1409.31	1093.33	1108.67	6342.67	1006.74	157.30	4721.58	2697.05	4527.73	7451.34	8582.67	1164.03	20561.74	13143.11
2019	797.85	1246.52	1415.11	1103.86	1119.62	6419.60	1020.43	159.35	4778.56	2721.61	4563.33	7539.22	8679.95	1179.78	20782.50	13282.33
2020	803.08	1258.99	1420.72	1113.54	1129.68	6488.76	1032.56	161.18	4829.82	2744.33	4596.33	7618.44	8767.89	1193.74	20982.66	13408.51
2021	808.59	1272.46	1426.64	1123.93	1140.50	6563.90	1045.87	163.18	4888.11	2768.71	4631.62	7704.40	8865.87	1209.05	21201.90	13545.08
2022	814.14	1286.08	1432.58	1134.41	1151.42	6639.92	1059.34	165.20	4944.48	2793.31	4667.22	7791.34	8962.34	1224.55	21420.91	13683.11
2023	819.73	1299.85	1438.55	1145.00	1162.45	6716.82	1073.00	167.25	5001.51	2818.12	4703.13	7879.27	9059.88	1240.25	21642.27	13822.64
2024	825.36	1313.76	1444.54	1155.68	1173.59	6794.60	1086.82	169.33	5059.19	2843.16	4739.34	7968.19	9158.50	1256.15	21866.03	13963.68
2025	830.66	1326.40	1450.33	1165.51	1183.81	6864.69	1099.13	171.18	5108.48	2866.30	4772.90	8048.50	9245.09	1270.31	22066.49	14091.71
2026	836.36	1340.60	1456.37	1176.38	1195.15	6944.81	1113.29	173.30	5167.40	2891.76	4809.71	8139.34	9345.76	1286.60	22294.81	14235.65
2027	842.10	1354.94	1462.44	1187.36	1206.60	7024.61	1127.64	175.45	5226.99	2917.45	4846.84	8231.20	9447.54	1303.09	22525.59	14381.14
2028	847.88	1369.45	1468.53	1198.43	1218.15	7105.96	1142.17	177.63	5287.27	2943.37	4884.30	8324.11	9550.45	1319.80	22758.85	14528.21
2029	853.71	1384.10	1474.65	1209.61	1229.82	7188.25	1156.89	179.83	5348.25	2969.52	4922.07	8418.07	9654.50	1336.72	22994.64	14676.87
2030	859.57	1398.92	1480.79	1220.90	1241.60	7271.50	1171.80	182.06	5409.93	2995.90	4960.17	8513.09	9759.70	1353.86	23232.97	14827.13
2031	865.47	1413.89	1486.96	1232.29	1253.49	7355.71	1186.90	184.32	5472.32	3022.52	4998.61	8609.20	9866.06	1371.22	23473.87	14979.03
2032	871.41	1429.02	1493.16	1243.79	1265.50	7440.89	1202.20	186.60	5535.43	3049.37	5037.37	8706.39	9973.61	1388.80	23717.37	15132.56
2033	877.39	1444.32	1499.38	1255.39	1277.62	7527.06	1217.69	188.92	5599.27	3076.46	5076.47	8804.68	10082.34	1406.61	23963.50	15287.76
2034	883.41	1459.77	1505.62	1267.10	1289.86	7614.23	1233.38	191.26	5663.85	3103.79	5115.91	8904.09	10192.29	1424.65	24212.28	15444.64
2035	889.48	1475.40	1511.90	1278.92	1302.21	7702.41	1249.28	193.63	5729.17	3131.37	5155.69	9004.62	10303.45	1442.91	24463.76	15603.22
2036	895.58	1491.19	1518.20	1290.85	1314.69	7791.61	1265.38	196.04	5795.24	3159.19	5195.82	9106.29	10415.84	1461.41	24717.95	15763.52
2037	901.73	1507.15	1524.52	1302.90	1327.27	7881.84	1281.69	198.47	5862.08	3187.25	5236.29	9209.12	10529.48	1480.15	24974.89	15925.56
2038	907.92	1523.28	1530.87	1315.05	1339.99	7973.12	1298.20	200.93	5929.68	3215.57	5277.12	9313.11	10644.38	1499.13	25234.61	16089.36
2039	914.15	1539.58	1537.25	1327.32	1352.82	8065.45	1314.93	203.42	5998.07	3244.14	5318.30	9418.27	10760.56	1518.35	25497.13	16254.93
2040	920.43	1556.06	1543.65	1339.70	1365.78	8158.86	1331.88	205.94	6067.24	3272.96	5359.84	9524.64	10878.02	1537.82	25762.50	16422.30

Table F-4

Employment Forecast From 2000 to 2040 by Year and by Coastal Subarea

Year	LA-1	LA-2	LA-3	MA-1	TX-1	TX-2	FL-1	FL-2	FL-3	FL-4	CGOM	WGOM	EGOM	EPA	GOM	Planning Areas
2000	388.98	576.13	786.25	512.97	459.15	3065.46	428.39	44.69	2205.80	1308.92	2264.33	3524.61	3987.80	473.08	9776.74	6262.02
2001	394.33	585.09	794.59	521.07	465.64	3119.84	436.89	45.32	2253.97	1330.10	2295.08	3585.48	4066.28	482.21	9946.84	6362.77
2002	399.52	593.55	801.90	528.79	471.69	3172.48	445.17	45.86	2300.39	1349.19	2323.76	3644.17	4140.61	491.03	--	6458.96
2003	404.46	601.57	808.21	536.17	477.20	3222.77	453.26	46.37	2344.20	1365.59	2350.41	3699.97	4209.41	499.63	--	6550.00
2004	409.45	609.70	814.57	543.65	482.77	3273.85	461.50	46.89	2388.84	1382.18	2377.37	3756.62	4279.40	508.39	--	6642.38
2005	414.34	617.64	820.85	550.94	488.23	3323.48	469.46	47.40	2431.93	1398.42	2403.77	3811.71	4347.21	516.86	--	6732.34
2006	419.39	625.89	827.75	558.56	493.92	3374.29	477.84	47.93	2475.73	1413.62	2431.59	3868.21	4415.13	525.78	--	6825.57
2007	424.50	634.24	834.71	566.29	499.67	3425.88	486.37	48.47	2520.32	1428.99	2459.74	3925.55	4484.16	534.85	--	6920.13
2008	429.67	642.71	841.73	574.12	505.49	3478.25	495.06	49.02	2565.72	1444.53	2488.23	3983.74	4554.32	544.08	--	7016.05
2009	434.91	651.29	848.81	582.06	511.38	3531.43	503.89	49.74	2611.90	1460.23	2517.06	4042.81	4625.80	553.64	--	7113.51
2010	439.60	658.89	855.38	589.06	516.68	3577.67	511.39	50.07	2651.06	1474.48	2542.93	4094.35	4687.00	561.46	--	7198.74
2011	444.68	667.51	863.16	596.81	522.62	3628.76	519.96	50.64	2694.87	1489.61	2572.16	4151.38	4755.08	570.60	--	7294.15
2012	449.82	676.25	871.01	604.66	528.64	3680.58	528.68	51.22	2739.40	1504.90	2601.73	4209.22	4824.19	579.89	--	7390.84
2013	455.01	685.09	878.93	612.62	534.72	3733.14	537.54	51.80	2784.67	1520.35	2631.66	4267.86	4894.35	589.34	--	7488.85
2014	460.27	694.06	886.93	620.68	540.87	3786.45	546.55	52.39	2830.68	1535.95	2661.93	4327.32	4965.57	598.93	--	7588.19
2015	465.01	702.02	894.30	627.83	546.42	3833.26	554.27	52.92	2870.22	1550.19	2689.16	4379.68	5027.60	607.19	--	7676.03
2016	470.11	711.16	902.90	635.68	552.66	3884.93	562.96	53.52	2914.05	1566.03	2719.86	4437.59	5096.56	616.48	--	7773.93
2017	475.27	720.42	911.59	643.64	558.97	3937.29	571.78	54.13	2958.56	1582.03	2750.92	4496.26	5166.50	625.91	--	7873.09
2018	480.49	729.80	920.36	651.69	565.35	3990.36	580.74	54.75	3003.74	1598.20	2782.34	4555.71	5237.43	635.49	--	7973.54
2019	485.77	739.31	929.21	659.84	571.81	4044.15	589.84	55.37	3049.61	1614.53	2814.12	4615.95	5309.36	645.22	--	8075.29
2020	490.56	747.78	937.36	667.14	577.65	4091.88	597.75	55.94	3089.63	1629.48	2842.84	4669.53	5372.80	653.69	--	8166.06
2021	495.70	757.57	946.76	675.11	584.23	4144.38	606.52	56.58	3133.55	1646.49	2875.13	4728.61	5443.14	663.10	--	8266.83
2022	500.88	767.49	956.25	683.17	590.88	4197.55	615.42	57.22	3178.09	1663.68	2907.79	4788.43	5514.42	672.64	--	8368.86
2023	506.13	777.53	965.83	691.34	597.60	4251.41	624.45	57.87	3223.27	1681.05	2940.83	4849.01	5586.64	682.32	--	8472.16
2024	511.43	787.71	975.52	699.59	604.41	4305.95	633.61	58.53	3269.09	1698.60	2974.25	4910.36	5659.84	692.14	--	8576.75
2025	516.25	796.75	984.37	707.01	610.55	4354.52	641.63	59.12	3309.35	1714.59	3004.38	4965.07	5724.69	700.75	--	8670.20
2026	521.65	807.18	994.24	715.46	617.50	4410.39	651.05	59.79	3356.39	1732.49	3038.53	5027.89	5799.72	710.84	--	8777.25
2027	527.11	817.75	1004.21	724.00	624.53	4466.97	660.47	60.47	3404.11	1750.58	3073.07	5091.51	5875.75	721.07	--	8885.64
2028	532.63	828.45	1014.27	732.65	631.64	4524.29	670.29	61.16	3452.50	1768.86	3108.01	5155.93	5952.80	731.45	--	8995.38
2029	538.21	839.30	1024.44	741.40	638.83	4582.33	680.13	61.85	3501.57	1787.32	3143.35	5221.17	6030.88	741.98	--	9106.49
2030	543.84	850.28	1034.71	750.26	646.11	4641.13	690.11	62.56	3551.35	1805.98	3179.09	5287.23	6110.00	752.66	--	9218.99
2031	549.54	861.41	1045.08	759.22	653.46	4700.67	700.23	63.27	3601.83	1824.84	3215.25	5354.13	6190.17	763.50	--	9332.89
2032	555.29	872.69	1055.56	768.29	660.90	4760.98	710.51	63.99	3653.03	1843.89	3251.83	5421.88	6271.42	774.49	--	9448.20
2033	561.10	884.11	1066.14	777.47	668.42	4822.07	720.93	64.71	3704.96	1863.14	3288.82	5490.49	6353.75	785.65	--	9564.96
2034	566.97	895.69	1076.83	786.76	676.03	4883.93	731.51	65.45	3757.63	1882.60	3326.25	5559.97	6437.19	796.96	--	9683.18
2035	572.91	907.41	1087.62	796.16	683.73	4946.59	742.25	66.19	3811.05	1902.25	3364.10	5630.33	6521.74	808.44	--	9802.86
2036	578.91	919.29	1098.53	805.67	691.52	5010.06	753.14	66.94	3865.22	1922.11	3402.39	5701.57	6607.42	820.08	--	9924.05
2037	584.97	931.32	1109.54	815.29	699.39	5074.34	764.19	67.70	3920.17	1942.18	3441.12	5773.73	6694.24	831.89	--	--
2038	591.09	943.51	1120.66	825.03	707.35	5139.44	775.40	68.47	3975.89	1962.46	3480.30	5846.79	6782.23	843.88	--	--
2039	597.28	955.86	1131.90	834.89	715.40	5205.38	786.78	69.25	4032.41	1982.95	3519.93	5920.79	6871.39	856.03	--	--
2040	603.53	968.38	1143.24	844.86	723.55	5272.17	798.33	70.04	4089.73	2003.65	3560.01	5995.72	6961.75	868.37	--	--

Table F-5

Employment by Major Industry Sector

Industrial Sectors	Agricultural Services	Mining	Construction	Manufacturing	Transportation and Public Utilities	Wholesale Trade	Retail Trade	FIRE	Services	Unclassified Establishments	Total
Geographic Area											
FL-1	1,859	326	18,283	19,777	9,978	9,525	67,525	14,101	94,589	120	236,083
FL-2	529	173	1,722	4,488	849	943	6,074	1,124	4,816	59	20,777
EPA Total Employment	2,388	499	20,005	24,265	10,827	10,468	73,599	15,225	99,405	179	256,860
EPA Percent in Category	0.93%	0.19%	7.79%	9.45%	4.22%	4.08%	28.65%	5.93%	38.70%	0.07%	100.00%
LA-1	1,713	10,742	23,664	37,934	28,534	24,339	79,738	17,725	123,261	161	347,811
LA-2	1,942	10,179	51,562	50,906	25,811	26,955	96,458	23,619	139,126	161	426,719
LA-3	1,092	11,533	12,988	24,470	26,309	12,590	64,256	18,624	131,158	125	303,145
MA-1	1,925	462	22,956	50,430	16,843	15,373	73,302	14,924	117,170	76	313,461
CPA Total Employment	6,672	32,916	111,170	163,740	97,497	79,257	313,754	74,892	510,715	523	1,391,136
CPA Percent in Category	0.48%	2.37%	7.99%	11.77%	7.01%	5.70%	22.55%	5.38%	36.71%	0.04%	100.00%
TX-1	1,649	3,171	15,983	35,054	13,025	12,777	65,689	12,944	91,194	134	251,620
TX-2	13,360	60,314	146,448	251,601	146,088	138,885	377,456	117,826	680,595	514	1,933,087
WPA Total Employment	15,009	63,485	162,431	286,655	159,113	151,662	443,145	130,770	771,789	648	2,184,707
WPA Percent in Category	0.69%	2.91%	7.43%	13.12%	7.28%	6.94%	20.28%	5.99%	35.33%	0.03%	100.00%
Impact Area Total Employment	24,069	96,900	293,606	474,660	267,437	241,387	830,498	220,887	1,381,909	1,350	3,832,703
Impact Area Percent in Category	0.63%	2.53%	7.66%	12.38%	6.98%	6.30%	21.67%	5.76%	36.06%	0.04%	100.00%

Table F-6
Payroll by Major Industry Sector
($000)

Industrial Sectors / Geographic Area	Agricultural Services	Mining	Construction	Manufacturing	Transportation and Public Utilities	Wholesale Trade	Retail Trade	FIRE	Services	Unclassified Establishments	Total
FL-1	34,161	10,403	384,460	651,139	313,497	236,691	860,238	341,618	2,020,760	1,450	4,854,417
FL-2	3,175	2,651	29,098	148,215	24,052	15,928	67,255	22,725	75,532	93	388,724
EPA Total Payroll	37,336	13,054	413,558	799,354	337,549	252,619	927,493	364,343	2,096,292	1,543	5,243,141
EPA Percent in Category	0.71%	0.25%	7.89%	15.25%	6.44%	4.82%	17.69%	6.95%	39.98%	0.03%	100.00%
LA-1	19,529	448,701	376,191	905,311	470,500	418,289	584,938	214,040	1,566,438	1,785	5,005,722
LA-2	21,953	382,330	1,363,188	2,084,861	843,256	742,912	1,057,018	655,316	2,883,188	1,837	10,035,859
LA-3	29,550	818,103	709,835	1,293,155	1,276,296	935,861	1,502,870	1,019,239	4,826,503	3,598	12,415,010
MA-1	31,659	18,833	538,004	1,650,816	505,933	429,120	888,117	416,075	2,528,555	1,629	7,008,741
CPA Total Payroll	102,691	1,667,967	2,987,218	5,934,143	3,095,985	2,526,182	4,032,943	2,304,670	11,804,684	8,849	34,465,332
CPA Percent in Category	0.30%	4.84%	8.67%	17.22%	8.98%	7.33%	11.70%	6.69%	34.25%	0.03%	100.00%
TX-1	20,667	104,061	392,197	1,121,882	386,798	335,981	847,264	321,642	1,910,799	2,332	5,443,623
TX-2	242,031	3,891,122	4,745,880	11,431,745	5,740,136	5,663,902	5,689,792	4,904,951	20,356,704	17,369	62,683,632
WPA Total Payroll	262,698	3,995,183	5,138,077	12,553,627	6,126,934	5,999,883	6,537,056	5,226,593	22,267,503	19,701	68,127,255
WPA Percent in Category	0.39%	5.86%	7.54%	18.43%	8.99%	8.81%	9.60%	7.67%	32.69%	0.03%	100.00%
Impact Area Total Payroll	402,725	5,676,204	8,538,853	19,287,124	9,560,468	8,778,684	11,497,492	7,895,606	36,168,479	30,093	107,835,728
Impact Area Percent in Category	0.37%	5.26%	7.92%	17.89%	8.87%	8.14%	10.66%	7.32%	33.54%	0.03%	100.00%

F-9

Table F-7

Employment Impacts Projected from BP's Joint Initial DOCD
(Peak employment is projected for the Year 2004 as shown)

Onshore Subareas	Direct Employment	Indirect Employment	Induced Employment	Total Employment	Baseline Employment	BP's Plan as a Percentage of Baseline
FL-1	1.0	0.9	0.6	2.5	461,500	0.00%
FL-2	0.1	0.1	0.0	0.2	46,890	0.00%
FL-3	1.5	1.2	0.9	3.5	2,388,840	0.00%
FL-4	0.4	0.3	0.2	0.9	1,382,180	0.00%
EGOM	1.2	1.0	0.6	2.7	4,279,410	0.00%
LA-1	142.7	38.9	55.4	236.9	409,450	0.06%
LA-2	115.1	43.8	47.0	205.9	609,700	0.03%
LA-3	218.5	79.7	84.6	382.9	814,570	0.05%
MA-1	11.7	4.4	4.7	20.8	543,650	0.00%
CGOM	487.9	166.8	191.7	846.4	2,377,370	0.04%
TX-1	19.2	6.6	7.2	32.9	482,770	0.01%
TX-2	292.9	171.9	169.6	634.3	3,273,850	0.02%
WGOM	312.0	178.5	176.7	667.2	3,756,620	0.02%
Total GOM	801.1	346.3	369.0	1,516	10,413,400	0.01%

Table F-8

Opportunity Cost -- Employment from a Hypothetical Oil Spill Scenario

Onshore Subarea	Direct Employment	Indirect Employment	Induced Employment	Total Employment	Baseline Employment*	BP Plan as a Percentage of Baseline
FL-1	69-143	48- 99	35-72	152-314	461,500	0.07%
FL-2	0	0	0	0	46,890	0.00%
FL-3	104-215	74-152	60-123	238-490	2,388,840	0.02%
FL-4	19- 39	11- 23	8- 18	38- 80	1,382,180	0.01%
EGOM	261-397	133-274	103-213	428-884	4,279,410	0.02%
LA-1	3,662- 7,974	763-1,636	1,884-3,861	6,309-13,471	409,450	3.29%
LA-2	4,956-10,395	800-1,684	2,206-4,412	7,962-16,491	609,700	2.70%
LA-3	6,820-13,352	1,455-2,865	4,176-8,028	12,451-24,245	814,570	2.98%
MA-1	2,654- 5,089	538-1,039	1,978-3,194	5,170- 9,322	543,650	1.71%
CGOM	18,092-36,810	3,556-7,224	10,244-19,495	31,892-63,529	2,377,370	2.67%
TX-1	3,432-6,599	734-1,433	1,753- 3,355	5,919-11,387	482,770	2.36%
TX-2	15,579-31,835	4,643-9,400	10,287-20,297	30,509-61,532	3,273,850	1.88%
WGOM	19,011-38,434	5,377-10,833	12,040-23,652	36,428-72,919	3,756,620	2.21%
Total GOM	37,364-75,641	9,066-18,331	22,387-433,601	68,748-137,332	10,413,400	1.32%

*Baseline employment is shown for the year 2004. Such a spill is most likely to occur during development drilling. The year 2004 is at the height of such activity.

The Department of the Interior Mission

As the Nation's principal conservation agency, the Department of the Interior has responsibility for most of our nationally owned public lands and natural resources. This includes fostering sound use of our land and water resources; protecting our fish, wildlife, and biological diversity; preserving the environmental and cultural values of our national parks and historical places; and providing for the enjoyment of life through outdoor recreation. The Department assesses our energy and mineral resources and works to ensure that their development is in the best interests of all our people by encouraging stewardship and citizen participation in their care. The Department also has a major responsibility for American Indian reservation communities and for people who live in island territories under U.S. administration.

The Minerals Management Service Mission

As a bureau of the Department of the Interior, the Minerals Management Service's (MMS) primary responsibilities are to manage the mineral resources located on the Nation's Outer Continental Shelf (OCS), collect revenue from the Federal OCS and onshore Federal and Indian lands, and distribute those revenues.

Moreover, in working to meet its responsibilities, the **Offshore Minerals Management Program** administers the OCS competitive leasing program and oversees the safe and environmentally sound exploration and production of our Nation's offshore natural gas, oil and other mineral resources. The MMS **Minerals Revenue Management** meets its responsibilities by ensuring the efficient, timely and accurate collection and disbursement of revenue from mineral leasing and production due to Indian tribes and allottees, States and the U.S. Treasury.

The MMS strives to fulfill its responsibilities through the general guiding principles of: (1) being responsive to the public's concerns and interests by maintaining a dialogue with all potentially affected parties and (2) carrying out its programs with an emphasis on working to enhance the quality of life for all Americans by lending MMS assistance and expertise to economic development and environmental protection.